D1200916

THE REFORMATION IN DENMARK

THE REFORMATION IN DENMARK

By E. H. DUNKLEY, D.D.

Published for the Church Historical Society

LONDON

S·P·C·K

1948

First printed . . . 1948

IN GRATITUDE TO

J. OSCAR ANDERSEN

HON. D.D. COPENHAGEN, OSLO, LUND,
SOMETIME PROFESSOR OF DIVINITY IN THE
UNIVERSITY OF COPENHAGEN

MADE IN GREAT BRITAIN

CONTENTS

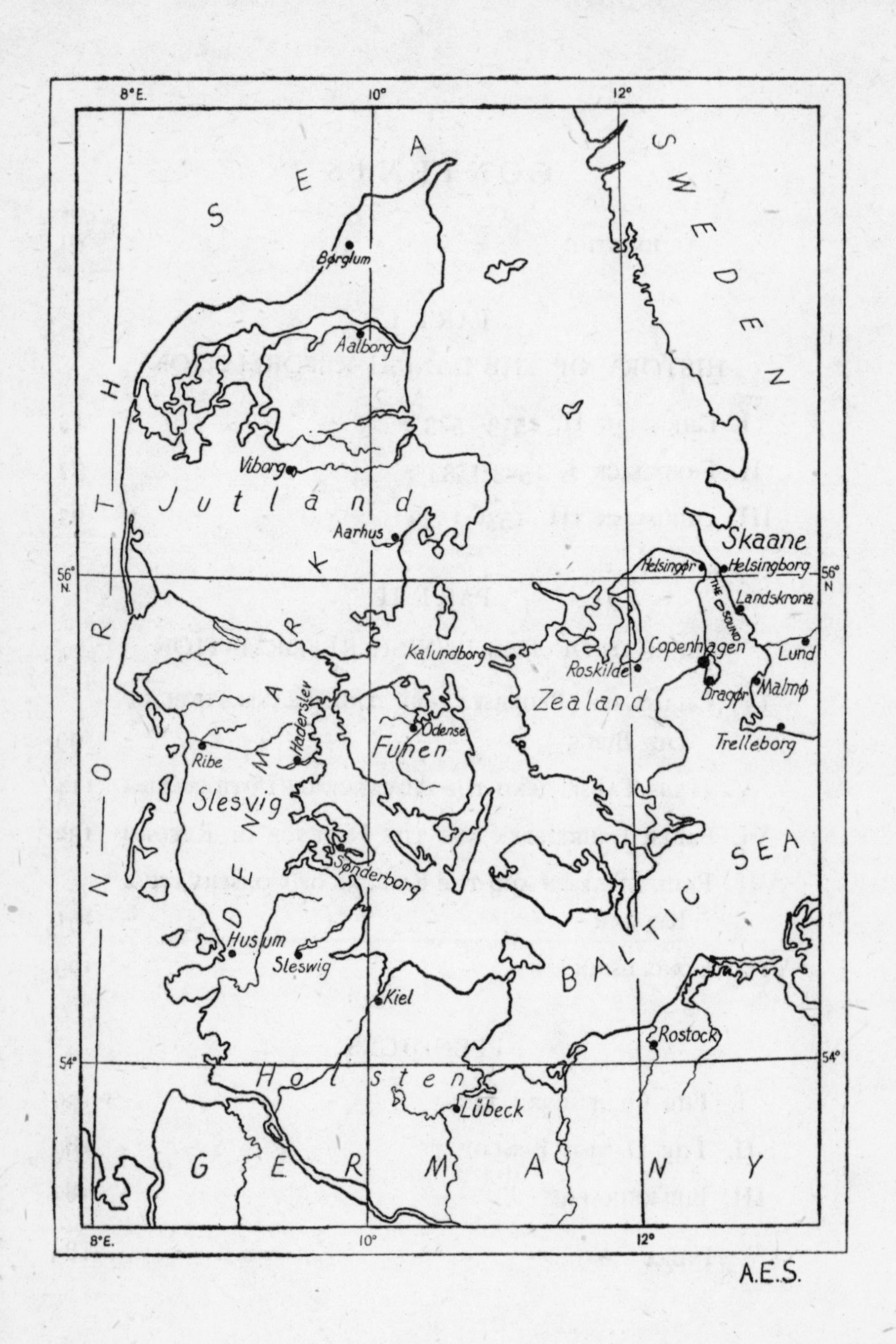

8°E.
10°
12°
NORTH SEA
SWEDEN
Børglum
Aalborg
Viborg
Jutland
Aarhus
DENMARK
Skaane
Helsingør
Helsingborg
THE SOUND
Landskrona
56° N.
Kalundborg
Copenhagen
Roskilde
Lund
Dragør
Malmø
Zealand
Haderslev
Odense
Funen
Ribe
Trelleborg
Slesvig
BALTIC SEA
Sønderborg
Husum
Sleswig
Kiel
Rostock
54°
Holsten
Lübeck
GERMANY
A.E.S.

INTRODUCTION

"THE civilization of Europe has spread in the main from the lands round the Mediterranean, and there is a tendency to neglect the history of the north of Europe. Yet great scenes in the drama of European history were enacted on the shores of the Baltic, which may well be called the northern Mediterranean."[1] To depict one of these scenes, that of the Reformation in Denmark, is the object of this book. Three reasons may be suggested why this subject should be of some interest to English readers. (1) Denmark has had many connexions, racial and royal, cultural and commercial, with this country. " Engle-land " appears to derive its name from the kingdom of " Angel " in southern Denmark, whence a large number of our Angle forefathers migrated with their wives and children in the fifth and sixth centuries to make their homes in the new " Engle-land ". One of the greatest of our early Kings was the Dane, Canute, who ruled over Denmark, Norway, the Hebrides and England and seemed about to found the earliest British Empire, had not his death at the age of forty brought about the collapse of this northern experiment in Empire-building. Most of the consorts of the long line of English Kings have come from the royal houses of France and Spain, the Netherlands and Germany, but Denmark at least gave us Anne, the wife of James I, and Alexandra, the beloved Queen of Edward VII. The cultural links between Denmark and Great Britain have been manifold, but mention can here only be made of Denmark's earliest poet of modern times, Thomas Kingo (1634-1703), a man of Scottish descent; Ludvig Holberg (1684-1754), called " the greatest poet of Scandinavia ", who studied at Oxford; Georg Brandes, the interpreter of Shakespeare; and Hans Christian Andersen, a name as honoured in this land as in his own. In the realm of commerce the two countries have in recent times been closely associated. Before the outbreak of war in 1939, about two-thirds of the total exports of Danish goods came to Great Britain, and though

[1] A. J. Grant, *A History of Europe*, p. 289.

Germany headed the list of countries importing into Denmark, the imports from Great Britain were almost as high. One further tie between us is to be found in the abolition of the slave trade, which Denmark enacted in 1792 and carried out in the Danish West Indies a few years later. " Denmark was the first nation to give this humane example to the world, and England the first to follow it."[1]

(2) The Reformation saw the mediæval Catholic Church in Denmark transformed into the national Church of Denmark, or, as it is called today, the Danish People's Church. Similar ecclesiastical transitions took place in the same period in Sweden, in Norway and in England. But National Churches were not the discovery of the Reformation age. Dr. F. Dvornik has reminded us in his valuable booklet, *National Churches and the Church Universal*, that in the early centuries of the Christian Church there existed beyond the borders of the Empire the three National Churches of Persia, of Armenia and of Abyssinia; and his contention is that " the problem of nationality and universality in the Church is as old as Christendom and the whole evolution of Christianity down to our own days is characterized by repeated attempts, more or less successful, at discovering the right balance between the national and the universal elements present in the Church founded by Jesus Christ " (p. 5). If, as Archbishop W. Temple said, " the Bible strongly insists upon the nation as existing by divine appointment, and it looks forward, not to the abolition of national distinctions, but to the inclusion of all nations in the family of nations,"[2] then the story of the Church of Denmark at its crisis in the sixteenth century is one of more than historical interest, for it provides a signal example of the mode by which the Church Universal was embodied in the people, culture and language of a particular nation, the Danes. The case of Denmark is an exceptionally clear one, since all but a few thousands of its inhabitants are members of the National Church. In England, on the other hand, two large sections of the population challenge the conception of a National Church: the Nonconformists, who stand for the principle

[1] J. H. S. Birch, *Denmark in History*, p. 297.
[2] *Church and Nation*, p. 51.

of free association in a denominational body, and the Roman Catholics, who claim membership in a supernational Church. But the visible weakening of denominational loyalties suggests that the day of National Churches is yet to come, and the hope that the Universal Church of the future may comprise the Churches of many nations is by no means an illusory one.

(3) To those who possess the forward-looking eye the story of religious change in Denmark which is here recounted is a reminder of the truth that " one Reformation always carries in it the seed of another."[1] When the Danish reformers effected the alterations in religion which they believed were necessary, they could not know that the future was to reveal a wealth of new knowledge which was to make their work incomplete. The discoveries of science, the advance of Biblical criticism, the study of comparative religion, and the immense growth of historical learning have rendered another Reformation overdue: perhaps, however, it should rather be said that the new Reformation is already in progress. It is impossible for us who are living within this process of religious reconstruction to foresee the issue of it: but it may not be unhelpful in these critical days to cast our thoughts back to the Reformation of an earlier day and to see how a country like Denmark, with a different history and culture from our own, and yet allied to us by racial stock, faced the challenge to inherited custom and belief which the new light of the sixteenth century brought.

Perhaps these pleas for a sympathetic reception of the subject of this book are superfluous: the true student of the age here depicted will read anything about it, however dry; for, as Sir Charles Oman has said with proper enthusiasm, " the sixteenth century was a wonderful time ".

[1] C. Beard, *The Reformation*, p. 406.

PART I

HISTORY OF THE DANISH REFORMATION

CHAPTER I

CHRISTIAN II, 1513-1523

1

"IN 1513 there came to the throne in Denmark the most extraordinary prince who had been seen in the north for many a generation ".[1] Christian II was a northern Renaissance prince, resembling in some points his contemporaries, Henry VIII and Francis I. An observer who saw him on his visit to the Netherlands in 1521 described him as " well formed, neither large nor small in person, with a black beard, and the face of an Italian ".[2] He was learned and interested in learning, gifted and ambitious, unscrupulous and capable of savage cruelty. His accession marks a new epoch in the development of Scandinavian history, and during his time a new set of actors appeared on the European stage. Henry VIII had succeeded his father in 1509, Leo X became Pope in 1513—the year in which Christian was elected to the throne of Denmark—Francis I became King of France in 1515, and Charles, soon to become Emperor, began his reign as Charles I of Spain in the year following.

The Scandinavian kingdoms, like Bohemia and Hungary, were elective monarchies, and on the death of King Hans on February 20, 1513, Christian, who had been acting as regent of Norway, became eligible for election as his father's successor. The custom was to demand from the new King, before his actual election, a charter (*Haandfaestning*), in which he should confirm the rights and privileges of the various classes of the community and give undertakings as to his future policy. Among other things, Christian promised not to interfere with a cathedral or monastic Chapter's freedom of choice in its election of a bishop or abbot; not to create new nobility from non-noble ranks, except for distinguished courage in the field; not to impose new taxes or to embark on war without consent of the Council (*Rigsraad*); and not

[1] Oman, *The Sixteenth Century*, p. 111.

[2] Brewer, *Letters and Papers of Henry VIII*, vol. iii, 1388. There are two portraits of him in existence: one painted in 1515, probably by a Netherlands artist, now in the Royal Picture Gallery, Copenhagen; the other cannot be earlier than 1521, since it depicts him wearing the Order of the Golden Fleece which he received in November 1520. It may have been painted on his visit to the Netherlands in 1521. It is now in the Brussels Museum. (See C. F. Allen, *De tre nordiske Rigers Historie*, ii, pp. 194, 538.)

to demand the recognition of an heir-presumptive in his own lifetime, unless the Council agreed. The charter concluded with the stipulation that if the King broke his agreements and refused to accept instruction from the Council, the inhabitants of the kingdom might take appropriate action without breach of their oath of fealty.[1]

It is probable that Christian never intended to observe the terms of his charter.[2] Since 1506 he had been acting for his father as regent of Norway and had gained insight into the peculiar difficulties confronting an elective monarchy with three kingdoms to rule. His own temperament and character made the restrictions involved in his charter most unwelcome: he was a passionate, sensitive, energetic, yet irresolute man, with a partiality for the middle and lower classes,[3] due perhaps to his having been brought up in the home of a Copenhagen burgher.[4] His policy may be briefly described as democratic and progressive.[5] He desired to limit the power and privileges of the nobles and higher clergy; to ease the peasantry of some of their burdens; to encourage the citizen class by educational reform and the expansion of commerce; and to accomplish these aims by breaking the power of the Rigsraad and making himself hereditary monarch of the three kingdoms.[6] No immediate difficulties to the accession of Christian presented themselves. At a joint meeting of the Danish and Norwegian Councils, at which representatives from Sweden and from the Hanse towns were present, the charter was finally agreed to on July 2; and in October he received homage from representatives of the two duchies, Slesvig and Holsten, as co-regent with his uncle, Duke Frederick. Thus Christian appeared to have attained without any serious difficulty his position as ruler of the northern kingdoms: but one outstanding question remained unsettled, his recognition as King by the Riksdag of Sweden. It was his deter-

[1] For a summary of the Haandfaestning see Paludan-Muller: *De første Konger af den Oldenborgske Slaegt*, pp. 289 ff.

[2] See C. F. Allen, *Histoire de Danemark*, i, p. 267.

[3] Arup, *Danmarks Historie*, ii, p. 542. "Christiern 2 havde uden hensyn til nationalitet eller stand taget de maend i sin tjenste, han ansaa for brugelige, og han havde fundet de bedst brugelige indenfor dansk borgerstand." ("Christian II had without regard to nationality or rank taken those men into his service whom he considered useful; and he had found the most useful men in the ranks of Danish citizens.")

[4] C. F. Allen gives a full account of Christian's boyhood and youth in his *De tre nordiske Rigers Historie*, i, pp. 223-237, and a lively portrait of his character in vol. ii, pp. 193 ff.

[5] Münter, *Den Danske Reformationshistorie*, i, pp. 232-234. He compares Christian II with the Emperor Joseph II.

[6] Helveg, *Den Danske Kirkes Historie*, iii, pp. 513, 589.

mination to win Sweden, and the violence and cruelty of the methods he employed which brought about his downfall ten years later.

2

The year after his election Christian was crowned King of Denmark at Copenhagen on June 11 and King of Norway at Oslo on July 29. Negotiations for his marriage with one of the granddaughters of the Emperor Maximilian had already been in progress, and on the day of his coronation at Copenhagen the betrothal and marriage ceremony between him and Princess Isabella took place by proxy at Brussels, Mogens Gjø, the future High Marshal of Denmark, acting for the King.[1] Owing to Isabella's youth—she was not yet fourteen—her journey to Denmark was postponed for a year. Since 1507 Christian had been living with his beautiful young mistress, Dyveke, who had come with her mother from Holland and was then residing at Bergen in Norway; on his accession Christian brought them to Denmark and established them in one of his houses. The mother, whose name was Sigbrit, was an able woman of masterful character, and Christian relied much on her help; she became, in effect, his Finance Minister, and the oppressive monetary burdens she laid on Danes of all ranks made her the best hated being in Danish history.[2] Yet her aim was to improve the position of Denmark in the north by developing commerce with her native Holland and thereby weakening the supremacy of the Hanseatic towns. In this she was supported by another of Christian's unofficial ministers, Hans Mikkelsen, formerly burgomaster of Malmø, an able and enlightened man, who became the King's confidential adviser and friend and a stalwart foe to the entrenched powers of the nobility.[3] Christian, moreover, showed his wisdom by attaching to himself the richest and most powerful of the Danish nobles, Mogens Gjø, a man of liberal views, whom he appointed in 1515 to be High Marshal of Denmark.[4]

The Princess Isabella, sister of the future Emperor, Charles V, did not arrive in Denmark till the summer of 1515. A Danish embassy, headed by Erik Valkendorf, Archbishop of Trondhjem,

[1] A full account of this ceremony and of the subsequent wedding is given by C. F. Allen, op. cit., ii, pp. 105 ff., 200 ff.

[2] Paludan-Müller, op. cit., p. 464.

[3] Particulars of Sigbrit and Hans Mikkelsen will be found in C. F. Allen, op. cit. ii, pp. 327 ff.

[4] Arup, *Danmarks Historie*, ii, p. 333.

was dispatched to the Netherlands to escort her to Copenhagen, and on August 12 she was married to Christian and crowned as Queen. Her life at first was not a happy one, for the King did not dismiss Dyveke, and Isabella felt the insult keenly. But the Dutch mistress died in 1517, and this had the effect of drawing the King closer to his consort. Sigbrit also learned to love the young Queen, an affection fully returned by Isabella, who had never known a mother's care. The strange trio, King and Queen and "Mother Sigbrit", continued happily together, and Isabella proved a faithful and affectionate wife. Three children were born of the marriage: a son, Hans, who died in 1532, and two daughters, Dorothea, who married Frederick, afterwards the Elector Palatine, and Christina,[1] who married, first, Francis II of Milan, and afterwards, Francis of Lorraine. The Queen herself accompanied Christian in his exile and became attracted to the Lutheran faith; she did not long survive the loss of her Danish home and died at Zwynaerde, near Ghent, on January 19, 1526.[2]

3

The first objective in Christian's policy was the subjugation of Sweden. In that country there were two parties: the nationalists, headed by Sten Sture, the Younger, who acted as administrator (*Rigsforstander*), and those who favoured the union with Denmark, of whom the leader was Gustav Trolle, Archbishop of Upsala.[3] These two men had only recently attained to power, Sten Sture being chosen as administrator the year before the accession of Christian II, and Trolle succeeding to the archbishopric two years later. "Thus the stage was cleared for a new company of actors, those young and sanguine ones, new to life and inclined to violent expedients; and thus the forces which had been gradually developing their strength in Sweden and Denmark came into vehement and more than usually tragic conflict. The destruction of the union [between Denmark and Sweden] and the breach with Rome were occasioned by the conduct of the new Archbishop and his allies and the hatred which they inspired."[4]

Trouble commenced soon after Trolle became Archbishop: he had hoped to be chosen administrator and he bore a bitter

[1] One of Holbein's happiest portraits is of Christina, the little widowed Duchess of Milan, now in the National Gallery, London.
[2] C. F. Allen, *Breve og Aktstykker*, p. 397.
[3] For these two men see C. F. Allen, *De tre nordiske Rigers Historie*, ii, pp. 168, 183 ff.
[4] Wordsworth, *The National Church of Sweden*, p. 163.

grudge against Sten Sture in consequence and refused to render him homage. In the autumn of 1516 the Archbishop was besieged in his castle at Staeket, near Stockholm, and refused to yield to Sture, since he relied on help coming from Christian. The latter sent a fleet the following year to harry the Swedish coast in support of Trolle and to threaten Sten's position on land; but the Danish force was defeated, and in November Sten summoned to Stockholm a Rigsmøde of all estates to which Trolle refused to submit. This recalcitrancy impelled the assembled estates to take strong measures, and it was decided to depose him from his office as Archbishop and to destroy his castle. His garrison at Staeket surrendered and he himself became a prisoner at the monastery of Vesterås. "The deposition of Gustav Trolle was a sensational measure", for "thus a formal breach was made with Rome by the civil power of Sweden a year before Luther burnt the papal bulls of indulgence at Wittenberg".[1]

At this point the Pope intervened; he approved of the sentence of excommunication which had been issued by Birgir, Archbishop of Lund, against Sten Sture for the deposition of Trolle, and called upon Christian to go to the rescue of the imprisoned Archbishop. The King was thus enabled to give his attempts at gaining the Swedish crown the character of a crusade, undertaken at the bidding of the Pope. In June 1518 a Danish force commanded personally by the King landed at Brunkebjerg and after a few weeks of fruitless campaigning was defeated at Brennkyrka; Christian was compelled by shortage of supplies to negotiate for an armistice which was to last till July 1520. Among the conditions it was agreed that hostages for Christian's security should be delivered over by Sten Sture to the King, among whom were Hemming Gad, Bishop of Linkøping, and the young Gustav Vasa; but Christian treacherously held them as prisoners and sailed away with them to Copenhagen, which he reached on October 12. This bad faith ultimately brought its own punishment, since through Gustav's absence from Stockholm at the time of the massacre in 1520 the life of the future liberator of Sweden was saved.

The situation in this year (1518) was made more intricate through the manœuvres of the legate, Arcimboldi, who had been sent by Leo X in 1514 to sell indulgences in the northern countries

[1] Wordsworth, op. cit., p. 164, and Svanström and Palmstierna, *Short History of Sweden*, p. 70.

for the rebuilding of St. Peter's, and had later received fresh instructions from the Pope to try to arrange peace between the opposed factions in Sweden. While in Copenhagen in 1517 protracted negotiations between him and the King took place, the legate endeavouring to gain permission for the sale of indulgences in Denmark, and Christian working to persuade Arcimboldi to act as his agent in the Swedish imbroglio. When King and legate had each gained, as he thought, his end, Arcimboldi proceeded to Sweden in the summer of 1518. He was received by Sten Sture with much courtesy and that able man soon won him over to his side. At a Herredag held at Arboga in December Arcimboldi, as legate, confirmed the previous sentence deposing Trolle, whereupon the latter formally resigned his archbishopric.[1] Christian's suspicions were at once aroused: he believed that the legate had been playing him false and that he had been scheming to secure the archbishopric for himself. As soon as Arcimboldi reached Lund on his way back to Denmark he was met with the news that all his goods and the money accumulated from the sale of indulgences had been seized by the King. Fearing his own life was in danger, he fled first to Lübeck and finally to Rome, where he endeavoured to put himself right with the Pope.

Meanwhile Christian was making preparations for a third attack on Sweden. In the summer of 1519 he sent his secretary, Didrik Slagheck,[2] a Westphalian priest, to Rome, with the twofold object of endeavouring to conciliate the Pope after the harsh treatment of his legate, Arcimboldi, and to persuade him to issue a bull of excommunication against Sten Sture. In this latter respect he was successful, and after the usual lengthy negotiations the bull was published by Bishop Lage Urne, of Roskilde, as papal commissary, in December 1519, on the very eve of the launching of the attack on Sweden. Christian meanwhile had been exerting himself to collect the necessary men and money. He applied for help, successfully to Francis I of France,[3] and unsuccessfully to his uncle, Duke Frederick; he had got possession of considerable sums from his seizure of Arcimboldi's booty, and he obtained, after continued demands, a part of the dowry promised on his marriage with Princess Isabella.[4] His own subjects were compelled to contribute under the varied forms of taxes, custom dues, loans and

[1] Münter, op. cit., i, p. 247.
[2] For Didrik Slagheck see Paludan-Müller, op. cit., p. 328.
[3] Brewer, *Letters and Papers*, iii, p. 1198.
[4] C. F. Allen, op. cit., iii, p. 108.

" free-will " offerings.[1] By the end of the year he had built up a considerable force which he placed under the command of Otto Krumpen and Karl Knudsen; and in the first week of January 1520, in the guise of champions of Pope and Church, and as vindicators of Christian's sovereignty, his army was ready to strike.

The advance was made into Sweden from Helsingborg, and on January 19 Otto Krumpen met and defeated the Swedish forces under Sten Sture at Lake Aasund; Sten was mortally wounded and died a few days later. His widow, Christine Gyldenstjerne, held out at Stockholm, and a force of Swedish peasants made a bold resistance at a bloody battle near Upsala; but in May the King himself arrived with his fleet before Stockholm and the city was invested by land and sea. By the end of the summer terms favourable to the Swedish nationalists were agreed to, the city surrendered, and on September 7 Christian entered the capital in triumph. Within a couple of months he had thrown away the fruits of his victory. He was crowned in Stockholm Cathedral on November 4 by Archbishop Trolle; after the coronation festivities the guests were invited on November 7 into a large room in the castle, where Trolle appeared before the King and demanded compensation for the injuries he had received at the hands of Sten Sture and his party. The next day the bishops and clergy who were present were assembled together and asked by Bishop Jens Andersen whether those who had conspired against the Church and Pope were heretics: after some hesitation they assented. Then the blow fell: the same day many of the assembled Swedish notables were hurried to their deaths, including Bishop Matthias of Strengnaes, Bishop Vincents of Skara, Erik Vasa, the father of Gustav, Erik and Eskild Gyldenstjerne, brothers of Christine, and other Swedish nobles, with members of the Stockholm Council; over ninety-four persons are said to have been slain that day. Christian continued the slaughter for some time afterwards: " more than six hundred heads had fallen before he quitted the Swedish territory, at the beginning of 1521 ".[2]

The effects of this atrocity—" the Bloodbath of Stockholm "—were lasting. Sweden never again accepted a Danish King and it led to the break of the Swedish Church with Rome. " It made the Swedes determined never to have again such a powerful Archbishop as Trolle, and, as two of the bishops had been his sup-

[1] Arup, *Danmarks Historie*, ii, p. 351.
[2] Geijer, *History of the Swedes* (Eng. trans.), p. 79.

porters, the whole order were objects of suspicion."[1] The responsibility for the crime must rest mainly on the shoulders of Christian II. Archbishop Trolle, though an accessory, does not appear to have been in full sympathy with the King's design. The actual instigator was probably Didrik Slagheck, for he seems to have suggested to the King that the Swedish insurgents could and should be treated as heretics. But it was the King who gave the order and it is upon him that the infamy of the deed rests.[2]

The reaction of the Roman Curia was characteristic. Leo X could not pass over in silence the murder of the two Swedish bishops and appointed a commissary, the Minorite, Giovanni di Potenza, to proceed to Copenhagen and to call the Danish King to account for his crime.[3] He was instructed, however, not to make things too hard for Christian, lest he should be driven farther along that road to Lutheranism which the Pope feared he had already begun to tread. A scapegoat was therefore found in Didrik Slagheck. This man, who succeeded to the murdered Bishop Vincents' see of Skara, was in conjunction with Jens Andersen (now bishop of the other vacant see of Strengnaes) left in charge of Swedish affairs on the King's departure. But Sweden was already in confusion, and Gustav Vasa had been chosen by the insurgent nobles as administrator and leader of the Swedish cause in August 1521. Slagheck, therefore, hurried back to Denmark to defend himself against charges of mismanagement, and succeeded so well that the King agreed to his appointment to the vacant archiepiscopal see of Lund. Entering with much pomp into Lund on November 25, 1521, the new Archbishop-elect soon quarrelled with Jens Andersen; fresh complaints of his conduct reached the King's ears, and on January 22, 1522, he was condemned and burnt as a heretic in the market-place at Copenhagen. The papal legate was present at the scene, and later absolved the King of his crimes. From these events neither Pope nor King emerged with credit. "If the Pope and his representative could act like that, must not the King think that everything was permitted him? However heavy a load of guilt rested on him, part of it must be placed on the Medici Pope and his counsellors. It is easy, therefore, to justify the severe judgment that Christian could never have gone to work

[1] Wordsworth, op. cit., p. 181.

[2] See Paludan-Müller, op. cit., pp. 356 ff., for a discussion of the motives prompting the Bloodbath.

[3] The Papal letter commissioning di Potenza is given in Münter, op. cit., i, p. 335.

in the way described if Leo X had fulfilled his duty of resolutely protecting the Church in the north against secular tyranny."[1]

4

In 1517 Erasmus had written to Capito: " polite letters, which were almost extinct, are now cultivated and embraced by Scots, by Danes and by Irishmen ";[2] his own writings, too, had penetrated into Denmark and found readers, especially among the higher clergy.[3] One of the most eminent of these was Christiern Pedersen, Canon of Lund, whose life and writings will be described in a later chapter.[4] Another humanist, though of lesser note, was Mathias Gabler of Stuttgart, a student at Wittenberg who had taken his bachelor's degree there in 1519. He was invited to Denmark by Christian II early in 1521 and was employed to lecture in Greek at the University of Copenhagen; he may have been the first to teach Greek in Denmark.[5] The King's flight, however, brought the arrangement to an end after a brief two years. Little more is known of him, but in a letter to Melanchthon he had spoken of Christian's regard for Luther, which had elicited from the cautious Melanchthon the remark: " That is fortunate; but I am not sure whether his favour is due to mature consideration or, like that of the populace, to a sudden fancy."[6] The only surviving trace of Gabler's activities is an epistle in Latin verse, with a few Greek words interspersed, which he composed in 1521 in praise of Christian II and which also contained laudatory references to scholars like Christiern Morsing and Paul Eliaesen.[7] Gabler was

[1] Pastor, *Geschichte de Päpste*, vol. iv, pt. 1, p. 605. " Wenn der Papst und sein Vertreter so verfuhren, musste da nicht der König denken, dass ihm alles erlaubt sei? So schwere Schuld er auch auf sich lud, einen Teil derselben trugen der Mediceer und seine Ratgeber. Es ist daher wohl das scharfe Urteil gerechtfertigt, dass Christian nie in der geschilderten Weise hätte zu Werke gehen können, wenn Leo X seine Pflicht erfüllt hätte, die Kirche im Norden gegen weltliche Willkürherrschaft entschieden zu verteidigen."

[2] P. S. Allen, *Erasmi Epistolae*, ii, p. 489. " Primum enim politiores literas pridem ad interitionem pene extinctas jamdudum et Scotti Danique et Hyberni colunt amplectunturque." To Capito, from Antwerp, February 26, 1516/17.

[3] Jørgensen, *Reformationen i Danmark*, p. 4. " Erasmus's Indflydelse naaede ogsaa til Danmark, og hans Bøger fandt Laesere navnlig blandt Domherrerne."

[4] Chapter IV.

[5] Helveg, *Den Danske Kirkes Historie*, iii, p. 546; Werlauff, *Kiøbenhavns Universitet*, p. 27.

[6] J. O. Andersen, *Overfor Kirkebruddet*, p. 103. " Det er heldigt; dog ved jeg ikke sikkert, om hans Yndest skyldes moden Overvejelse eller—som Hoben plejer—et vist Indfald." For Christian's relations with the Wittenbergers Andersen's work is specially valuable: see pp. 63-138.

[7] Andersen, op. cit., p. 108; Werlauff, op. cit., p. 67.

not the only lecturer at the University who was a foreigner: in the faculty of law was the German, Amelungus Amelungi; in medicine the Scotsman, Alexander Kinghorn; and in philosophy Thomas Skotte, a compatriot of Kinghorn's. The other leading teachers in the University were men of Danish birth: Anders Christiernsen and Paul Eliaesen in theology, Vincenz Lunge in law, and Mathias Petersen and Christiern Morsing in philosophy.[1]

The invitation to Mathias Gabler may have formed part of the King's plans for the reform of the University by obtaining from abroad a teacher in Greek. A more important and more fruitful measure was the foundation of the Carmelite College at Copenhagen[2] and the appointment of Paul Eliaesen as its first principal.[3] It was natural that the King should turn to the Carmelite Order for help in his plans, for their Provincial Prior, Dr. Anders Christiernsen, had himself been a professor in the theological faculty at the University.[4] About 1517 the Carmelites had founded a college, where young men could be educated, at Copenhagen on a piece of land belonging to the Helsingør community. In a letter dated August 3, 1517, Christian II promised the Helsingør brethren the reversion of the St. George's chapel and hospital, situated outside the northern gate of the capital. This promise was made good the following year when the King on December 8 confirmed the gift, to which, however, certain conditions were attached. Interest in learning was a characteristic of Christian II, and in his gift to the Carmelites he made the stipulation that the community should maintain at the University of Copenhagen a doctor or bachelor of theology who should there deliver theological lectures. The Provincial Chapter which met at Landskrona a few months later made arrangements for the opening of the college and appointed as its first principal Paul Eliaesen.[5] Unfortunately the arrangement scarcely lasted three years. Paul Eliaesen relates in his *Skibykrøniken* that on St. John Baptist Day 1522 he was summoned to preach before the King at the castle in Copenhagen, and that some allusion he made to the cruelty of Herod and Herodias angered the King, who suspected the preacher of hinting at Dyveke or Sigbrit. The result was that the King at once withdrew his gift of St. George's chapel and hospital, and Eliaesen had to fly to Jutland to escape the King's wrath. Thus

[1] Werlauff, op. cit., p. 27.
[2] Werlauff, op. cit., pp. 22-24.
[3] See Chapter VII.
[4] Werlauff, op. cit., p. 60.
[5] Heise, *Skibykrøniken*, p. 62.

Paul's work at the college came to an end after a brief three years; but that time had been long enough for his teaching to make its mark on the ablest of the students, some of whom rose to eminence in the reformed Church of Denmark.[1]

Christian's interest in the University is further illustrated by the regulation, which was indeed a repetition of a similar prohibition issued by his father, King Hans, in 1498, that no one should proceed to a foreign university unless he had first taken a bachelor's degree at Copenhagen: infringement of this rule entailed a fine of a hundred marks.[2] The King's encouragement of learning extended also to the patronage of men who were sympathetic with Luther. A German priest, Martin Reinhard, from the diocese of Würzburg, who had studied for a time at Wittenberg, became in December 1520 a theological student at Copenhagen, probably to take advantage of Paul Eliaesen's lectures.[3] It is thought that he came on the King's initiative; at any rate, a few months later he became a royal chaplain. A surviving document of the time indicates the duties expected of him.[4] There were to be three such chaplains: two for the King's service, one for the Queen's. They were to be learned in the New Testament and be able to preach; they must be men of good voice so that they could lead in the singing and read aloud at table at mealtimes. These provisions are in accord with the interest in the new learning which the King had shown by his foundation of the lectureship filled by Paul Eliaesen, and also with subsequent regulations which he issued with the aim of making the Danish clergy more familiar with the Scriptures. Reinhard was permitted to preach publicly in the church of St. Nicholas, Copenhagen, besides preaching to the Court, and it is possible that Queen Isabella was influenced by him, for she later became a Lutheran. The effect of his preaching may perhaps also be seen in the subsequent conversion to the new faith of such leading members of the Court circle as Mogens Gjø, the High Marshal, Hans Mikkelsen, the King's confidential friend, and Christiern Vinter, his secretary.

It has been suggested[5] that Reinhard's preaching was made ineffectual by his ignorance of Danish, a handicap which was

[1] Heise, op. cit., pp. 62-64, 117.

[2] Münter, *Kirchengeschichte von Dänemark und Norwegen*, iii, p. 61; Werlauff, op. cit., p. 28.

[3] Andersen, op. cit., p. 80.

[4] Andersen, op. cit., p. 83.

[5] By Bishop W. E. Collins in the *Cambridge Modern History*, ii, p. 606; and by Dr. J. P. Whitney in his revised (1940) *History of the Reformation*, p. 104.

partly remedied, so it has been said, by Paul Eliaesen acting as his interpreter. But it is very improbable that Eliaesen would have interpreted for a man with whose views he could have little sympathy; and in any case Reinhard's speaking in German would not have deprived him of hearers, for the active commerce then existing with German ports meant that there were sufficient people in Copenhagen who understood that tongue.[1] The chief limitation of his influence would have lain in the brevity of his stay in Denmark, for he arrived in December 1520 and was back in Germany in the following March. However, the intention was he should return to Denmark; he was sent meanwhile by the King as an envoy to the Elector of Saxony to procure the sending of Carlstadt, and if possible of Luther himself, for work at the Copenhagen University. Reinhard himself was to graduate at Wittenberg (which he had not yet done) and was then to return to Denmark for further service. These schemes were not, however, fully carried out, and there is no information that Reinhard ever visited Denmark again. On the other hand, Carlstadt accepted the King's invitation and arrived at Copenhagen at the close of May 1521. His stay, however, lasted only three weeks. With his impetuous nature and extremist outlook he had arrived with great expectations of assisting in the reform of the Danish Church: but such was not the King's design in his employment. Carlstadt soon realized that he could effect nothing radical as a reformer, and he left hurriedly, and nothing would ever persuade him to return.[2]

This was the end of Christian II's connexions with Wittenberg for the time—until two years later, when he appeared there himself in the character of an exile. Much discussion has taken place among historians of the Danish Reformation as to the significance of these invitations which were issued to German scholars and reformers, and as to their somewhat abrupt cessation. Did this mean a change in the King's attitude to the new learning? Was it evidence of inconstancy on the part of the King, or a sign of an unexpected development in the views of the reformers? It is to be noted that Christian travelled to the Netherlands in June 1521 to visit his brother-in-law, the Emperor, and perhaps to consult with him on the question of religion, for he carried with him a box full of Luther's books.[3] While at Bruges he met Cardinal Wolsey[4] and

[1] Andersen, op. cit., pp. 94, 95.
[2] Andersen, op. cit., p. 114.
[3] Andersen, op. cit., p. 135.
[4] Brewer, *Letters and Papers*, iii, 1494.

Erasmus, and the latter has referred to his conversation with the King in a letter to Archbishop Warham of August 23, 1521. "Would it were true what Christian, the victorious King of the Danes, once said to me as we talked—he meant it as a joke, I imagine—that nothing can be done with mild medicines, but it is characteristic of effective remedies that they start by shaking up the whole body."[1] This remark shows that the King's mind was occupied with the religious question, though it would be hasty to conclude from it that he was actually contemplating violent measures. The visit to the imperial Court at Brussels may not have been without its effect in deciding him not to go farther in his relations with the Wittenbergers. Luther himself was absent from Wittenberg for the period of his voluntary incarceration at the Wartburg, May 1521 to March 1522, and this was just the time when Carlstadt and the radicals were making unheard-of innovations. This may have decided the King to cease direct relations with Wittenberg and to go his own way. His own conception of reform is disclosed in the remarkable code of regulations which, if completely carried out, would have reformed the Church in discipline and worship, while leaving it Catholic in doctrine and constitution. For comprehensiveness it is perhaps unique among the legal documents of the age.

5

It is not clearly known how these laws were drawn up, or who precisely was their author; but a recent view[2] is that Hans Mikkelsen, assisted by Fru Sigbrit and Niels Lykke, one of the Rigsraad, were mainly responsible, although they could not have brought these laws into being if the King had not given his approval. The work was begun early in 1521, and the first regulations, issued on February 10, concerned the market towns; then followed, on May 26, laws affecting strand rights and wrecks, and a code of regulations for schools, now known only in an undated draft. Finally, towards the end of the year appeared the two larger codes, known as the *Landretten* and the *Byretten*, or, as they were formerly called, the *Geistlige Lov* and the *Verdslige Lov* (the ecclesiastical and civil laws). They are printed in Danish in P. H. Resen's edition of

[1] Allen, *Erasmi Epistolae*, iv, p. 568. "Atque utinam verum esset quod invictus Danorum rex Christiernus mihi simile quiddam dicenti respondit—ludens, opinor—levibus pharmacis nihil agi, sed illud esse remediorum efficacium, ut primum corpus omne concutiant."

[2] Arup, *Danmarks Historie*, ii, p. 360.

Christian II's Law Books.[1] *The Byretten* collection, dated January 6, 1522, bore considerably on the Church's life; it was issued on the King's authority, and though it claimed to have the Council's assent there is some doubt whether it had ever been referred to the Rigsraad. Among its more important provisions were the following. (*a*) The clergy are forbidden to send appeals to Rome, and a court of four doctors is to sit at Roskilde to judge all spiritual causes: the only appeal from this court is to the King and Rigsraad.[2] (*b*) The bishops' own courts are forbidden to concern themselves with any cases except those relating to matrimony and adultery: disobedience to the Church's sentence in these latter causes will involve punishment by the civil authorities.[3] (*c*) Land in the towns which is owned by churches and monasteries and not actually used by them is to be conveyed to the citizens, who shall possess them by a kind of inheritance. The possessors may sell or mortgage such property, but the rent must be secured to the ecclesiastical owners unchanged.[4] (*d*) Ecclesiastical persons, secular or regular, may not for the future buy land or receive it under testamentary disposition.[5] Bequests made in wills must take the form of actual money if bequeathed to the Church.[6] In the *Landretten* an exception to the rule against the clergy inheriting land is allowed by the provision that they may not thus inherit land " unless they will follow St. Paul's advice, given in 1 Tim. 3, and take a wife and live in holy matrimony, as their forefathers did ".[7] (*e*) Mendicancy is forbidden to the regular Orders or to monasteries with landed property, except by special permission of the King. Only the four Orders of Friars (Dominicans, Franciscans, Carmelites and Augustinians) may beg.[8] (*f*) Country clergy must not move to the towns, thereby neglecting their parish, and the obligation is to be enforced under threat of loss of office.[9] (*g*) Careful control of the property and income of parish churches is enjoined; in towns the burgomaster and council must appoint each year two new churchwardens who shall be responsible for the church accounts.[10]

In addition to these directions affecting the clergy in general the *Landretten* sets out further duties incumbent on the bishops.

[1] *Kong Christian den Andens Geistlige oc Verdslige Danske Lov-Bøger*, by P. H. Resen: Copenhagen, 1684. For an account of these regulations and a discussion of their significance see also J. O. Andersen, *Overfor Kirkebruddet*, pp. 139 ff.; H. Matzen, *Forelaesninger over den danske Retshistorie*, Inledning, pp. 251 ff.

[2] Resen, p. 65.
[3] Resen, p. 66
[4] Resen, p. 68.
[5] Resen, p. 69.
[6] Resen, p. 69.
[7] Resen, p. 6.
[8] Resen, p. 67.
[9] Resen, p. 70.
[10] Resen, p. 70.

(*a*) They must perform their ministry at all the great festivals and themselves preach, and only sickness or similar mischance may be recognized as valid excuse for absence on such occasions.[1] (*b*) They must supervise the lives of all their clergy, and punish where anything is amiss: and all monasteries and convents must submit to episcopal visitation.[2] (*c*) Their own personal appearances in public must be seemly and proper: they must not be accompanied by pipes and drums or by a large following.[3] (*d*) Deacons must not be ordained before the age of twenty-five, nor priests before the age of thirty, and no one must be ordained without a title. Ordinands must be masters or bachelors in Holy Scripture, or else give proof that they are competent to preach and to read the Service: the bishop is to refuse ordination if they do not reach that standard.[4] (*e*) The bishop must not institute to a benefice anyone who has not been ordained; and a priest must not say more than one Mass on Sundays and must preach on the Epistle or Gospel.[5] (*f*) In cathedral churches a succentor is to be appointed who shall be responsible for the music of the Services; he is to be acquainted with the new mode of music (" den nye Mensur ") and able to train the choir in it.[6]

Other provisions in these regulations relate to education. The rule that students may not proceed to a foreign university unless they have taken their bachelor's degree at Copenhagen has been already mentioned.[7] Begging for maintenance at school is absolutely forbidden: only those may attend school whose parents can provide for them. Those who wish to educate their children must send them first to the parish priest, who shall teach them the Paternoster, Ave Maria, Credo, etc., in Danish and also to read and write; they may then be sent to the town school, if their parents can afford their maintenance.[8] Since the ordering of schools comes under the care of the bishops, they are required to see that the stipends of schoolmasters are improved, and if possible to provide them with a benefice or curacy.[9]

Numerous directions also are given for the ordering of social and economic life, and among them may be noted a few regulations having a humanitarian tone in advance of the time, as, *e.g.*, the one which forbids the practice of " selling and giving away peasants and Christian souls, like irrational creatures ";[10] or the

[1] Resen, p. 1. [2] Resen, p. 1. [3] Resen, pp. 1, 2.
[4] Resen, pp. 2, 3. [5] Resen, p. 3.
[6] Resen, p. 4. On " den nye Mensur " see Andersen, op. cit., p. 191.
[7] Resen, p. 8. [8] Resen, p. 37. [9] Resen, p. 2. [10] Resen, p. 34.

provision that wrecked seafaring men were to be humanely treated;[1] or, finally, the direction to schoolmasters to "have a much greater consideration for their pupils than they have hitherto had, giving them good and blameless instruction and seeking to teach them with equal care, the poor as well as the rich".[2]

It is not surprising that one of the older historians of Denmark speaks in warm praise of these laws and of their royal author: he calls it "a noble and beneficent plan, which provides convincing proof of the uncommon intellectual powers of the King and at the same time speaks very much in favour of the purity of his intentions".[3]

Two questions naturally arise in considering the general character of these reforms: did the King intend to separate the Danish Church from Rome? Were these reforms ever really carried into effect?

The most significant step was the setting up of a court for ecclesiastical causes at Roskilde and the prohibition of appeals to Rome; but this was probably not intended as implying a complete breach with the Pope, but only as a disciplinary measure to prevent large sums of money leaving the country. There is no evidence in the laws of any departure from Catholic doctrine or of any violent alteration in the inherited constitution of the Church. The reforms were mainly in the sphere of ecclesiastical discipline; doctrine was untouched and worship only slightly affected. The King's attitude has been described as that of "pre-Lutheran Humanism".[4] This is the view taken by most Danish historians. "However much of a reformer Christian II appears in Church affairs, it was by no means his intention to break with the existing Church order, so far as it was authorized by canonical rule. He would abolish the abuse and encroachments which had crept in in the course of years, even if they had attained legal validity in royal charters; but further he would not actually go."[5] "The

[1] Resen, p. 40.

[2] Resen, p. 2.

[3] Münter, *Kirchengeschichte von Dänemark und Norwegen*, p. 41. "Ein edler und wohlthätiger Plan, der ein überzeugender Beweis von den seltenen Verstandeskräften des Königs ist und zugleich sehr zum Vortheile für die Reinheit seiner Absichten spricht."

[4] Heise, cited by Andersen, *Overfor Kirkebruddet*, p. 131.

[5] Helveg, *Den Danske Kirkes Historie* iii, p. 591. "Hvor reformatorisk end Christian II traadte op i Kirkesager, saa var det dog slet ikke hans Agt at bryde med den bestaaende Kirkeorden, forsaavidt denne var hjemlet i den kanoniske Ret. Han vilde afskaffe de Misbrug og Overgreb, der havde indsneget sig i Aarenes Løb, selv om disse havde vundet Lovskraft ved at optages i de kongelige Haandfaestninger; men videre vilde han egentlig ikke gaae."

ecclesiastical standpoint represented in the laws by no means indicates any breach with Catholic doctrine or with the Roman Church as an institution. If there is any question of ' a reforming outlook ' in the *Landretten* or of a ' Lutheran ' influence upon it, at any rate that Lutheranism is quite excluded which gives to the secular authorities a right of reform within the Church's own inner sphere, or which thinks of building the Church afresh on the foundation of the priesthood of the laity with the rejection of the rights of the hierarchy."[1] On the other hand, it has been maintained that the legislation represents an attempt at ecclesiastical independence. " The main thing, however, was that Christian here assumed supremacy in the Church whose bishops had hitherto been able to say that they had no superior over them in the land. This was the result of that movement begun by Christian I's journey to Rome and later consistently pursued with the object which the new law now presented as accomplished—viz., that supremacy in the Danish national Church should be taken from the Pope, who had arbitrarily assumed it from Denmark's own Archbishop, and should be placed in the King's hand."[2] Even so it is admitted that this was not the result of a break with Catholic doctrine.

In regard to the question whether Christian's reforms actually took effect, it has been flatly asserted that " Christian's new code never came into operation ".[3] But a letter of Bishop Lage Urne, dated February 6, 1522, provides evidence that the laws did have some effect; for it speaks of a serious rising among the peasants of Zealand occasioned by the democratic principles of the new legislation.[4] If its effect on the peasants was some evidence that the laws actually were for a time in force, so also was the anger which their promulgation stirred up among the privileged classes. It

[1] Andersen, *Overfor Kirkebruddet*, p. 163. " Det kirkelige Standpunkt, som lovene repraesenterer, paa ingen Maade betegner noget Brud med katolsk Laere eller med Romerkirken som Institution. Naar der er blevet talt om ' reformatorisk Opfattelse ' i Landretten eller om ' luthersk ' Indvirkning paa den, er i hvert Fald den Lutherdom ganske udelukket, der tilkender verdslig Øvrighed en Reformationsret paa de indre kirkelige Omraader, eller som taenker paa at nybygge Kirken paa det almindelige Praestedømmes Grundlag med Forkastelse af Hierarkiets Ret. "

[2] Paludan-Müller, *De Første Konger af den Oldenborgske Slaegt*, p. 392. " Men Hovedsagen er dog, at Kong Christien her tiltager sig Herredømmet i den Kirke, hvis Biskopper hidtil kunde sige, at deres Dommer ikke fandtes i Riget. Det er Resultatet af den Bevaegelse, der forberedtes ved Kong Christiern den Førstes Romerreise, og som siden i stadig Fremgang har peget mod det Maal, denne Landslov nu fremstillede som naaet: Suprematet i den danske Nationalkirke skulde herefter tages fra Paven, der egenmaegtigen havde taget det fra Landets egen Aerkebiskop, og laegges i Kongens Haand."

[3] *Camb. Mod. Hist.*, ii, p. 607.

[4] Helveg, op. cit., iii, p. 610.

has been held[1] that it was the new legislation of Christian, even more than his treacherous and savage conduct in Sweden, which raised up the opposition against him among the nobles and their adherents, and which soon brought about his downfall. When Christian had fled, on the day the new King was receiving the homage of the nobles, they burned the hated code.[2]

The legislation which thus appeared to end in fire and smoke was in reality prophetic of reforms which later Danish history was to achieve. "As Christian II's reign, regarded simply from the point of view of chronology, is the central point in the eight hundred years' history of Denmark, so Hans Mikkelsen's citizen government is also the central point in the Danish people's political development. Its ideas came again victoriously to the fore in 1536, in 1660, in 1788, in 1848—yes, even in 1919. Anyone who considers the political evolution of the Danes must recognize that an essential feature of it is the constant emphasis on equality. . . . The Danish people belong to one of that small class of nations in the world in which the outward conditions have formed a definite desire that equality of citizenship should be the fixed foundation of society. To this Hans Mikkelsen's citizen rule contributed in the highest measure. . . . It had raised the Danish citizen to a state of equality of rights with the Danish nobleman: it had checked the Danish peasants' gloomy progress towards serfdom.

Styge Krumpen and Jørgen Friis, Predbjørn Podebusk and Tyge Krabbe might rejoice to see the flames consuming the condemned law books: but their deed was ineffectual, for the law which proclaimed equality and human worth remained written in the Danish people's hearts."[3]

6

The troubles of Christian II's reign were now coming to a head. Sweden had thrown off his rule and Gustav Vasa had become the acknowledged leader of the Swedes in their struggle for indepen-

[1] By Helveg, op. cit., iii, p. 611.

[2] Arup, *Danmarks Historie*, ii, p. 395.

[3] Arup, op. cit., ii, p. 396. See also C. F. Allen, *De tre nordiske Rigers Historie*. "Den Fordommelsesdom, som hans seirende Fjender faeldede over disse Love, formaaede ikke at berøve dem deres virkning; imod hine Modstanderes Villie, og uden at de selv ret vidste af det, traengte deres Inflydelse i mange Punkter igjennen i den følgende Tid, fordi de svarede til Samfundets Tarv og Trang og vare grundede i Fornuft og Retfaerdighed" (III, ii, p. 4). "Som vi have antydet fik Christiern den Anden Opreisning af den følgende Tid, som godkjendte og optog mange af hans Lovbud. For nogles Vedkommende skete det rigtignok kun altfor seent. Hans Villie med Hensyn til Bondens personlige Frihed maatte vente paa sin Fuldbyrdelse indtil 1788" (III, iii p. 31).

dence. Gustav received help from Lübeck and the Hanseatic towns, which had been antagonized by Christian's policy of raising the Sound tolls and his violation of the privileges of the Hansa. The relations between Christian and his uncle, Duke Frederick, never very cordial, had become strained after Christian had obtained investiture of the duchy of Holsten directly from the Emperor on his visit to the Netherlands, and as this was done without Frederick's knowledge or consent he felt personally affronted.[1] The heavy taxes Christian had been forced to impose and the loans he had raised had roused widespread discontent at home. He had angered the nobles by his concessions to the peasants and alienated the bishops by his encouragement of the Wittenberg scholars. His only supporters were members of the citizen and peasant classes and they could not give him much help. By the end of 1522 the discontent began to harden into conspiracy: Jutland, as the part of the kingdom farthest from the capital and the nearest to the territory of Duke Frederick, was the scene of action. On December 21 some eighteen of the leading nobility of Jutland, including the Bishops of Børglum, Viborg, Aarhus and Ribe, together with Mogens Gjø, Erik Banner, Tyge Krabbe, Mogens Munk and other prominent nobles, met at Viborg and entered into negotiations with Frederick, whom they desired to come to their help. Urged by his two chief counsellors, Wulfgang von Utenhof and Johann Rantzau, he agreed to do so, concluded an agreement with Lübeck and, marching into Jutland, he received homage at Viborg on March 26 at a gathering of the estates of Jutland, the nobles, the representatives of the towns and two peasants from each district (*Herred*).[2] Meanwhile Christian was endeavouring to rally forces to his side, but, while hesitating whether to attack the rebels or not, the defection of the most notable of the bishops, Lage Urne of Roskilde,[3] and the news he received of the alliance Frederick had made with Lübeck decided him to leave the country for a time. With his wife and three children and a few friends, including Hans Mikkelsen and Fru Sigbrit, he went on board on April 13 and sailed for the Netherlands. It is unlikely that he visualized his exile as permanent: he believed he had powerful friends abroad; his brother-in-law, the Emperor, would be on his side; his withdrawal from Denmark was necessary for the moment,

[1] Paludan-Müller, op. cit., p. 403. The Duke of Holsten was a Prince of the Empire; see Steinberg, *Short History of Germany*, p. 73.
[2] Arup, op. cit., pp. 385 ff.
[3] For Lage Urne see C. F. Allen, *De tre nordiske Rigers Historie*, ii, pp. 251-253.

but soon he would return with an army, and when he had recovered his kingdom he would make the crown hereditary and so liberate himself and his successors from the power of the nobility.

Such seems to have been his plan, and during the nine years of his exile he plotted and schemed to regain his throne. He lived mostly in the Netherlands, under the suspicious eye of the Regentess Margaret, the Emperor's aunt; sometimes in Germany, in the territory of his uncle, the Elector Frederick of Saxony; and once he visited England, where he and his Queen were for a few days welcomed and feasted at Greenwich.[1] At length in November 1531 he landed near Arendal in Norway with a small force, endeavoured to come to an understanding with Frederick I, was tricked into yielding himself up by the King's agent, Knud Gyldenstjerne, and then made a close prisoner in the castle of Sønderborg. In 1549 he was removed to the castle of Kalundborg, where he was better treated; and here he remained till 1559, when death at length released him.

7

Of the need of reform in the Church there can be no doubt in the minds of those who know the state of Christendom in the early sixteenth century, and Denmark was no exception. Good contemporary evidence is provided by the writings of Paul Eliaesen, who, though he had a keen eye for the faults of the Church, was a sincere Catholic and a patriotic Dane. A few extracts from his *Svar paa Kong Gustavs Spørgsmaal* ("Answer to King Gustav's Questions") will give his views on the darker side of contemporary church life. "Some of the Church's prelates have indeed used their riches sinfully, and for the most part they have been those who have been brought in and intruded into the benefices and sees of the Church by secular power. . . . Since Princes have thus advanced their friends and servants whom they had long employed on affairs of ambition and evil-doing, the property and wealth of the Church have been used ill; because neither the wise nor the good have attained to the Church's high offices, but rather those who are the Princes' flatterers and creatures."[2] "I will not

[1] Brewer, *Letters and Papers*, iii, 3153.

[2] C. G. Secher, *Povel Eliesens Danske Skrifter*. "Nogre kirckens Prelater haffue syndelige brughet rigdom, tha er thet mest giort aff thenom som werdslig magt haffuer weldelige trengdt oc indsaet wdi kirckins laen oc prelatedømme. Men siden at Fursterne framdroge sijne wenner oc tienere, ther the haffde lenge brughet wdi homodt oc møghen syndig handell, tha bleff rigdom och gotz ijlde brughet wdi then hellige kircke, fordi ther komme tha huerckin the wijse eller the gode til kirckins prelatedømme, men the mendt allersnarisk som mest hengde hooss Fursterne oc wore thenom till sinde oc metfeldige" (p. 199).

defend the negligence of some bishops. God gives them the wisdom and grace to enable them to preach His Word and nourish therewith the common people who now, by reason of these melancholy and sceptical times, are so detached from the Christian faith."[1] From the books of his favourite St. Bridget it is evident, he declares, that " God sorely punishes the avarice, pride and unchastity which now unfortunately exist among many of the clergy ".[2] " We see now, and ought to see it with tears, how shameless is the present unchastity, since the Church's ban has neither respect nor power, and is neither loved nor feared; we see how many poor maidens are dishonoured by abandoned and perjured priests, monks and other evil-living Christians. And this happens for the most part because the bishops may not now use their ancient authority which they have by God's law."[3]

The root cause of this unsatisfactory state of the Church was its great wealth; a large proportion of the land of Denmark was in ecclesiastical hands, and was thus exempt from taxation. The bishops were feudal magnates, with their own castles and retainers,[4] and lacking, for the most part, a sense of spiritual vocation; they were thus unable or unwilling to correct what was amiss in the lower ranks of the clergy. Christian II's ecclesiastical legislation was both evidence of the need of reform and a gallant attempt at bringing it about. But the King's attitude to the Church was inconsistent: while appearing to desire its welfare, his dealings with individual bishops were arbitrary and tyrannical. Apart from the murder of the two Swedish bishops in the Stockholm Bloodbath, he twice imprisoned and seized the goods of Jens Andersen, Bishop of Odense; he plundered the see of Trondhjem while the Archbishop, Erik Valkendorf, was absent in Rome seeking protection from the Pope against Christian's demands; his creature, Didrik Slagheck, soon after becoming Archbishop of Lund, was

[1] " Thette er tha icke sagt wdi saadan mening, at ieg wil forantworde nogre bispers orsømmilse, Gudt giffue thenom alle then wiisdom oc naade, at the kwnne selffue tractere Gudtz ordt oc ther met spijse then menige cristhen mandt som nw henger saare løslige hooss then cristhen troo for then mistrøst oc twijlsmaal the ere nw bestedde vdi " (p. 203).

[2] " Gudt hardelige straffer then gerighedt, homodt oc wkyskhedt som nw (dess waer) brugis hooss mange aff klerckeriidt " (p. 231).

[3] " Wij thet nw see oc thet burde att sees mett graedindis øghen, huore wbluelige hoor thet nw brugis sidhen att kirckins bandt haffuer huerkin agt eller magt, nar thet nw huerckin elskis eller raedis, oc huore manghen fattig pijge ther nw forgeffnis beliggis aff forløben oc forsoorin skalke, prester oc mwncke oc andre onde Cristen. Oc helst fordi at prelaterne maa icke nw bruge theris gamble ret som the haffue aff Gudz low " (p. 239).

[4] H. Matzen, *Forelaesninger over den danske Retshistorie*, i, p. 43.

burnt at the stake; while his treatment of the archiepiscopal see of Lund illustrates the flagrant methods employed in filling such high offices. On the death of Archbishop Birgir, December 10, 1519, the Chapter immediately chose their dean, Aage Sparre, as his successor, but under pressure from the King they afterwards cancelled this and elected instead the royal secretary, Jørgen Skodborg, Archdeacon of Aarhus. Leo X, however, promised the see to one of his favourites, Cardinal Paolo de Ceci, and placed it under his administration. When Skodborg and the Chapter refused to cede to the Crown the island of Bornholm and two manors in Skaane belonging to the see, Christian in revenge gave the archbishopric to the infamous Didrik Slagheck, who had perhaps been the instigator of the Stockholm Bloodbath. Slagheck, however, hardly held the office for two months, and was ignominiously and brutally put to death on January 24, 1522.[1] On this de Ceci again demanded the see, but Christian insisted on the appointment of his German secretary, Johann von Weze, who was consecrated February 23, 1522. His tenure was, however, very brief, for he left Denmark with the King in April 1523. Meanwhile, von Weze, Skodborg and Cardinal de Ceci carried on their own negotiations in person at Rome, working one against the other; but the first claimant to the see, Aage Sparre, was recognized as Archbishop by the new King, Frederick I, on the understanding he did not seek confirmation from Rome.[2] Christian II was responsible for some of these discreditable appointments, but the action of the Pope in nominating by provision an Italian cardinal to the wealthiest and most powerful post in the Scandinavian kingdoms caused great offence, and warrants the opinion that "this daring act of Leo's, more than anything else, caused the eventual loss of Denmark to the Papacy".[3]

8

In strong contrast with his dealings with the bishops while he was in power in Denmark was Christian's behaviour towards Lutheranism during his exile. It may be that misfortune and sorrow had softened his heart, and his conduct certainly appeared

[1] Paludan-Müller, op. cit., p. 405.

[2] Von Weze entered the service of Charles V and died as Bishop of Constance in 1548. Skodborg lived to see the archbishopric again vacant on the resignation of Aage Sparre in 1532, and died as bishop suffragan to the famous Hermann, Archbishop of Cologne, in 1551. See Jørgensen, *Reformationen i Denmark*, p. 52; and Münter, *Kirckengeschichte von Dänemark und Norwegen*, pp. 117 ff.

[3] A. J. Mason in *Church Quarterly Review*, April 1891, p. 156.

to show attachment to the new faith.[1] He arrived in Saxony in October 1523 to visit the Elector, and during his stay of a year the King and his Danish following came into touch with the leaders of the German Reformation. For a few months he resided at Wittenberg with the painter Lukas Cranach.[2] Christian heard Luther preach[3] and was deeply impressed; later Queen Isabella arrived, and she and the King were drawn closer to the new movement. In 1524 the Queen went to Nuremberg and there, at the King's desire, she received the Communion, in the evangelical manner, in both kinds.[4] While in Wittenberg Christian determined to have the New Testament translated into Danish, after the example of Luther's German translation which had been published in 1522. His motives were probably both religious and patriotic. He had sufficiently adopted the reformed outlook to desire the Scriptures to be obtainable in the language of his people; and, with all his faults, he was a patriotic Dane, who throughout his life preferred to speak Danish rather than Latin or German.[5] He therefore commissioned his loyal follower, Hans Mikkelsen, who had become a sincere adherent of Luther, to undertake the task—an unsuitable appointment, since Mikkelsen, though a capable lawyer and financier, was no scholar. He translated, however, St. Paul's Epistles from Luther's German version, and then handed over the rest of the New Testament for Christiern Vinter to complete. The latter was a scholarly humanist and used Erasmus' Latin version as his basis.[6] The work was completed in August 1524, the volumes being sent to Antwerp for trans-shipment to Denmark. In thus encouraging the production of a Danish New Testament Christian was acting in conformity with his character as a patron of sacred learning: his interest in scholarship had already been shown by his support of Christiern Pedersen and Paul Eliaesen and by the educational requirements of his laws. Though interested in Luther and the new movement, and willing also to promote the reading of the Bible, it cannot be said that during his reign in Denmark he supported the Lutheran cause.[7] The reforms he desired lay in the sphere, not of doctrine, but of the moral and intellectual life of the clergy. It was not Lutheranism

[1] Münter, op. cit., iii, p. 84.
[2] Brandt, *Om Lunde-Kanniken Christiern Pedersen*, p. 169.
[3] *Luthers Werke* (Weimar) xv, p. 466.
[4] Allen, *Breve og Aktstykker*, pp. 173, 179.
[5] Allen, *De tre nordiske Rigers Historie* III, ii, p. 39.
[6] Allen, *De tre nordiske Rigers Historie*, iv, p. 459.
[7] L. P. Fabricius, *Danmarks Kirkehistorie*, ii, p. 69.

as a spiritual movement which attracted him, but rather the type of reform for which the great name of Erasmus stood. As it has been said of Henry VIII, with whom Christian had some points of resemblance, that for all his opportunism in religion " he never went back from " the point " which had been gained: he never closed the open Bible ":[1] so it might be said of Christian II that both in his regnal years and in his early years of exile he sought—along with the recovery of his kingdom—the advancement of Christian learning. The Reformation made little progress in Denmark in his days, but at least the new learning gained an entrance.

[1] H. Gee, *The Reformation Period*, p. 129.

CHAPTER II

FREDERICK I, 1523-1533

1

CONSIDERABLE light is thrown on the situation in Denmark during the first months after Christian's flight by a letter of Paul Eliaesen which fortunately survives, written September 30, 1523.[1] It was addressed to a friend, Hans Lavridsen, Canon of Roskilde, and contains such frank speaking that at the conclusion Paul says he knows he can rely on his friend's honour, if he has written indiscreetly; for he discloses, not only the state of unrest that followed Christian's exile, but the reasons for it—viz., the selfish and tyrannical behaviour of the nobility, on which Paul speaks plainly. After saying that the change on the throne had not turned out as he had hoped, and that there was more unrest in the country than ever, he went on: "The people now speak with far greater temerity of the bishops and nobles of the whole kingdom than they have ever done of King Christian, who, to his own great shame, was expelled because of his evil rule. There are even those who think that Christian was only driven out in order that those in power might be able to pursue their own private interests. . . . There are, besides, many who think that it would have been better to endure the tyranny of one rather than of many. The avarice of one man is not difficult to content, but to satisfy the insatiable desires of a number is an impossibility. . . . The majority now long with greater ardour for King Christian's return than they formerly wished for his departure."[2]

The effect of Christian's exile outside Denmark was considerable. That a King should thus easily lose his throne shocked even hardened politicians like Henry VIII and Wolsey;[3] it was a blow both to the prestige and to the influence of the Emperor; and it may

[1] Heise, *Skibykrøniken*, pp. 191 ff.

[2] Heise, op. cit., p. 193. "Almuen taler nu med langt større Dritighed om hele Rigets Praelater og Adel, end den nogensinde har gjort om Kong Kristiern, der for sin slette Regerings Skyld blev fordreven til saa stor Skam for sig selv. Ja der er endogsaa dem, som mene, at Kong Kristiern kun blev fordreven, for at de store kunde sørge for deres egne private Fordele. . . . Der er fremdeles mange, som mene, at det havde vaeret bedre at finde sig i eens Tyranni end i saa manges. Eens Gerrighed er det ikke vanskeligt at maette, men at tilfredsstille manges umaettelige Begaerlighed er en Umulighed. . . . De fleste attraa derfor ogsaa nu Kong Kristierns Ankomst med større Iver, end de før ønkede hans Bortgang."

[3] Brewer, *Letters and Papers*, iii, 3153, 3155.

be presumed to have been most unwelcome to Christian's two other powerful relations, his uncle, Frederick, the Elector of Saxony, and his brother-in-law, Joachim, the Elector of Brandenburg.[1] The general effect was to draw the northern powers closer together and to isolate them from the rest of Europe. Gustav Vasa had gained Sweden by the expulsion of Christian II; Holsten and Slesvig, Lübeck and the Hanse towns had supported Frederick in his seizure of the Danish crown; it was, therefore, to their common interest to keep together and to uphold the new King of Denmark in the face of possible threats from the Emperor, from north Germany, or from Christian II.

The character of the new King was indeed in striking contrast with that of his brilliant, violent and ill-fated nephew. The latter, by his position as brother-in-law of the Emperor and in his rôle as a progressive Renaissance Prince, possessed a standing among contemporary monarchs which Frederick could not equal. The uncle resembled rather his nearest neighbours, the north German Princes. In temperament quiet and reserved, he had a good brain for the work of kingship, a keen eye for what was politic, and a nature thrifty to the point of parsimony. If Christian possessed some of the marked characteristics of Henry VIII, Frederick was not unlike the first Tudor. Since coming of age he had ruled Slesvig and Holsten in conjunction with his brother, King Hans, and on the death of the latter he had shown prudence and restraint in not challenging the election of his nephew to the throne of Denmark. Some of the Jutland nobles, headed by Neils Stygge, Bishop of Børglum, Iver Munk, Bishop of Ribe, and Predbjørn Podebusk, a member of the Rigsraad, made a tentative offer of the crown to Frederick, but he had a better appreciation of the real situation than these discontented councillors and refused the offer.[2] When he did finally attain the crown at the age of fifty-two he naturally relied mostly on his Holsten counsellors, and the prominence of Holsteners in his reign became a source of grievance to the Danes. Two of the most eminent of his advisers were Johan Rantzau,[3] a distinguished general, whose aim was to unite Holsten and Slesvig, Denmark and Norway under the rule of

[1] Christian's father, King Hans, had married Christina, sister of Frederick the Wise, of Saxony; and his sister, Isabella, had married Joachim I, of Brandenburg. See Appendix I.

[2] C. F. Allen, *De tre nordiske Rigers Historie*, ii, p. 16.

[3] Paludan-Müller, *De første Konger af den Oldenborgske Slaegt*, pp. 466, 467; C. F. Allen, op. cit., v, pp. 44-48.

Frederick; and Wulfgang von Utenhof,[1] who, after acting as tutor to Frederick's eldest son, Christian, became chancellor of the Danish kingdom, and held that post for twenty-four years.

Frederick's position as the elected successor to a deposed King was thus far from strong: it was not he but the insurgent nobles and bishops who had won the victory;[2] it was they consequently who were in a position to dictate terms. The King's election charter (*Haandfaestning*) was agreed to at an assembly of notables held at Roskilde on August 3, 1523. Not only was the assent of the Rigsraad declared to be necessary in all the usual business of government, but the 75th article enjoined that even the *Haandfaestning* itself might be amended by the Rigsraad with the King's consent, but not by the King with the Rigsraad's consent—an unprecedented addition to the power of the Council.[3] Christian's attempt at ecclesiastical reform embodied in his new laws was abandoned and the code itself declared to be null and void, and strict provisions were laid down to prevent the further infiltration of Lutheranism. The King was compelled to promise, among other things, (*a*) not to allow heretics to preach or teach openly or secretly within the kingdom; (*b*) not to nominate foreigners to Danish sees, except with the Council's consent; (*c*) not to permit cases to be sent to Rome unless they had been first dealt with by the Danish bishops. According to one recent interpretation, these provisions constituted an attempt to establish a Danish national Church. " The ecclesiastical constitution which was in the minds of the Danish bishops was, by these regulations, the formation of a national Church, with Roman Catholic doctrine, but independent of the Pope. These were the ideas of the great Church Councils of the fifteenth century still showing themselves to be alive."[4] It may be added that they were for a time the ideas of Henry VIII, with the proviso that in his case the royal Headship was to crown the edifice of this non-Papal Catholicism. But no more in Denmark than in England was this attempt at a national Catholicism to succeed: Frederick's reign saw the gradual spread of Lutheranism; its victory was assured when Frederick was succeeded by Christian III, his Lutheran son. The bishops' conception of a Danish national

[1] Heise, *Wulfgang von Utenhof* in *Historisk Tidsskrift*, 4 R. 6 B., pp. 163 ff.

[2] Paludan-Müller, op. cit., p. 471.

[3] Paludan-Müller, op. cit., p. 472.

[4] G. Jørgensen, *Reformationen i Danmark*, p. 32. " Den Kirkeordning, so foresvaevede de danske Biskopper, var efter disse Bestemmelser at dømme en national Kirke med romersk-katolsk Laere, men frit stillet till Paven. Det var Tankerne fra de store Kirkemøder i det 15. Aarhundrede derstadig gjorde sig gaeldende."

Church, independent of Papal control and free from Lutheranism, thus proved illusory; their plans were wrecked by the inflowing tide of Lutheran ideas and by the opposition of some of the nobles and citizens, who were covetous of the Church's wealth and critical of its system.[1] Lacking the support of the Pope, the bishops failed also to win the united aid of the Crown and nobility. The ten years of Frederick's reign depict the process by which this occurred.

2

On August 7, 1524, Frederick was crowned in Copenhagen as King of Denmark. The ceremony was performed by Gustav Trolle, the former Archbishop of Upsala, the only Archbishop available, for the see of Lund was still vacant. In the same month the Norwegian Rigsraad elected Frederick to the throne of Norway, but stipulated that their country should stand on an equal footing with Denmark as an elective monarchy. Frederick was not crowned as King of Norway nor did he ever visit it. While preparations for the coronation were going forward in Copenhagen, Frederick demanded an extraordinary levy of 100,000 gylden with which to pay his mercenaries; as he would not lessen his demand and refused to be crowned till it was granted, the assembled Herredag was compelled to yield. But the occasion was used by the bishops to extract from the King and Rigsraad a fresh undertaking to resist the encroachments of Lutheranism, and they specified in particular the need to take action against " the thousands of books in Danish full of Luther's heresy which King Christian has caused to be printed for the destruction of the Christian faith in Denmark."[2] They were probably referring to the Danish *New Testament* which was completed in August, and rumours of which may have already reached their ears. Having obtained fresh assurances, the bishops agreed to contribute a fourth part of their episcopal incomes as their share of the general levy and the King was thus enabled to get the sum he had demanded.

The Lutheranism which the higher clergy and many of the nobility feared was not only the spiritual movement so called, but also the movement among the peasants for better conditions of life which was a characteristic of the time: for over most of Europe de-

[1] Münter, *Kirchengeschichte von Danemark und Norwegen*, p. 147. " Die Reformation selbst, so weit sie unter seiner Regierung fortschritt, war nicht sowohl sein Werk, als das Werk der Nation, besonders des Adels und der Burger in den grosseren Stadten."

[2] Helveg, *Den Danske Kirkes Historie*, iii, p. 641.

mands for religious and for economic reform were rising and mingling together. In Denmark, as elsewhere, the peasants laboured under irritating restrictions, such, *e.g.*, as being compelled to sell their produce to their master at his own price; and the feudal rights of the lords over woods and fisheries were resented as an unjust exclusion of the common man from the chance of game and extra food. Combined with these grievances was the discontent aroused by the compulsory payments to the clergy, not so much the tithes, which were regarded as warranted by Scripture, as the extra contributions in kind demanded on special occasions, which were felt to be troublesome and unwarranted exactions. In addition, there was widespread dissatisfaction with the state of the clergy, who too often were ignorant and unequal to their duties.[1] At length, while the Peasants' War in Germany was at its height, the unrest among the depressed classes in Denmark culminated in a rising which broke out early in 1525 in the province of Skaane—*i.e.*, the southernmost portion of what is now Sweden, a province which then belonged to Denmark. The rising was supported by one of the most prominent of Christian's adherents, the sea-captain Søren Norby, but was crushed by Frederick's general, Johan Rantzau, at a battle in which thousands of the peasants are said to have been slain.[2] In July a Herredag was held at Copenhagen to bring about peace and order after this popular rising, but some of the nobility seized the occasion to demand from the bishops concessions which they could hardly be expected to grant.[3] One concerned the purchase of land by the bishops and higher clergy: where this had occurred in the case of clerics not of noble birth who had sold it subsequently to citizens or peasants, the demand was that such land should be restored to the nobility. Another demand was still less likely to meet with acceptance: it was that the bishops should surrender their disciplinary authority over the peasants and retainers of the nobles and allow the nobles themselves to exercise such authority over their own servants. These demands were rejected at the time, but they were renewed on subsequent occasions and were significant of the growing dissatisfaction with the system of the Church among a section of the nobility.

The King's attitude to religion had, up to the time of his accession, been that of a conventionally Catholic Prince, and for the first two years of his reign his religious policy was one of caution

[1] Helveg, op. cit., p. 656.
[2] Jørgensen, op. cit., p. 35.
[3] Helveg, op. cit., p. 662

and reserve. The first open sign of an impending change was the betrothal, in February 1526, of his daughter, Dorothea, to Albert, Duke of Prussia. The latter's position as head of the Teutonic Knights and his renunciation of Catholicism the previous year made this alliance a significant one, and it was rendered more so by the fact that just previously the King's eldest son, Duke Christian, had married Dorothea, the daughter of the Lutheran Duke Magnus of Saxony-Lauenberg. Christian made no secret of his convictions and encouraged the spread of Lutheranism in southern Jutland, where he resided. In June the King himself took the decided step of breaking with the Catholic rule of fasting, in which he was followed by Mogens Gjø, now the High Steward of Denmark, and others of the royal circle. In the same month Paul Eliaesen was summoned to preach before the Court in Copenhagen Castle in order that the King might learn his views on the new doctrines. According to his own account he " freely but temperately spoke his opinion of Lutheranism and unreservedly admitted that neither of the two parties possessed true moderation, and consequently one side ought not to be called to account for its faults without the same happening to the other ".[1] Such an attempt at a middle course met with no success, for not only did Paul get abuse and mockery from the soldiery and by-standers as he left the castle, but he had shown himself to be not the man the King needed in his further contemplated changes. Within a short while that man had been found in Hans Tausen, " the Danish Luther."[2]

3

The new ideas on religious and social reform gradually percolated from Germany into Denmark through the activities of trade and commerce, the medium of books, the intercourse of students at the universities. It is not possible to fix a precise date for the first entry of such Lutheran influences into Denmark, but it is less difficult to locate the district where such influences began actually to prevail. " Among the towns of Denmark it was not particularly the cathedral cities which became the starting-point of the Reformation movement. The many Catholic clergy, especially those on the cathedral chapters, were in a position to

[1] Heise, *Skibykrøniken*, p. 116. " Povl frit, men dog maadeholdent, havde sagt sin Mening om Lutheriet, idet han uforbeholdent tilstod, at intet af de to Partier besad det rette Maadehold, og at saaledes den ene Part ikke burde kaldes til Regnskab for sine Fejl, uden at det samme skete med den anden."

[2] See Chapter V.

offer some resistance, and this was the case with some of the bishops. Viborg formed an exception, for right from the beginning it became a focal point of the Reformation in Jutland. On the Viborg Chapter, which then consisted of three 'prelates' and twelve canons, were several adherents of King Christian, and some of them soon took the side of the Reformation."[1]

It was at Viborg that Hans Tausen began his labours as a reformer. He was born in Fünen in 1494, became a monk of the Order of St. John in their wealthy house at Antvorskov, and from there was sent to study for five years (1516-21) at the University of Rostock. This was followed by a period of residence first at the University of Copenhagen and then at Wittenberg, where he was won over to the Lutheran faith. His superiors then sent him to their house at Viborg, in the belief, probably, that the Prior, Peder Jensen, a man of learning, would be a wholesome influence with Tausen in the direction of orthodoxy. When Tausen came to Viborg in 1525 he was allowed to preach in the monastery church and visitors from the town came to hear him. These increased in numbers, and in the following year he appealed for protection to the citizens, as his residence at the monastery, he declared, was no longer safe. The burgomaster and citizens obtained from the King (October 23, 1526) a letter of protection on Tausen's behalf, and the King made him his chaplain with instructions to continue to preach at Viborg.[2] For a time he was allowed the use of the small church of St. John's, but when the accommodation here became insufficient he preached out of doors, until one day his hearers made a forcible entrance into the large church of the Greyfriars, and here he continued to preach to large congregations.[3]

While thus engaged Tausen obtained an assistant in Jørgen Sadolin, who subsequently became the first Lutheran bishop in Fünen.[4] Born in 1499, he had studied for three years (1521-23) at Wittenberg, and soon after his arrival at Viborg a royal letter of protection was obtained for him, permitting him to open there a school for students who were unable to go to the University.[5]

[1] Jørgensen, op. cit., p. 78. " Blandt de danske Købstaeder var det ikke saerlig Stiftsbyerne, der blev Udgangspunkter for Reformationsrøret. De mange katolske Gejstlige, navnlig i Domkapitlerne, var her i Stand til at gøre nogen Modstand, og det samme var Tilfaeldet med nogle af Biskopperne. En Undtagelse dannede Viborg, der lige fra Begyndelsen af blev Braendpunket for Reformationen i Jylland. I Viborg Domkapitel, der paa denne Tid bestod af 3 Praelater og 12 Kanniker, fandtes flere af Kong Christierns Tilhaengere, og nogle af dem sluttede sig snart till Reformationen."

[2] Heise, *Diplomatarium Vibergense, Breve og Aktstykker*, p. 161.

[3] Karup, *Geschichte der katholischen Kirche in Dänemark*, Appendix ,p. 9.

[4] Heise, *Skibykrøniken*, p. 112.

[5] Münter, op. cit., p. 172; Werlauff *Kiøbenhavns Universtet*, p. 31.

Among other steps taken for spreading the new doctrines was the setting up of a printing-press in Viborg in 1528, which was at once put to use by the reformers.[1] For a time Tausen held an afternoon service in the Greyfriars' church, while the Mass and the old services continued as before.[2] The conjunction of the old and the new worship in the same building was a compromise continually threatened by the violent of both parties, but the situation was eased by the fact that Tausen was conservative in his attitude to the old ceremonies. Though he celebrated the Lord's Supper in the evangelical manner, he nevertheless retained the vestments, lights and the elevation of the Elements. His one great desire was that the pure Word of God should be preached, he cared not by whom.[3]

Somewhat similar occurrences were taking place at Malmø, an important town on the Sound, opposite Copenhagen. Here also a printing press was set up by the Swedish priest, Oluf Ulriksen,[4] and here the new movement had the support of the burgomaster, Jørgen Kock, who encouraged Klavs Mortensen to commence his ministry at Malmø. Mortensen,[5] born *c.* 1500, was a native of the town, who, though a poor man's son, had been educated at the University of Copenhagen and ordained to the priesthood. While in Copenhagen he used to preach in the church of Our Lady, and his sermons had such a Lutheran cast that Bishop Lage Urne forbade him to preach in the diocese. He then returned to Malmø and with the burgomaster's support began his ministry in a small, disused chapel outside the town; from there he removed to a small church within the city which had formerly belonged to the Greyfriars. His hearers increased, and it was not long before he was celebrating the Lord's Supper in the Lutheran manner and using Danish hymns in the services.[6] When the congregations grew too large for the small building an arrangement was made with the rector of the parish church of St. Peter's for Mortensen to have the use of the church for an afternoon service. The arrangement did not last long, for Archbishop Aage Sparre raised objection to the use of the parish church in this manner, and Mortensen consequently withdrew for a time to Haderslev. In August 1528, how-

[1] Helveg, op. cit., p. 770.
[2] Karup, op. cit., Appendix, p. 9.
[3] Helveg, op. cit., p. 777.
[4] The printing press had belonged to Hans Brask, Bishop of Linkøping, but Gustav Vasa had compelled him to get rid of it, as he had used it against the Reformation. Oluf Ulriksen, however, bought it and conveyed it to Malmø, where it did good service for the reformers. See H. Kent, *Braendpunkter i Reformationstidens Gudtjeneste-ordning*, p. 83, *note*.
[5] Heise, *Skibykrøniken*, p. 121.
[6] Karup, op. cit., Appendix, p. 14.

ever, he returned to Malmø, armed with a letter of protection from the King, and thus was enabled to continue his ministry. Mortensen is remembered in history as "the father of Danish hymnology". He brought out in 1528 a collection of hymns for use in church, some being translations of Luther's hymns and others versifications of the Psalms.[1] It may be regarded as the earliest complete Danish hymnary.[2]

The changes taking place at Viborg and Malmø spread to other towns in Denmark, and gradually also into the country districts; but except in north Slesvig and in Salling (North Jutland) very little is known as to the way ideas of reform took effect in the country parishes. There survives, however, among other popular verses of the time a satirical poem called "A History of Peter the Smith and Adser the Peasant". It gives a lively picture of the conversation of four men—a craftsman, a peasant, a priest and a monk—who are found chatting together in an inn over their beer. The talk ranges over most of the controverted points in the life and teaching of the Church, and the morals and manners both of the parish clergy and of the monks and friars come in for bold criticism. The work was published in 1529 and it indicates the ferment which was working in the minds of country people in the years preceding the actual Reformation.[3]

4

The Reform movement had thus made some progress in Denmark by the end of 1526, but it had not received formal recognition or approval from either the Crown or the Rigsraad.[4] A meeting of this powerful body, which had placed Frederick on the throne of Denmark, was summoned to be held at Odense in December 1526.[5]

[1] C. J. Brandt, *Vore Danske Kirke-Salmebøger*, pp. 3, 4. No copy of Mortensen's first edition nor of the second edition survives; but Ludvig Dietz reprinted at Rostock in 1529 the second edition, of which one copy is extant. It contains 69 hymns, 22 of them being Luther's.

[2] C. Bruun, *Psalmebøger fra Reformationstiden*, i, p. 193.

[3] Published for *Samfundet til udgivelse af gammel nordisk litteratur* by S. Grundtvig. A short account of this poem, with extracts, is given in Jørgensen, *Reformationen i Danmark*, pp. 100-111.

[4] See J. E. Larsen, *Om Rigsdage og Provindsialsamlinger samt Rigsraadet i Danmark*, p. 299 (*Historisk Tidsskrift I*). "Hvert Aar havde ordentligviis en almindelig Sammenkomst Sted, for at tage Beslutninger om offentlige Anliggender og paadømme de indstaevnte Retsager; dog kunde Raadet ogsaa flere Gange i samme Aar sammenkaldes, naar Omstaendighederne giorde det fornødent. En saadan Forsammling af Rigsraadet kaldtes 'Herredag' eller 'almindelig Herredag', og kunde ordentligviis alene finde Sted, naar Køngen befalede saadant."

[5] Helveg, op. cit., iii, pp. 688 ff.

It consisted of some thirty to forty nobles, headed by the bishops:[1] apart from a small Lutheran minority led by Mogens Gjø,[2] the majority were opposed to religious changes and ill-disposed towards the King.[3] Frederick's strength lay in his indispensability: if the nobles disliked his government, still more did they dread the return of Christian II.

The most urgent matter before the Herredag was the King's need of money, and Frederick believed he saw a way by which he could both enrich himself and render the Danish Church independent of Rome. He sent a proposal (the business of the Herredag was mostly conducted by an exchange of letters between the King and the Rigsraad)[4] that in future a bishop should seek confirmation, not from the Pope, but from the Archbishop of Lund, and that the money usually sent to Rome to obtain this confirmation should be paid into the King's treasury for the defence of the kingdom. Strangely enough, the bishops as well as the nobles agreed to this, although it was, as has been said, " a proposal of far-reaching importance, for thereby the Danish Church was in effect separated from the Pope of Rome ". The same writer offers an explanation of this conduct of the bishops. " The two proposals were a resumption of the Church polity of which the Danish bishops made themselves the advocates at the time of the great Councils. It meant a breach with the Pope, but not with the Catholic Church and its doctrine, and it was in accordance with the old ecclesiastical law which was in force in Denmark until Christian I concluded a pact with the Pope."[5] It may be that one or two of the more learned bishops, like Lage Urne and Ove Bilde, took this view, but probably to the majority the King's proposal did not seem as decisive a step as posterity now sees it to have been; in any case, all of them were men of noble birth, and would view the matter, not simply as bishops, but as Danish noblemen.

The bishops' chief concern was the spread of Lutheranism,

[1] For the bishops see Appendix II.

[2] For Mogens Gjø see Heise, *Skibykrøniken, passim.*

[3] The leader of the lay nobility opposed to reform was the High Marshal, Tyge Krabbe, for whom see *Skibykrøniken*, pp. 102-108.

[4] Larsen, op. cit., p. 300.

[5] Jørgensen, op. cit., p. 51. "Disse Forslag var af vidtraekkende Betydning; thi derved løsreves den danske Kirke i Virkeligheden fra Paven i Rom. . . . De to Forslag var en Genoptagelse af den Kirkepolitik, som de danske Bisper selv havde gjort sig til Talsmaend for paa de store Konciliers Tid. Den betegnede et Brud med den romerske Pave, derimod ikke med den katolske Kirke og dens Laere, og den stemmede med den gamle kirkelige Ret, som stod ved Magt her i Danmark, indtil Kong Christiern I sluttede Forbund med Paven."

which they feared, not only for its dissemination of heretical doctrines, but for the popular unrest which accompanied it, and for the political machinations of Christian II and his adherents which they believed it screened. They demanded, therefore, that the King should not grant letters of protection to anyone to preach in cathedrals, parish churches or elsewhere, and that those who desired to preach God's Word should obtain permission from the bishop of the diocese. As the King had promised in his election charter not to encourage Lutheranism he was placed in a difficult position; but he evaded the difficulty by replying that it was his duty to protect everyone against violence, and that he had not ordered anyone to preach anything except God's Word and the Gospel. With this the bishops had to be content. To strengthen their hands against Lutheranism the bishops had also tried to secure the support of the lay nobility, but this could only be at done at the price of concession. The nobles repeated the demand made at the Herredag at Copenhagen in 1525 that the bishops should cease to exercise disciplinary authority over the peasants on the nobles' estates. As this closely affected their powers of ecclesiastical discipline the bishops were unwilling to agree; but they promised to consider a new ordering of the matter which should be mutually satisfactory. A further demand made by the nobles was that land which during the previous twenty years had been bought by the Church from the estates of the nobles should be returned back to the original owners. To this the bishops would not consent, but they agreed that for the future land so bought should be returned without retrospective effect. In return for this the bishops asked the nobles to act with them in resisting Lutheranism.

The bishops thus emerged from the Herredag a weakened party: they had not been able to prevail on the King to withdraw his letters on behalf of the evangelical preachers, and they secured the promise of lay support against Lutheranism only at the cost of material concessions. "The King had maintained his right by his own letters to authorize priests 'who could preach God's Word and the Gospel' in spite of the bishops' objection; and the bishops themselves had, at least in part, conceded to him the right to nominate bishops without regard to the Pope."[1] It was not long before the latter right began to be put into effect; indeed, a crucial

[1] Helveg, op. cit., iii, p. 698. "Kongen havde jo her haevdet sin Ret til ved sine Breve at kalde Praester, 'som kunde praedike Guds Ord og Evangelium', trods Bispernes Indsigelse, og disse havde jo selv, idetmindste halvveis, indrømmet ham Ret til at kalde Biskopper, uden Hensyn til Paven."

step in the appointment of bishops had already been taken before the Herredag at Odense. Aage Sparre, who had been the original choice of the chapter for the vacant see of Lund in 1519, had so far not been able to secure his position as Archbishop elect owing to the various rival condidates put forward by Christian II and the Pope. For some time after his accession Frederick had hesitated about the filling of the archiepiscopal see. He had corresponded with the Pope on the matter, and at first had recommended Jørgen Skodborg for Papal confirmation; Clement VII had agreed to this and, ignoring other claimants, had confirmed Skodborg in the primacy by a letter of November 29, 1525.[1] For some reason the King subsequently changed his mind, and in a letter of August 19, 1526, he promised the archbishopric to Aage Sparre, for which the latter paid the King 1,000 gylden in consideration of the royal confirmation. Thus the greatest see in the north was disposed of without Papal consent and a decisive step taken in the severance of the Danish Church from obedience to the Pope.

Shortly after the dismissal of the Herredag the King obtained another opportunity to appoint his own nominee to an impending vacancy. Jens Andersen, Bishop of Odense, was desirous of resigning on the grounds of age, or it may have been under royal pressure or persuasion; and Knud Gyldenstjerne, the Dean (*Domprovst*) of Viborg, was allowed (January 6, 1527) to become his coadjutor, with the promise of succeeding him in the see, on payment of a sum of money to the King equivalent to what he would have had to pay to Rome.[2] This policy of filling up vacant sees with men congenial to the Crown and of using the confirmation fees for the benefit of the royal treasury was pursued throughout the reign. Its excuse was the King's need of money; its aim was the strengthening of the royal power.

After the closure of the Herredag in December 1526 the unrest in the country increased, expressing itself particularly in resistance to the collection of episcopal tithes. By an arrangement dating from the middle of the fifteenth century it had been settled that the tithes should be paid to the bishops on corn and cattle, but that the lesser offerings on such things as butter, altar bread, etc., known as bishop's gifts, should cease.[3] Complaints were now being made that the bishops were demanding both contributions. At the same time other grievances in regard to the

[1] Helveg, op. cit., iii, pp. 661, 685.
[2] Helveg, op. cit. ,iii, p. 699.
[3] Helveg, op. cit. ii, pp. 320 ff.

state of the Church were being brought forward: that, *e.g.*, in many churches Mass was said only once in three or four Sundays, and that in the diocese of Aarhus there was a district of about fifteen parishes with only two or three priests to serve them.[1] Again, the bishops were accused of allowing their officials, as an expedient for increasing their fees, to draw to the bishop's court cases which should really be tried before the manorial or other civil courts. In this, as in other complaints, the peasants had the support of many of the nobility, who were jealous of the wealth of the bishops and resented claims made on their tenants as an infringement of their own rights. Mogens Gjø, in particular, told the King that the peasants were within their rights in resisting the demand for both tithe and bishop's gifts and advised a sympathetic handling of their complaints. In the towns, the considerable property belonging to the friars, their large churches, buildings and gardens, roused the cupidity of the civic authorities and contributed to the growing ill-will felt by so many towards the begging Orders. In truth, many of the friars were poor enough, and their increasing unpopularity led to a serious decline in their income from voluntary offerings. The position, in fact, looked so grave in Jutland that the four bishops—Jørgen Friis of Viborg, Iver Munk of Ribe, Styge Krumpen of Børglum and Ove Bilde of Aarhus—realizing that the root of all these discontents lay in a deep spiritual unrest, determined to seek help from abroad. They addressed a letter (May 19, 1527) in fulsome terms to the famous Catholic controversialist, Johann Eck, beseeching him to come to the help of the Church in Denmark. Johann Cochlaeus was also invited, but both refused, and perhaps the explanation is to be found in a remark dropped by Erasmus in a letter to Cochlaeus (August 25, 1527): "iter perlongum est, et gens fera dicitur."[2]

Meanwhile it was decided to summon again a Herredag at Odense to consider the problems of the Church, and in August 1527 assembled the Herredag which was to be of crucial importance in the history of the Reformation in Denmark. The bishops at once brought forward a list of their grievances. They declared that the peasants and common people of Jutland were conspiring "against Holy Church and the prelates of the realm of Denmark", possibly in collusion with Christian II. They complained of the ill-treatment meted out to the friars, who not only were not supported, but were even ill-used when they asked for food and alms.

[1] Jørgensen, op. cit., p. 56.

[2] P. S. Allen, *Erasmi Epistolæ*, vii, p. 146.

They demanded that the new doctrines proclaimed by relapsed monks should receive no encouragement from the King by the issue of letters of protection, but that such men should either return to their monasteries or quit the realm. The King's cue was to act as an impartial judge between bishops and nobles, people and peasants.[1] It was his duty to defend all classes from oppression: it was not only the peasants who believed themselves wronged by the bishops; the nobles also complained of the fines imposed by the Church on their tenants. On this the bishops offered to withdraw their demand for the lesser gifts and to surrender their jurisdiction over the servants of the nobility, on condition that King and nobles alike would protect the Church, ensure the payment of lawful tithe and refuse to countenance the activities of " Lutheran priests and apostate monks ". This concession seems to have induced a majority of the Rigsraad to urge the King to satisfy the bishops by withdrawing his letters of protection. This he refused to do. He maintained that the Christian faith was free; that he himself could not compel anyone to any form of belief; neither could he see what belief every man had in his own heart. " His grace is King and Judge over life and property in his kingdom, but not over souls; therefore every man must form himself inwardly as he will answer for it before Almighty God at the Last Day ". To this the King will adhere until " there shall be brought about a final settlement thereof in the whole of Christendom, according to God's dispensation and permission ". He refused, therefore, to withdraw the letters of protection he had issued to Hans Tausen and others, but promised that he would not for the future issue any more. The bishops then turned to the question of clerical marriage[2] and demanded that those priests and monks who married should within a fixed time either return to their monasteries, or leave the kingdom, or else submit to the bishop's judgment. To this the King's final rejoinder was that it was no new thing for monks to leave their cloisters, and that he would not force them to return; if they married, " that was their own business, for which they must answer to God: he would neither bid it nor forbid it ".[3]

[1] Paludan-Müller, op. cit., p. 524.

[2] It is not known who was the first Danish priest to marry, but Hans Tausen was one of the first. The fact that the question of clerical marriage came before the Herredag suggests that such marriages were already not infrequent. See Münter *Den Danske Reformationshistorie*, i, p. 489.

[3] Helveg, op. cit., iii, pp. 741, 743. "Hs. N. er Konge og raader over Liv og Gods i Riget, men ikke over Sjaele; derfor maa hver skikke sig derudi, som han vil forsvare det

The actual results of these exchanges of view were embodied in writing in the Recess of August 20, 1527.[1] This enjoined afresh the duty of paying tithes and confirmed the jurisdiction of the bishops in the courts spiritual. On the other hand, the fines imposed by the Church on the servants of the nobility were awarded to the latter. No order was taken with regard to the marriage of the clergy or the renunciation of the conventual life by the monks, and no withdrawal of his letters of protection on behalf of the evangelical clergy was made by the King. Thus the most important points of contention were left unsettled and the Herredag seemed to end indecisively for both parties; yet the reformers had this advantage that the Herredag had closed without outlawing their views or punishing those who held them, and thus the cause of Lutheranism was free to go forward and gain fresh adherents.

Danish historians of an older generation have deduced more from the decisions of the Herredag than the facts really warrant. One speaks of a Constitution agreed on by the Herredag granting, among other things, freedom of conscience to all.[2] Another declares that " the Odense Herredag ended with the establishment of full religious and doctrinal freedom for the Lutherans. . . . In accordance with the preceding article a mandate repealed the obligation of celibacy or placed under the protection of the King the clergy and religious desirous of marrying ".[3] A contemporary, however, like Paul Eliaesen,[4] who may have been at Odense at the time of the Herredag, makes no mention of such a formal declaration of complete religious liberty, which would indeed have been far ahead of the ideas of the time. A far more accurate summary is expressed in the following words: " When we look at the Herredag as a whole and ask what was its essential result we find the answer to be that the bishops certainly seemed to have gained something,

---

for Gud paa den yderste Dag . . . der skeer en endelig Forening derom i all Christendom efter Guds Skikkelse og Tilladelse. . . . Hvem som vil enten gifte sig eller løbe af kloster, maa det gjøre, som han vil forsvare det for Gud paa sit egen Eventyr, og vil Hs. N. det hverken byde eller forbyde."

[1] Paludan-Müller, op. cit., p. 525.

[2] Münter, *Den Danske Reformationshistorie*, i, p. 508; and *Kirchengeschichte von Dänemark und Norwegen*, p. 207. He has been followed in this by Kidd, *Documents of the Continental Reformation*, p. 234.

[3] Engelstoft, cited in Schmitt, *Paulus Heliä*, p. 46. " Der Odenser Herrentag endete damit, dass den Lutherischen vollkommene Religions-und Lehrfreiheit in Dänemark zugestanden wurde. . . . Ein Mandat hob infolge der vorhergehenden Artikel die Verpflichtung des Cölibatsgesetzes auf oder stellte die heiratssüchtigen Geistlichen und Ordensleute unter den Schutz des Königs."

[4] *Skibykrøniken*, pp. 118, 119.

but that what they gained they did so by compromise with the King and Council; and further they were forced to tolerate the King continuing to appoint clergy who acted under his authority and thus were free to preach the Gospel and to enter on matrimony."[1] Two main results, indeed, issued from these meetings of King and Rigsraad in 1526 and 1527. At the earlier session a decided step in the separation of Denmark from the Papal see was made by the determination that the bishops should no longer seek for confirmation from the Pope nor pay the accustomed fees to the Curia. The later session was noteworthy for the failure of the bishops to secure united action by the King and Council against the inroads of Lutheranism. The result was that the reformers were able to go forward without serious opposition in their work of proclaiming the Gospel and reconstructing the Danish Church.

Almost simultaneously with these Danish conferences two other assemblies outside Denmark issued pronouncements on the new faith and the treatment of its adherents. In Sweden Gustav Vasa summoned a Riksdag to meet at Vesterås in June 1527, at which, among other changes affecting the life of the Church, " a general though indefinite liberty of preaching was conceded to the reformers, but no mention was made of Luther or Lutheranism ". In the Recess put forth at the end of the Riksdag it was agreed that there should be " liberty for the preachers to proclaim the pure Word of God ".[2] The liberty to preach the new faith which was thus officially recognized in Sweden was in Denmark only won by the refusal of the Government to penalize its followers. The other pronouncement was made at the Imperial Diet of Speier and had reference, not to the liberty of individual preachers, but to the responsibility of individual Princes for the provisional settlement of the religious question. The Recess issued on August 27, 1526, asserted: " We, the Electors, Princes, Estates of the Empire . . . unanimously (have) resolved . . . each one is so to live, govern, and carry himself as he hopes and trusts to answer it to God and his Imperial Majesty."[3] These words must have been known to Frederick when a year later he made the notable utterance that

[1] Helveg, op. cit., iii, p. 749. "Betragte vi da denne Herredag i sin Heelhed og spørge hvad der var dens vaesentlige Udbytte, saa er Svaret, at Prelaterne nok tilsyneladende havde vundet noget, men hvad de vandt, det vandt de efter Overeenskomst med Kongen og Rigens Raad, og desuden nødtes de til af finde dem i, at Kongen fremdeles vedblev at beskikke Praester, der stode under hans Dom, og altsaa frit kunde praedike Evangelium og indgaae Aegteskab."

[2] Wordsworth, *The National Church of Sweden*, pp. 194, 199.

[3] Kidd, *Documents of the Continental Reformation*, p. 185.

each man was to answer to God for his religious life until a final settlement was reached at a General Council of Christendom.

5

After the meetings of the Rigsraad at Odense the reform movement, during the next two or three years, began to spread more rapidly. One sign of this was the increasing interest in the new religious ideas shown among the students at the University of Copenhagen. Paul Eliaesen records in his *Skibykrøniken* the names of several of those who had attended his lectures at the University who afterwards turned to Lutheranism.[1] Perturbed by the growing religious dissension, the Chancellor of the University, Bishop Lage Urne, addressed a letter (June 25, 1527) to the Senate, complaining of the numbers of the students who had fallen away to heresy, and directing that for the future theological lectures should only be open to those who were in Orders and had proceeded to a bachelor's degree.[2] This injunction, though intended to prevent the spread of Lutheranism, had really the effect of damaging the University itself, for it excluded the younger students (who had not attained the required status) from attending lectures in the theological faculty. A further significant occurrence was the delivery of a lecture, attacking the Catholic clergy and composed in a completely Lutheran spirit, by Oluf Gyldenmund, at that time (1529) a teacher at the Malmø College. The lecture was delivered in the church of Our Lady, Copenhagen, on the invitation of Claus Urne, a nephew of the bishop, Lage Urne, and Rector of the University, who later himself became a Lutheran.[3]

While the new teaching was thus penetrating into the very citadel of the Danish Church by winning converts among the teachers and students of the University, it had already won a position for itself on the outskirts of the kingdom, in the duchies of Slesvig and Holsten.[4] This was due largely to the influence of Frederick's eldest son, Duke Christian, who was a convinced and zealous Lutheran. Born in 1503, he had been present as a lad of eighteen at the Diet of Worms, and had surrendered to the attrac-

[1] *Skibykrøniken*, p. 63.

[2] His letter to the University is printed in Münter, *Den Danske Reformationshistorie*, i, p. 535.

[3] Werlauff, *Kiøbenhavns Universitet*, p. 78.

[4] Some account of the progress of Lutheranism in Slesvig and Holsten is given by G. J. T. Lau, *Geschichte der Einführung und Verbreitung der Reformation in den Herzogthümern Schleswig-Holstein*, pp. 97-119.

tion of the popular Saxon hero. "His mind and character were profoundly penetrated with the religious and moral spirit of the German reformation."[1] He had married Dorothea, the daughter of the Lutheran Duke Magnus of Saxony-Lauenberg, and the young couple lived mostly at Haderslev, the Duke ruling in his father's name over the surrounding district. At Haderslev he caused an evangelical clergy school to be opened under two approved Lutheran theologians from Germany, Ederhard Weidensee and Johann Vandal, to which the parish priests of the neighbourhood were bidden to attend, in order that they might hear "God's pure Word and the Gospel". They were required also to take an oath renouncing all errors, and if they refused they were removed from their parishes and new ministers, ordained by Dr. Weidensee, acting as Superintendent, were instituted in their place. All clergy were encouraged to take to themselves wives, and in each district a visitor, or provost, was appointed to supervise the teaching and conduct of the clergy.[2]

This Lutheranizing policy of Duke Christian had the double effect of inclining his father to countenance the religious changes already proceeding in both the kingdom and the duchies, and of strengthening the Catholic members of the Rigsraad in their opposition to Duke Christian as the probable successor to the Crown. In the larger towns of Slesvig the presence of Lutheran influences is shown by the activities of Herman Tast at Husum and Melchior Hofman at Kiel, both of whom had the King's sanction for their ministry; at Kiel also Frederick gave permission for a press to be set up "to print copies of the Old and New Testament and other religious books."[3] The King's policy was to allow the free preaching of the Gospel, without forcible suppression of the old ways; but his son's greater zeal would not tolerate what he regarded as the errors of the old faith, with the consequence that sporadic acts of violence broke out both in the duchies and in Denmark itself. Growing fear of Duke Christian's influence led the Rigsraad in 1529 to request the King to have his second son, John, then a boy of eight, brought to Denmark, in order to get the young Prince away from the influence of his elder brother and to have him brought up in the Catholic faith.

The compromise reached at Viborg by which the services both

[1] Ranke, *History of the Reformation in Germany* (Eng. trans.), p. 767.
[2] Helveg, op. cit., iii, pp. 763-766; *Kirkehistoriske Samlinger*, i, p. 390.
[3] Helveg, op. cit., iii, p. 768.

of the old and of the new order were held in the same church of the Greyfriars did not last long. The feeling amongst the citizens against the old clergy and the friars was growing, and no doubt the preaching of Tausen and Sadolin hastened the crisis which was evidently approaching. Early in 1529 the burgomaster and council sought permission of the King to demolish some of the churches which were declared to be superfluous. Frederick, in a letter of February 3, 1529,[1] departed from his policy of abstention from the use of force which he had hitherto followed, and gave the required permission on condition that half of the lead and of the bells should be reserved for the Crown. Demolition was proceeded with at once and the number of churches in Viborg thus destroyed is said to have been twelve.[2] The cathedral was spared, and the two largest churches, next to the cathedral, the Greyfriars and the Blackfriars, were preserved as parish churches. The bishop, Jørgen Friis, complained bitterly to the King about these acts of destruction, but he was unable to stem the tide of violent innovation which was sweeping through the city. The cathedral Chapter itself contained members not unfavourable to reform, among them the bishop's own brother, Niels Friis. Some of the Lutheran-minded canons composed a new order of service, consisting of the Lord's Supper, or Danish Mass, with sermon, and hymns in the vernacular, and sent it to the King for his approval.[3] These changes led to disturbances in the cathedral, but the clergy who advocated reform were supported by the burgomaster and council, and were able to maintain their position in spite of the opposition of the bishop. Tausen continued to minister and preach in the church of the Greyfriars, and Sadolin was appointed to the other parish church, that of the Blackfriars, after being 'ordained' by Tausen to preach the Gospel and minister the sacraments. The friars themselves had left their monasteries some time before this, probably early in 1530.

On the other side of the kingdom, in the important city of Malmø, there were two monasteries, that of the Greyfriars and a house of the Order of the Holy Spirit, which soon began to feel the effects of the increasing unpopularity of the mendicants. The leading spirit among the citizens, Jørgen Kock, personally re-

[1] Heise, *Diplomaterium Vibergense: Breve og Aktstykker*, p. 170.

[2] *Eine alte Chronik über die Vertreibung der Graubrüder, apud* Karup, *Geschichte der katholischen Kirche in Dänemark*, p. 9.

[3] Helveg, op. cit., iii, p. 801; H. Knudsen, *Bidrag til den Danske Reformationshistorie*, in *Annaler for Nordisk Oldkyndighed og Historie*, p. 132.

quested the King to allow the dissolution of the two communities, proposing that the estates of the Greyfriars should be converted into a hospital and clergy school, and the property of the house of the Holy Spirit should be used as a Town Hall. The King consented to this on the condition, expressed in a letter of October 10, 1528,[1] that the monks should not be compulsorily ejected from their homes. But the position of the two communities was becoming untenable; the civic authorities were determined to put a stop to what they regarded as "superstition", and the brethren were consequently given the choice either of conforming to the new faith or of vacating their premises. By the end of 1529 the house of the Holy Spirit was in the hands of the magistrates, who used it as a *Raadhus*, or Civic Hall, and in the following year they seized the property of the Greyfriars and therewith founded a hospital and clergy school. The movement of reform had been strengthened by the arrival (February 3, 1529) of two of Eliaesen's former colleagues at Copenhagen, Frans Vormordsen and Peder Laurenssen, the latter becoming a lecturer at the new clergy school which was opened in June of that year. Malmø, indeed, had become the Wittenberg of Denmark, the centre of Lutheran activity and the home of its most zealous protagonists. Here appeared in 1529 the new *Danish Mass*, based on the old Latin service, but translated into Danish, and with provision for preaching and for the singing of hymns.[2] The names of Frans Vormordsen, the future Lutheran Bishop of Lund; Clavs Mortensen, the "father of Danish hymnody"; Peder Laurenssen, who, besides lecturing at the clergy school, acted as secretary to the city council and was the author of several important Lutheran writings; Oluf Gyldenmund, later Professor of Rhetoric at the University; Jep Nielsen, burgomaster of Malmø; and Jorgen Kock, the master of the Mint, were prominent throughout these years as the leaders of the Lutheran and democratic party in this important mercantile city on the Sound, with its trade connexions with the Netherlands and the Hanse towns of the Baltic.[3]

Both Malmø and Copenhagen possessed liberal civic constitutions, for Frederick I had granted to each of them (November 29, 1526) the right to possess four burgomasters and twelve councillors elected by the whole body of citizens. This gave them a constitu-

[1] Published in Knudsen, op. cit., p. 153.
[2] Reprinted in C. Bruun, *Psalmebøger fra Reformationstiden*, i, pp. 93-120.
[3] For these men see notes in Heise, *Skibykrøniken*, pp. 120-128.

tion in advance of all other Danish towns at that time.[1] In Copenhagen, Lage Urne, as bishop of the diocese and as Chancellor of the University, had succeeded so far in preventing Lutheranism from becoming predominant in the capital; but when his strong hand was removed the new forces gained impetus. The Rector of the University was an annual appointment, and in the years 1529 and 1530 was held in succession by two men—Claus Urne, nephew of Lage Urne, and Peder Svave, a Pomeranian[2]—both of whom were favourable to Lutheranism; and the same can be said of two of the four burgomasters of the city—viz., Niels Stemp and Ambrosius Bogbinder. It was to Niels Stemp that Paul Eliaesen had addressed, in 1528, his little work on *The Care of the Sick and Poor*, suggesting ways in which the sick and needy of the city could be provided for by the establishment of a hospital.[3] Ambrosius Bogbinder became a burgomaster in 1529, but lost the position two years later on suspicion of plotting in favour of Christian II, whose adherent he was. A decisive step in the advance of the new faith in Copenhagen was the removal of Hans Tausen, at the King's request, from Viborg to the capital. On his arrival (August 1529) he was allowed to occupy the pulpit of the church of St. Nicholas, one of the four parish churches of the city, and soon introduced the Lutheran mode of worship with the singing of psalms and hymns. The result was serious dissension among the citizens which in due course led to the summoning of the important Herredag of Copenhagen in the summer of 1530.[4]

6

The later years of Frederick I saw the dissolution of many of the monasteries in Denmark.[5] The proceedings took a different course from that which happened in England, and the suppression of religious houses was not carried out on the same widespread scale. In England the great change occurred in definite stages and continued over a number of years—from 1524, when Wolsey began it, to the wholesale surrender of monasteries and nunneries between the years 1537-40. In Denmark the evidence indicates the gradual disappearance of some of the monasteries and the survival of others after the actual Reformation had been carried through. A

[1] C. F. Allen, *De tre nordiske Rigers Historie*, v, pp. 232-233.
[2] Werlauff, op. cit., pp. 70, 78.
[3] *Danske skrifter*, ed. C. E. Secher, p. 143.
[4] *Skibykrøniken*, p. 136.
[5] See Daugaard, *Om de danske Klostre i Middelalderen*; and Fabricius, *Danmarks Kirkehistorie*, ii, pp. 155-165.

contemporary document (*En gammel Krønike om Graabrødrenes Udjagelse*)[1] describes the fall of fifteen Franciscan houses during the years 1528-32. There can be no doubt that the mendicant Orders were becoming increasingly unpopular, and their large buildings and great wealth, in sinister contrast with the ideals of their founders, aroused feelings of indignation and of cupidity in the breasts of both nobles and citizens. At Viborg the large church of the Greyfriars, as has been said, was seized and converted into a parish church in which Tausen ministered and preached. But this was followed by further tribulation for the brethren. The citizens arranged that soldiers should be quartered in the monastery, and according to the *Chronicle* this led to acts of violence. The prior journeyed to Copenhagen to appeal to the King for redress; he returned with a sealed letter which was read in the presence of the brethren and of some of the citizens, and contained the royal order for the expulsion of the friars by New Year's Day 1530.

At the monastery of Tønder in South Jutland the brethren began to experience difficulties in the autumn of 1530 because the castle bailiff commandeered part of the monastic buildings, leaving the friars the use of only the choir, the dormitory and a small refectory. During a visit of the King he caused a Lutheran service to be held in the monastery church, and after the service the prior humbly requested the King that they might be allowed to continue to serve God in this place. The King's reply was curt and evasive, and after his departure the bailiff seized the remainder of the buildings and their contents. The monks are believed to have betaken themselves to the Greyfriars' house at Ribe.

The authors of the old *Chronicle* relate in some detail the events which occurred at the Franciscan house at Malmø. Difficulties had begun in 1528, and in the autumn of the following year the monks were excluded from the chancel and forbidden to say Mass there, although allowed to do so in the sacristy. The following Easter, stones were thrown at the brethren as they sang their choir office. A party of citizens tried by threats or by flattery to persuade them either to accept the new teaching or to allow their monastery to be converted into a theological college. A few weeks later disturbances occurred when another party of citizens invaded the monastery, seized the keys of the cellar and helped themselves to food and drink. The next day the burgomaster arrived and ordered the

[1] Printed as appendix in W. J. Karup, *Geschichte der katholischen Kirche in Dänemark*; and also in *Kirkehistoriske Samlinger*, i, pp. 325 ff., with notes by H. Knudsen.

brethren to leave the premises. The prior was thrown into prison, but soon after released on his promising to receive instruction in the Lutheran faith. He later became warden of the hospital which was erected within the monastery precincts. The sub-prior also abandoned his habit, married and settled down to a citizen's life in Malmø.

At Ystad on the eve of the feast of the Annuciation 1532 the burgomaster and a number of citizens presented themselves at the monastery gate and demanded admittance: they had, they declared, a letter from the King authorizing the conversion of the monastery into a hospital. When the letter was read it was found that it ordered the expulsion of the monks, first because they did not preach the Gospel, and secondly because they had no means of livelihood. When they protested, scenes of violence occurred, and two of the monks were so badly mauled that they subsequently died: but whether this was in consequence of their ill-treatment or not the writers of the *Chronicle* do not make clear.

The instances so far mentioned illustrate the way the Greyfriars suffered at the hands of the burgher class; but the nobility were also active in securing the suppression of some of the houses of religion. The authors of the *Chronicle* attribute the dissolution of the monasteries at Flensburg, Randers, Kalundborg and Naestved to the influence of Mogens Gjø, whom they regarded as the great protector of heretics; and behind him was the King himself, who openly or secretly, as circumstances fell out, sanctioned the closing of the monasteries and the dispersal of their occupants.

Besides the fifteen houses of the Greyfriars mentioned in the *Chronicle* there were eleven others[1] whose dissolution is not described, some of them continuing for a time longer. The Greyfriars at Odense, *e.g.*, elected a new prior as late as 1534; but in 1539 their buildings, together with those of the Blackfriars, were taken over as a hospital.[2] Probably the other mendicant Orders received much the same treatment as the Greyfriars. Paul Eliaesen mentions[3] the dissolution of the Carmelite monastery at Assens in 1530 and states that its property was handed over to the town; in the same year he was compelled, as Provincial of his Order, to assent to the surrender of the house at Landskrona to the civic authorities.[4] Two years later the King gave the Carmelite monastery at Skel-

[1] C. F. Allen states that in at least twenty-nine Danish towns there were houses of the Greyfriars (*De tre Rigers Historie*, i, p. 217).
[2] C. T. Engelstoft, *Odense Byes Sognehistorie* (*Nythistorisk Tidsskrift*, vi, pp. 29, 33).
[3] *Skibykrøniken*, p. 120.
[4] *Ibid.*, p. 64, note 1.

skør to Johan Urne, a member of the Rigsraad, on the ground that the brethren were too poor to maintain it. The parent house at Helsingør survived Eliaesen's time, but was dissolved in 1541 and replaced by a hospital.[1]

If it be asked what happened to the monks thus compelled to leave their homes, no completely satisfactory answer can be given. Probably some in the larger towns took to ordinary work and married, adopting the new faith, or at least renouncing the old. Others became evangelical clergy and were put in charge of parishes. Others, again, continued their old life in some much reduced community, and when that was no longer possible, left Denmark to seek refuge abroad. Traces of Danish Franciscans have been found at places as distant as Lüneburg, Lyons and South Holland.[2]

7

In these years in which the tide of reform was gathering force the Catholic Church in Denmark was weakened by a series of changes among the bishops. It has been noted that Knud Gyldenstjerne became the coadjutor of Jens Andersen at Odense; in March 1529 the latter resigned the see, and Gyldenstjerne became bishop, though he had not been consecrated, nor had his appointment received Papal confirmation. He seems rather to have favoured than hindered the advance of Lutheranism, and in 1532 summoned Jørgen Sadolin from Viborg to aid him in the administration of his diocese.[3] A greater blow to the Church was the death a few weeks later (April 29, 1529) of Lage Urne, the most distinguished of the Danish bishops of the Reformation period. His death gave the King the opportunity of selecting a successor who would be in agreement with the royal policy. The choice fell on Joachim Rønnov, a member of a Danish noble family, who had travelled in France and Italy, but appears not to have had the usual clerical education.[4] Before his name was submitted to the Chapter for election he was required by the King to promise to be loyal to himself and his heirs, and not to hinder the preaching of the Gospel or allow the clergy who married to be molested. On his election he was confirmed as bishop of the see by the Crown, but

[1] Schmitt, *Paulus Heliä*, p. 133. For the position of religious houses under Christian III see *post.*, Chapter III, sect. 10.
[2] Fabricius, *Danmarks Kirkehistorie*, ii, p. 160.
[3] *Skibykrøniken*, p. 112. See *post.*, sect. 9.
[4] *Ibid.*, p. 141.

since he lacked episcopal Orders[1] he appears to have addressed himself to Jørgen Skodborg, the one-time Archbishop of Lund, then residing at Lübeck, with a view to obtaining his help towards rectifying his position; but Skodborg could only advise him to apply to the Pope for confirmation—a thing Rønnov in Frederick's lifetime dared not do.[2]

In 1532 the see of Lund again became vacant. The Archbishop, Aage Sparre, troubled with the difficulties caused by the spread of Lutheranism in his diocese, especially in Malmø, resigned the see in July, to become once again its dean. In his place the King appointed Torben Bilde on the same conditions as those imposed on Rønnov—viz., that he should promise obedience to the Crown and protect those clergy who preached the Gospel or wished to marry. Thus in the course of the three years 1529-32 the King had been able to secure that the occupants of the three most important bishoprics in the kingdom—Lund, Roskilde and Odense—were men who owed their appointment to himself and had promised not to impede the course of reform. None of them were in episcopal Orders or had been confirmed by the Pope. The bishops of the four Jutland sees—Viborg, Aarhus, Ribe and Børglum—were all Catholic prelates in the sense that they had been duly consecrated, but, except in the case of Ove Bilde of Aarhus, were men of unchaste life, and wanting in the qualities of spiritual leadership.[3] The Church of Denmark was thus not in a state to respond to the popular demand for reform: its official leaders, the bishops, were divided into two groups, those who opposed and those who were prepared to favour the new movement; while the archiepiscopal see of Lund, which should have produced a man capable of uniting the bishops and leading the Church, was treated as a prize in the game of international politics.

8

On July 2, 1530, there met in Copenhagen, in response to the royal summons, a notable assembly of the estates of Denmark.[4] Besides the King himself and the ecclesiastical and lay members of the Council, there were present many of the lesser nobility, representatives of the towns, and—a remarkable innovation—

[1] Knudsen, *Joachim Rønnov*, p. 71. His episcopal duties were carried out for him by Vincentius, titular Bishop of Greenland, a Franciscan in episcopal orders.

[2] Paludan-Müller, op. cit., p. 529.

[3] Schmitt, *Paulus Heliä*, p. 66.

[4] A good account in Fabricius, *Danmarks Kirkehistorie*, ii, pp. 136-151.

"Master Tausen and his company". The latter comprised about a score of the most prominent Lutheran preachers in the country,[1] and their summons to this official assembly is significant of the growth of the movement in Denmark. The reasons for the holding of this Herredag were the increasing dissensions among the different classes of the community, which were aggravated by the religious quarrel and the fear of an invasion by Christian II. The King hoped that it would lead to a settlement of the religious difficulty and to a closer union among the estates of the realm; and he intended to use it as an opportunity to refute the charges brought against himself of breaking the promises given in his coronation charter.

The first business of the Herredag was the presentment by the Rigsraad of some general grievances against the Crown, such as the heavy taxation, the seizure of Church tithes, and the unrest and discontent prevailing through the land. The bishops then sent to the King a list of their complaints with regard to the spread of heresy and the encouragement given by Frederick to the evangelical preachers. Meanwhile Tausen and his brethren had been sitting together in conference composing a statement of their faith which they intended to present to the Herredag. When completed, this consisted of the Forty-three Articles which later came to be known as the *Copenhagen Confession* (*Confessio Hafnica*).[2] It coincided in time with the *Augsburg Confession*, from the pen of Melanchthon, which the German Protestant Princes presented to the Emperor at the Diet of Augsburg on June 25, and with Zwingli's *Fidei Ratio* and the *Confessio Tetrapolitana*, which were presented to the Emperor on July 8 and July 11 respectively;[3] but the Danish Confession appears to have been drawn up quite independently of these German and Swiss doctrinal statements. The Forty-three Articles were not brought before the Herredag for discussion; but they obtained a far wider hearing from the fact that Tausen and his brethren preached on them, successively and in detail, in the

[1] Their names are thus given by Fabricius, op. cit., ii, p. 138. Hans Tausen from Copenhagen; Peder Laurensen, Frans Vormordsen, Oluf Chrystomos, Claus Mortensen and Hans Olufsen from Malmø; Jacob Skønning and Jørgen Sadolin from Viborg; Morten Hegelund from Aalborg; Peder Thomesøn and Peder Jensen from Salling; Mogen Gjø's chaplain, Niels Christensen, and Anders Liung from Landskroma; Christiern Skrok from Assens; Hans Nielsen from Falsterbo; Tyge Christensen, Anders Nielsen, Anders Madsen, Jacob from Ystad; and Mads Jensen and Rasmus from Trelleborg.

[2] Printed in full in Latin translation in Münter, *Kirchengeschichte von Dänemark und Norwegen*, pp. 308 ff., and in the original Danish in the same author's *Den Danske Reformationshistorie*, ii, pp. 109 ff.

[3] Kidd, *Documents of the Continental Reformation*, pp. 259, 468.

church of the Holy Spirit before interested and excited congregations.

Alarmed by this publication of heretical views, the bishops drew up a list of twenty-seven errors with which they charged the reformers.[1] These included such erroneous views as the denial of free will; the denial of purgatory; the displacement of the seven sacraments by the two Gospel sacraments only; the marriage of the clergy; the abolition of life vows; and the claim to ordain to the ministry. To these accusations of heresy the evangelical preachers replied point by point, and then added twelve counter-charges specially addressed to the bishops.[2] The chief heads in the indictment were: that they neither preached themselves nor appointed learned Christian preachers in their dioceses; that they persecuted those who tried to preach the Gospel; that they allowed begging monks and indulgence mongers to go about deceiving the people; that they kept many benefices in their own hands and left one priest to look after several parishes; that they forbade the clergy to marry and thus encouraged profligacy.

While these controversial exchanges were proceeding the King and Rigsraad on July 10 issued a Recess which contained the following important provision: " Concerning God's Word and the Gospel, we will that each one who has the grace may clearly proclaim it and publicly teach the common people in all our towns and elsewhere in this kingdom. . . . Whosoever shall preach or teach anything other than what he can prove is agreeable with Scripture shall be brought to justice."[3] This gave the Lutheran clergy legal covering for their ministry, but it also exposed them to prosecution if their preaching was proved to be inconsistent with Scripture. Both sides were now anxious to meet at a conference, so that the issue might be settled by public debate; but this was never held, because agreement could not be reached on the two preliminary questions: in what language, Latin or Danish, was the debate to be conducted, and who should be the judge in the controversy? The Herredag closed on August 2 without further result,

[1] Summary in Schmitt, *Paulus Heliä*, p. 83. They are also summarized and discussed in Münter, *Den Danske Reformationshistorie*, ii, pp. 121 ff.

[2] Both these are reprinted in *Danmarks christelige Praedikanters Gjensvar*, by H. F. Rordam; and are also in Münter, *Den Danske Reformationshistorie*, ii, pp. 139 ff.

[3] Rørdam, op. cit. p. iii, " Om Guds Ord og Evangelium ville vi, at hvilken som Naaden havde, maa det klarligen praedike og aabenbar laere for menige Almue, udi alle vore Købstaeder og andensteds over alt Riget. . . . Dersom nogen praediker eller laerer noget andet, end han bevise kan med den hellige Skrift, da skall den samme stande derfor til Rette."

and both sides were disappointed at its meagre outcome. The bishops had failed to secure the prohibition of heretical preaching, and their opponents had not obtained, as they had hoped, " a Christian reformation ". The King's policy had been to mediate between the two, and in consequence he had succeeded in pleasing neither. It is probable that he feared to go farther with reform, lest he should alienate the Catholic majority among the nobles; their support was increasingly necessary to him as the threat of invasion by Christian II drew nearer. But it is also possible that he had begun to be seriously alarmed by the growth of religious disturbances; he could not risk the unity of the nation by undertaking a complete recasting of its religious faith and corporate life.

The King's caution seemed to be justified by the events which followed the dissolution of the Herredag. Before he left Copenhagen he had arranged with Rønnov, the Bishop of Roskilde, that the clergy of the church of Our Lady in Copenhagen should continue to say Mass as heretofore, but that on Sundays an evangelical minister should celebrate the Mass in Danish and preach.[1] This attempt at a compromise, which had failed at Viborg, did not succeed here, for on November 2 the magistrates[2] wrote to the King to say that the preachers were denouncing the Latin Mass and stirring up the people against the old services, so that they feared rioting would ensue: they asked that either the bishop should prohibit the offending services or else that they themselves should be allowed to resign. The King made no reply, but let things take their course. The result was an outbreak of violence. On December 27 a crowd, headed by the burgomaster, Ambrosius Bogbinder, broke into the church of Our Lady, damaged crucifixes and holy images, and kept up a tumult until Tausen himself came and restored order. As a consequence of this riot the church was closed, by order of the King, to both the rival parties, and so it remained until November 15 in the following year, when the Catholics were allowed to take possession again and resume their services.

9

The last years of Frederick's reign saw the final appearance of Christian II on the Scandinavian scene before he disappeared into the darkness of his lifelong imprisonment.[3] He had been present at Augsburg when the Diet assembled there in June 1530, and had

[1] Knudsen, *Joachim Rønnov*, p. 164. [2] Paludan-Müller, op. cit., p. 536.

[3] Paludan-Müller, op. cit., pp. 542 ff. A detailed account of Christian's invasion and mprisonment is given in Heise, *Kristiern den anden i Norge og hans Faengsling*.

tried to secure the Emperor's help in the recovery of his kingdom. To win Charles's support he had renounced the Lutheran faith and been absolved by the Pope. The death of the Regentess Margaret on November 30 of this year seemed to clear a way for his venture, for she had always viewed him with suspicion and opposed his plans. During the next few months he busied himself collecting money and arms from some of the rich merchant houses of the Netherlands for his campaign against Frederick. On October 26, 1531, he sailed from Medemblik, a small port on the Zuyder Zee, with a fleet of twenty-five ships carrying 7,000 men, but unluckily for him the ships were dispersed in a storm in the North Sea; he lost most of his artillery and much of his money. What was left of his force succeeded in landing at points on the southern coast of Norway. He was welcomed by the exiled Archbishop of Upsala, Gustav Trolle, who tried to enlist support for Christian among the Norwegian bishops and nobles by presenting him as their rightful King and as a bulwark against Lutheranism; but months were spent in negotiation and desultory campaigning without achieving any considerable result. Meanwhile Frederick had entered into an agreement with Lübeck for the supply of men and ships, and in May 1532 he dispatched a strong Danish-Hanseatic fleet to Oslo. Christian, whose forces were now unequal to the struggle, was compelled to negotiate. He was persuaded by Knud Gyldenstjerne, Bishop of Odense, Frederick's leading commissary, to throw himself on his uncle's goodwill and to accept a safe conduct. On Christian's arrival at Copenhagen on July 24 the King refused to honour his commissary's arrangement and ordered Christian to be held as a prisoner. A few days after reaching the castle of Sønderborg, which was to be his prison for the next seventeen years, Christian received the news that his only son, Hans, had died at Regensburg (August 11, 1532): thus all hope of himself or his heirs ascending the throne of Denmark seemed finally to be extinguished. Yet within eight months Frederick himself had passed away, and the hopes of Christian and of his still considerable following again revived.

Before Gyldenstjerne left Fünen to go as one of the commanders of the army to Norway he called Jørgen Sadolin to come and work in his diocese; and during his absence in Norway Sadolin acted as the bishop's suffragan and used his powers to advance the cause of reform.[1] On Gyldenstjerne's return he supported Sadolin in the

[1] Helveg, op. cit., iii, pp. 921 ff.

changes he had made. The latter issued in 1532, on the authority of Gyldenstjerne, a Danish translation of Luther's *Small Catechism*,[1] which the clergy were instructed to use in their parishes, and he prepared a series of questions, based on the *Augsburg Confession*, for the clergy to answer and thus satisfy Sadolin that they were exercising their ministry on Lutheran principles. Later he translated into Danish and published in Copenhagen in 1533 the *Augsburg Confession* itself, and was thus the means of giving to the Danish Church two of the primary documents of the German Reformation, the *Confession* of Augsburg and Luther's *Small Catechism*.[2]

In the last year of the King's life occurred the change, already alluded to, in the primacy at Lund, when Aage Sparre, with Frederick's consent, resigned the archbishopric in favour of Torben Bilde. The latter undertook, in a letter to the King, July 15, 1532,[3] to allow the preaching of "the true Word of God", and not to oppress or restrain those who desired so to preach or who wished to marry. Though this promise may not have meant the deliberate encouragement of the new faith, it yet weakened the resistance of the old order: the holder of the greatest see in the north had now undertaken not to oppose the advance of the new creed.

With the tide of reform thus slowly but surely creeping over the land, the King, whose policy had been to let reform take its course without himself taking steps likely to cause upheaval, passed quietly away at his castle at Gottorp on April 10, 1533. His character has been very differently assessed. Paul Eliaesen passed a severe judgment on him in his *Skibykrøniken*, accusing him of breaking his coronation oath, of encouraging heresy and of plundering the Church; and in his private life being given to low pleasures. A more charitable and probably more accurate estimate is that of his chancellor, Wolfgang von Utenhof, who described him as an intelligent, patient man, handling his affairs with wisdom and ability, good-natured and tolerant in disposition, and compassionate to the poor.[4]

[1] Printed in A. C. Bang, *Den lutherske Katechismus Historie.*
[2] Kolderup-Rosenvinge, *Grundrids af den danske Kirkeret*, pp. 2 & 30.
[3] Printed in Rørdam, *Malmøbogen*, pp. xlv-xlvi.
[4] *Skibykrøniken*, pp. 155-159. Heise, *Wulfgang von Utenhof* in *Historisk Tidsskrift*, R.4, B.6, p. 205.

CHAPTER III

INTERREGNUM, 1533-1536—CHRISTIAN III, 1536-1559

1

THE death of Frederick I exposed Denmark to the miseries of a disputed succession, and this at a time when large areas of the north, in Scandinavia and Lower Germany, were seething with unrest. In Lübeck the demagogue Jørgen Wullenwever became burgomaster in 1533 and thus " united the power of a popular leader with that of a lawful magistrate ".[1] In Münster, Anabaptists seized the reins of power (1534) and attempted to carry into effect their revolutionary doctrines. Sporadic risings of Anabaptists occurred throughout North Germany and the Netherlands. In Denmark, the two chief cities, Copenhagen and Malmø, each had democratic leaders in Ambrosius Bogbinder and Jørgen Kock. It was fear of this revolutionary spirit which kept the late King from advancing farther along the path of reform, and now his restraining hand was gone.

He had left four sons, of whom the eldest, Christian, was a man of thirty, and the second, Hans, a boy of twelve. Christian had already disclosed his strong Lutheran convictions, and it was not likely that he would be chosen by the Catholic majority of the Rigsraad. Their inclination was to elect Hans, in the hope that they could thereby ensure him being brought up as a Catholic, and in the meantime that they would retain control of the country during his minority. A Herredag was summoned to meet at Copenhagen in June 1533;[2] there were present some thirty-seven members, who were grouped into three parties: the stricter Catholics, under Bishop Ove Bilde; a small Lutheran section, led by Mogens Gjø; and a middle party, of which the chief figure was Bishop Joachim Rønnov. In the debates which followed they were unable to reach agreement and decided to postpone the election till the following year, when a joint meeting of the Danish and Norwegian Councils should meet to elect a King for both countries. When they turned their attention to ecclesiastical affairs their

[1] Ranke, *History of the Reformation in Germany*, p. 761.
[2] Heise, *Herredagen i Kjøbenhavn*, 1533, in *Historisk Tidsskrift*, R.4, B.3, pp. 222 ff.

disunity became more marked: a majority wished to restrict the activities of the evangelical preachers, to restore the old services, to maintain the surviving monasteries, and to give each bishop complete jurisdiction over the clergy in his own diocese. A Recess enjoining this was issued on July 3,[1] but Mogens Gjø and his following refused their consent and left the Herredag. A further Recess of July 13[2] announced the intention of the remainder to hold together and not to recognize any King without the consent of all. Meanwhile the government of the country was to be conducted by the bishops, assisted by members of the Council, acting in their respective dioceses; but as this was signed by only thirteen out of the thirty-seven members it was evident that true unity and agreement had not been reached and that the peaceful government of the country was imperilled.

Abroad the situation was ominous: foreign claimants to the throne were known to be contemplating action, among them Count Frederick of the Palatinate,[3] Joachim, the Elector of Brandenburg,[4] and Henry VIII of England.[5] The powerful city of Lübeck had its representative in Copenhagen in the person of its ambitious burgomaster, Wullenwever,[6] who came to seek an alliance with the Danish government. When, however, the Rigsraad, reversing the late King's settled policy of union with Lübeck, joined in alliance with the Netherlands, with whom Lübeck was at war, Wullenwever left Copenhagen in anger, determined to revenge himself by turning the critical situation in Denmark to his own advantage. Meanwhile Duke Christian, wisely refusing to intervene at this juncture, was biding his time; and in the castle of Sønderborg was the old King, not forgotten by the common people, for whose welfare he, with all his faults, had shown sincere concern. The match which set this combustible material alight was the decision of Count Christopher of Oldenburg[7] to free his kinsman and restore him to the throne of Denmark. A man of knightly qualities and attached to the evangelical faith, he was the very instrument needed by Wullenwever to head a coalition

[1] Karup, *Geschichte der katholischen Kirche in Dänemark*, p. 242.

[2] Paludan-Müller, *De Første Konger af den Oldenborgske Slaegt*, pp. 577, 578.

[3] He married in 1535 Dorothea, daughter of Christian II, and in 1544 became the Elector Palatine.

[4] Joachim I, Elector of Brandenburg, married in 1502 Isabella, sister of Christian II. He died in 1535.

[5] *Letters and Papers of Henry VIII*, vol. vii, 1030, 1272, etc.

[6] Ranke, op. cit., p. 761.

[7] Count Christopher, b. 1504, younger son of Count John of Oldenburg, and second cousin to Christian II. See *Skibykrøniken*, p. 180.

against the Danish state; and in May 1534 Count Christopher entered into an engagement with Lübeck to lead a force of mercenaries into Holsten and Denmark with the object of reinstating Christian II.

The war[1] which now broke out developed rapidly in its early stages in favour of Count Christopher. With ships loaned by his Hanseatic ally he landed at Dragør in Zealand on June 21, 1534, was welcomed by the city of Malmø, now under the control of Jørgen Kock, and by July was in possession of Copenhagen. No serious resistance was offered by the nobles of these provinces of Zealand and Scaania, and on August 10 the Count was accepted at a gathering of representatives at Lund as governor on behalf of Christian II. The island of Fünen was the next portion of the kingdom to yield to the Count, and this was followed by a successful rising of the peasants of Jutland under the leadership of the old sea captain, Klement; except the southern part of the peninsula, almost the whole of Denmark was by this time in the hands of the Count and his allies.

Meanwhile, under the leadership of Mogens Gjø, the nobles in Jutland gathered at a Herredag at Skanderborg, where, after some opposition from the bishops, it was decided on July 4 to offer the crown to Duke Christian. In return for their homage the new King issued a declaration that on the return of peace a settlement of the religious question should be made in consultation with the members of the Council and the nobility. Johan Rantzau was then dispatched to crush the rising in northern Jutland, and by the end of the year (1534) and with the fall of Aalborg he had brought the north under the rule of Duke Christian. Count Christopher was at this time contending with a new foe who had appeared on his eastern flank, no less redoubtable an antagonist than Gustav Vasa of Sweden, who had decided both to assist his kinsman,[2] Duke Christian, and to help himself by striking a blow at the ally of Lübeck. Wullenwever retaliated by securing a promise of help from Albert, Duke of Mecklenburg, who was married to a niece of Christian II. An agreement was reached on November 14 between the Duke and the city of Lübeck by which, on the release of Christian II from prison, the Duke would act as his regent and succeed him to the throne. Thus, through the failure of the Rigs-

[1] A full account of " the Count's War " is given by Paludan-Müller, *Grevens Feide*.

[2] Christian III married Dorothea and Gustav married Katherine, both daughters of Magnus I, Duke of Saxe-Lauenberg. See *Letters and Papers*, vii, 710.

raad to elect a strong King on the death of Frederick, the whole state of Denmark was on the brink of dissolution and the land itself was divided up among the competing interests. Jutland was held by Duke Christian; Fünen by the forces of Count Christopher; Zealand was under the uneasy dual control of the Count and Duke Albert; and Copenhagen and Malmø were held by their citizens in independence of all higher authorities.

Early in 1535 the tide turned in favour of Duke Christian, largely by reason of a series of swift strokes which he made in conjunction with his able general, Rantzau. In March a force was dispatched to Scaania to unite with the nobles of that province and with the Swedish army and to lay siege to Malmø. At the same time Rantzau crossed over into Fünen and attacked and routed an army of insurgent peasants. A month later Christian dispatched a fleet to join with the ships of Gustav Vasa and threaten the naval supremacy of Lübeck in the Baltic. The decisive action of the war was fought two months later at Oksnebjerg in Fünen, where on June 11, 1535, Rantzau, commanding the royal army, defeated a combined force raised by Count Christopher, Albert of Mecklenburg and the city of Lübeck. At the same time a naval engagement near Bornholm ended in a success for the royal fleet and the destruction of many of the Hanseatic ships. Denmark thus had to yield to the victorious power of Duke Christian; only Copenhagen, Malmø and Landskrona still held out. The last two surrendered on easy conditions; but Copenhagen had to endure a severe siege and was finally starved into surrender on July 29, 1536.

2

When Christian had entered his capital in triumph his greatest need was for money to pay the troops by whose aid he had won his kingdom. At Copenhagen was an army of over 10,000 men, besides a fleet manned by Danish, Swedish and Prussian crews, all of whom had to be paid before they could be discharged.[1] The richest men in the country were the bishops, but they showed themselves unwilling to assist the King in his straits. Christian therefore determined to seize by force what he could not gain by persuasion. On August 11 he assembled a meeting of his army commanders, together with Johann and Melchior Rantzau, to consult how to meet the crisis, and it was decided forthwith to arrest and imprison the bishops. At 4 a.m. on the following day Torben Bilde, Arch-

[1] Arup, *Danmarks Historie*, ii, p. 478.

bishop of Lund, Rønnov, Bishop of Roskilde and Oluf Munk, Bishop of Ribe, were seized and lodged in the castle at Copenhagen. Four hours later the King summoned his remaining councillors together to approve what had been done. The same day forces were dispatched to Fünen to seize Gyldenstjerne, Bishop of Odense, and to Jutland to arrest the Bishops of Viborg and Børglum. The remaining Bishop, Ove Bilde of Aarhus, who was in Copenhagen, was allowed a few days of freedom, but he, too, soon found himself a prisoner.[1]

This *coup d'état* meant the end of the old episcopate of Denmark, but the view that it was unavoidable would probably represent the general opinion of Danish historians. "Had the King on that August night entertained for a moment any doubt as to the moral justification of the step he was about to take, the doubt was quickly dispelled. Necessity compelled him to get money where it was to be had, and it was to be had first and foremost from the bishops. And they no longer had any legitimate claim on the nation's wealth; for the Catholic episcopacy had in fact ceased to be. The bishops' own behaviour, and the proclamation of the Gospel, had brought it down; Catholicism was vanquished, and with that 'the bishops' times' were over."[2] Although the step was a violent one, it must be recognized that there was no bloodshed and that the bishops, apart from the loss of their freedom and the forfeiture of their estates and possessions, were not harshly treated. Only one of them, Rønnov, died in prison;[3] the others were released after a year or two's detention and were given small properties for their maintenance.[4] But they were set free only on the condition that they did not try to recover their position or to interfere with the new order in the Church. For the step was a great deal more than an expedient for obtaining money. The bishops' property and estates certainly provided the royal treasury

[1] See the letter of the Prussian Admiral Pein to Albert, Duke of Prussia, in Paludan-Müller, *Den Første Konger af den Oldenborgske Slaegt*, p. 620; and *cf.* Kidd, *Documents of the Continental Reformation*, p. 324.

[2] Jørgensen, *Reformationen i Danmark*, p. 229. "Hvis imidlertid Kongen i hin Augustnat et Øjeblik har naeret Tvivl om den moralske Berettigelse af det Skridt, han stod i Begreb med at foretage, er den hurtig bleven overvunden. Nøden tvang ham til at tage Pengene, hvor de var, og de var netop først og fremmest hos Biskopperne. Og disse havde ikke mere noget retmaessigt Krav paa Nationens Rigdomme; thi det katolske Bispedømme havde i Virkeligheden ophørt at vaere. Bispernes egen Holdning og Evangeliets Forkyndelse havde bragt til Fald, Katolicismen var overvunden, og dermed var 'Bispernes Tid' udrundet."

[3] Rønnov died a prisoner in Copenhagen Castle on May 1, 1544, while negotiations for his release were proceeding. Knudsen, *Joachim Rønnov*, p. 144.

[4] Helveg, *Den Danske Kirkes Historie*, iv, pp. 12, 13.

with the resources it needed; but Christian III's intention was to abolish the bishops' temporal power as well as to seize their wealth. Christian was a convinced Lutheran, and the Augsburg Confession had declared that a bishop's duty was to preach the Gospel and administer the sacraments, to remit or retain sins, and to banish erroneous doctrine, and that he was not to mingle secular duties with these supreme spiritual tasks. But the Danish bishops had exercised immense secular authority. Therefore those who showed reforming sympathies were sacrificed equally with those who clung to the old order. "Christian not only desired to separate the Danish Church from Rome and amend its doctrine and practice. It was his design to abolish the rule of bishops in its old form, and therefore bishops like Joachim Rønnov and Knud Gyldenstjerne had to go, although they had long before agreed to advance the Gospel."[1]

The success attending this stroke of the King is the measure of the unpopularity of the bishops. The Prussian admiral, Pein, reporting the events to his master, Albert, Duke of Prussia, declared that "most of the young nobility, the citizens of Copenhagen and other places and the Bønder, are well satisfied, and greatly rejoice at these doings; and the military also are very well pleased".[2] The lack of resistance on the part of the older Catholic nobles can be partly accounted for by the fact that some of the most stalwart supporters of the bishops had been taken prisoner in the war and were now in Germany. They were not to be released until they had paid homage to the King and promised to be loyal to the new régime. The submission of the members of the Council to the King's high-handed action is hardly surprising: some, like Mogens Gjø, welcomed the suppression of the bishops; others, like Tyge Krabbe, were Catholics and disliked the revolutionary change. But both sections of the Rigsraad, immediately after the seizure of the bishops, were compelled to sign a declaration by which they engaged themselves never to assist in the restoration of episcopal rule and not to oppose the preaching of the Gospel.[3] A similar declaration was readily made by the civic authorities of

[1] Jørgensen, op. cit., p. 229. "Kong Christian vilde ikke blot rive den danske Kirke løs fra Rom og aendre dens Laere og Skikke. Det var hans Hensigt at afskaffe Bispedømmet i dets gamle Skikkelse, og derfor maatte ogsaa Biskopper som Joakim Rønnov og Knud Gyldenstjerne falde, skønt de forlaengst var gaaet ind paa at fremme Evangeliet."

[2] See p. 71, note 1.

[3] Helveg, op. cit., iii, p. 1021. A transcript of the original declaration is published in Kornerup, *Reformationen i Danmark*, pp. 5, 6.

Copenhagen, Malmø and other towns. Thus the bishops fell, unbeloved and little lamented, and no champion appeared to defend or succour them.

Immediately after the surrender of Copenhagen the King issued a writ of summons to the Rigsdag, or national Diet,[1] which was to meet in October. Before this took place there assembled in Copenhagen a gathering of " preachers and ministers of God's Word from Zealand, Scaania and Jutland ", as part of the preparations for the Rigsdag. They presented an address[2] to the King in which they asked that the preaching of the Gospel might be freely allowed throughout the whole kingdom; that a superintendent should be placed over each diocese, with a man of marked gifts over the whole clergy to direct them in all spiritual matters; that a university of proper standing should be established in Copenhagen or elsewhere; that schools should be opened in all districts; and that hospitals for needy students, for widows and orphans, for the sick and aged, should have capable wardens appointed in charge of them. Most of the reforms underlying these proposals were to be the subject of regulation at the forthcoming Rigsdag, and as the clergy were not summoned to the Rigsdag[3] it was at least fitting that their views should be thus presented to the King beforehand.

3

On October 15, 1536, the Rigsdag assembled at Copenhagen, consisting of 19 members of the Council, 403 nobles, representatives from 81 towns and from every district—in all not less than 1,200 persons.[4] The proceedings lasted a fortnight, and on the concluding day a speaker addressed the assembly on behalf of the King, thanking them for their attendance and announcing that it was his desire to submit to them a new ecclesiastical and civil constitution. There was then read out a long list of complaints[5] against the imprisoned bishops intended as a justification of their seizure, among which were the following charges: (*a*) that they had agreed not to elect a King, but to rule the kingdom themselves; (*b*) that they had persisted in this policy even when the

[1] A Rigsdag was a meeting of representatives of the four estates of the realm—nobles, clergy, citizens and peasants—or at least of a majority of the four estates. See J. E. Larsen, *Om Rigsdage og Provindsialsamlinger*, pp. 303 ff.

[2] Helveg, op. cit., iii, p. 1024; Kornerup, op. cit., p. ix.

[3] Paludan-Müller, op. cit., p. 626.

[4] Paludan-Müller, op. cit., p. 629.

[5] Published in H. F. Rørdam, *Monumenta Historiae Danicae*, i, pp. 143-199.

flames of rebellion had spread throughout the land; (*c*) that they had divided up the estates of the Crown among themselves and their relatives and friends; (*d*) that the archbishopric of Lund had passed from hand to hand, so that there were now four or five men claiming to be Archbishop; (*e*) that every man knew how intolerably overbearing they were towards noble, citizen or peasant when they fell foul of them in some dispute. To general charges such as these were added specific complaints against individual bishops, not all, perhaps, fully warranted; but the main accusation, that when the throne was vacant they had postponed the election of a King and thereby plunged the country into war, was substantially just.

The next step was the settlement of the terms of the electoral charter (*Haandfaestning*) between the King and the Rigsraad.[1] The terms, which were drawn up on October 3, were less stringent for Christian III than they had been for Frederick I, in proportion as his position was much stronger than his father's had been. Frederick had had to renounce his claim to demand the election of his son as his successor in his own lifetime; this was omitted in Christian's charter, and in lieu thereof it was enacted that on the King's death his son, if of full age, or the regent, if the King's son was a minor, should retain possession of the royal castles. This in effect meant that the Council abandoned its complete freedom of choice and was a step in making the Crown hereditary. All reference to the rights and privileges of the Church or the bishops was omitted, and Christian III simply promised to reverence Almighty God, His Holy Word and doctrines, and to promote the advancement of the Christian faith. The nobles were allowed to retain their patronage of churches where it could be shown that this right of patronage was of ancient standing; and it was agreed that a nobleman's chief estate should be free of tithe on condition that his dependents paid their tithe in full. A question of wider issue was the relation of Norway to the Danish Crown, and it was decided that from henceforth Norway should be subject to the Danish monarch in the same way as Denmark itself, and should no longer have the status of an independent kingdom, electing its own King. Such were the far-reaching changes which the *Haandfaestning* effected and recorded. They have been shortly stated thus: the fall of the old Church; the abolition of the bishops' authority; the concentration of all civil and ecclesiastical power in the hands of

[1] Paludan-Müller, op. cit., pp. 626 ff.

the King and Council; the strengthening of the monarchy and its partial conversion into an hereditary office; the limitation of the power of the Rigsraad[1] as against that of the King; and the incorporation of Norway into the Danish state.[2]

At a general meeting of all the estates of the Rigsdag held in the market-place at Copenhagen on October 30 the representatives of the people confessed that they had committed wrong in rising up against those in authority, and the members of the Rigsraad and of the nobility admitted that they had been moved to act against the peasants and the commons. All ranks being now reconciled to one another and united in the defence of their country, there followed the adoption of the General Recess, the chief provisions of which were the following:[3] (*a*) The bishops being held responsible for the disorder, anarchy and war of the previous three years, they are to be deposed from their position, and other bishops, or superintendents, of Christian character are to be appointed, whose duty it shall be to preach the Word of God and instruct the people in the Christian faith. (*b*) The property of the bishops in each diocese, their castles, manors, lands and houses, are to be forfeited to the King and held by him in perpetuity for the maintenance of the Crown and the good of the kingdom. (*c*) Monasteries, cathedral Chapters and canonries are to continue until the King, in consultation with wise and learned men, shall make other provision. Monks and nuns are to be free to leave their convents; but if they prefer to remain they must live worthily of their vocation, and must have the Word of God preached to them. (*d*) The episcopal tithes are to be handed over to the King for the support of learned men and the setting up of schools; the other tithes, which the people are to continue to pay according to custom, are to be divided into three parts, one going to the parish priest, one for the maintenance of the parish church, and the third to the Crown for the support of scholars. (*e*) Hospitals are to be maintained and furnished with what is necessary; and in every town respectable and prudent

[1] E. Arup, however, considers that the Rigsraad gained in power from the fact that the King was expected to choose his ministers from among the Danish-born members of the Rigsraad (*Danmarks Historie*, ii, p. 486.)

[2] Paludan-Müller, op. cit., p. 628. "Disse vare de store og gjennemgribende Aendringer, Grevens Fejde medførte i Danmarks Statsret: Den gamle Kirkes Fald, Biskopsmagtens Afskaffelse, al Magt i Stat og Kirke lagt i Kongens og et verdsligt Raads Haand, Kongemagten styrket, Kronens Arvelighed halv indført, Rigsraadets Magt ligeoverfor Kongen indskraenket, Norge indlemmet i Danmarks Rige."

[3] Cited from N. Cragii, *Annales Daniae*, by Kidd, *Documents of the Continental Reformation*, No. 132. The Great Recess is printed facsimile in Kornerup, *Reformationen i Danmark* No. 22.

men are to be appointed to look after the sick and those who have no work. Begging by the able-bodied is punishable with death, though allowed to the sick who have no other resource. Most of the constructive proposals in this Recess for the reform of Church life were embodied in the Ordinance of 1539.

One clear result of the Rigsdag was the strengthening of the authority of the Crown. Not only had the King, in conjunction with the Lutheran minority of the Council, organized the ecclesiastical revolution, but he had secured its recognition and acceptance by the numerous and powerful assembly of the Rigsdag. Further, he had won for himself and his successors the vast wealth of the episcopal estates; he had no longer to fear the influence of the bishops, often exercised, as it had been, to the disadvantage of the Crown; and he had obtained a concession from the nobility which went some way towards weakening the electoral privileges of the Rigsraad. It had been agreed by the terms of the *Haandfaestning* that, in view of the evils which had arisen on the death of Frederick I, the election of the heir to the throne should be made in the lifetime of the reigning King, and in this the King's eldest son was to have the preference. Thus the aim of Christian II, in which he had failed—to make the monarchy hereditary—was in some measure accomplished by his cousin, Christian III.[1]

4

It would be wrong to regard the King's suppression of the bishops as inspired by a desire for self-aggrandizement. Christian III was a sincerely religious man; perhaps of all the European sovereigns in the age of the Reformation he, with Edward VI of England, were the only Kings who showed disinterested zeal for the recovery of religion.[2] Consequently his next step was to obtain from

[1] Heise, *Herredagen i Kjøbenhavn*, 1533, pp. 471-472. " Bisperfraenderne og Bispervennerne gik det navnlig ud over. Vel blive flere af dem senere atter optagne i Raadet; men dette kom i den følgende Tid kun til at bestaa af nogle og tyve Medlemmer ligesom i Kristiern den andens Dage, og det fik heller ikke i laengere Tid den politiske Myndighed, som det havde haft i Kong Frederik's Tid. Hertug Kristian havde sejret i Forening med den menige Adel, og dennes sociale stilling blev end mere udviklet paa de lavere Staenders Bekostning; men Rigsraadets Magt og Betydning have foreløbig lidt et Knack, medens Kongemagten atter var bleven staekkere, idet Anarkiets Grundpiller, det ubundne frie Kaar uden Tronfolgervalg i Kongens Levetid og Retten til vaebnet Modstand mod Kongerne, vare gaaede ud af Haandsfaestningerne. Det blev Følgerne af den tilsyneladende Sejr, som Bispearistokratiet vandt paa Herredagen 1533. Det var forbeholdt Hertug Frederiks Søn at knaekke dets Magt; det var den Nemesis, som ramte Oprørerne fra 1523."

[2] H. M. Gwatkin, *The Reformation*, in Hastings' *Encyclopædia of Religion and Ethics*, x, p. 618.

Germany one of the outstanding Lutheran divines to enable him to complete the work of reform in Denmark. For this purpose he applied to the Elector of Saxony for the loan of the services of Johann Bugenhagen, and in July 1537 this well-known assistant and friend of Luther arrived in Copenhagen.

Born at Wollin in Pomerania in 1485, and a member of the Premonstratensian Order (a branch of the Augustinian Canons), Bugenhagen,[1] though alive to the need of reform, had not at first approved of Luther's attack on the indulgence system; but after reading his treatise *On the Babylonish Captivity of the Church* he had become a whole-hearted supporter of the new movement. In 1521 he took refuge in Wittenberg, and was later elected by the Town Council as parish priest of St. Mary's, the town church. The remainder of his life was spent in visits to the newly-founded reformed communities of northern Germany in order to organize them on a Lutheran basis, periodically returning to his spiritual home at Wittenberg. In 1528, *e.g.*, he went as Superintendent to Brunswick and there issued a Church Order, the precursor of many such formularies; and from there he went to Hamburg to organize its Lutheran community, returning to Wittenberg the following year. In subsequent years he paid visits to Lübeck, where he arranged for the translation of the Bible into Low German, and to his native Pomerania, having between times returned to Wittenberg to become doctor of divinity. His zeal, learning and administrative ability made him one of the outstanding figures of the German Reformation, inferior only to Luther himself and his great colleague Melanchthon. When, therefore, he received the summons to proceed to Denmark, it was as no obscure Lutheran preacher that he arrived in Copenhagen, nor was the work to which he was called new to him.

His first task was to crown the King and Queen.[2] The ceremony took place with much pomp in the church of Our Lady, Copenhagen, on August 12, the King's thirty-fourth birthday. There were present Albert, Duke of Prussia, and his Duchess, Christian's sister, besides the ambassadors and representatives of foreign states and cities. The occasion aroused great interest, both in and beyond Scandinavian lands, not only by reason of the splendour of the festivities, but also because the actual crowning was performed, not by the Archbishop of Lund, but by Dr. Bugenhagen, parish priest of Wittenberg.

[1] Hering, *Johannes Bugenhagen.*

[2] Helveg, op. cit., iv, p. 5.

Some days later, on September 2, the church of Our Lady was the scene of another remarkable ceremony—the ordination of seven Lutheran clergy to be Superintendents, or 'bishops', of the reformed Church of Denmark.[1] In the presence of the King and Queen and members of the Rigsraad Bugenhagen laid his hands on the heads of the men who had been selected for the office and work of Superintendent. Their names and future dioceses were: Frans Vormordsen (Lund), Jørgen Sadolin (Odense), Mads Lang (Aarhus), Jakob Skjønning (Viborg), Peder Tomesen (Børglum), Hans Vandal (Ribe) and Peder Palladius (Zealand). The last-named was the only one not well known in Denmark, but he owed his promotion to the senior bishopric (often called Zealand rather than Roskilde) mainly to the recommendation of Luther and Bugenhagen, who had known him for some years in Wittenberg and had marked his great abilities. The others were prominent Danish clergy of the Lutheran faith, with the exception of Hans Vandal, who was of German or Slavonic origin. The fact that the name of the most distinguished Danish reformer, Hans Tausen, was not among those of the new Superintendents must probably be attributed to the desire of the King that he should undertake special work at the University.

The ordination of these seven men by a divine from Wittenberg was a deliberate act on the part of Christian III and his Lutheran advisers. It would have been possible to have found a regularly consecrated bishop, such as Hans Reff, of Oslo,[2] a man of few scruples, or, as has been suggested, one of the older bishops might have been prevailed upon to help. "It was not, on the one hand, a case in which no true episcopal consecration could be had; in all probability a very slight pressure would have brought the older bishops to consecrate Gyldenstjerne, Rønnov, and others who might have carried the ancient succession on. Nor was it, on the other hand, a case of deliberate preference for presbyterian ordination, as in some countries; the men now set apart—or almost all of them—were already presbyters, and they were to be made something more, and for the future to have sole authority to ordain. The act was intended distinctly to mark a new beginning."[3] It was, moreover, a new beginning, not only for the

[1] Helveg, op. cit., pp. 6 ff.

[2] Hans Reff had studied in Paris, became canon of Trondhjem, consecrated Bishop of Oslo in 1525, and was reinstated as Bishop or Superintendent of Oslo by Christian III in 1537. He died in 1545. See Willson, *History of Church and State in Norway*, pp. 312, 348.

[3] Canon A. J. Mason in *Church Quarterly Review*, April 1891, p. 186.

Church of Denmark, but for the Christian Church as a whole; for, as Bishop Stubbs noted, " up to the period of the Reformation there was no other idea of episcopacy except that of transmission of apostolic commission: that the ministry of the episcopal government could be introduced without such a link was never contemplated until Bugenhagen reconstituted a nominal episcopate in Denmark ".[1]

A noteworthy contrast exists between this decisive step thus taken in Denmark and similar arrangements which had been made some years before in Sweden. A Swedish scholar, Petrus Magni, was confirmed and consecrated as Bishop of Vesterås by authority of Pope Clement VII in 1524, " a fact ", writes Bishop John Wordsworth, " very important for Sweden, since through him the ' apostolic succession ' was maintained and transmitted at this critical epoch in its history ".[2] In 1527 Gustav Vasa was making preparations for his coronation, and in accordance with his wishes three new bishops[3] were consecrated by Petrus Magni with the old ritual in order that they might assist at the coronation, the King believing that the people would not be content unless he was crowned by anointed bishops. Thus while in Sweden an effort was made to maintain some continuity with the past, in Denmark the intention seems to have been to emphasize the commencement of a new order. But the Danish view of this step is different from the Swedish and the Anglican. " The Danish Church, which has always regarded ordination from the right standpoint and has maintained the principle that at the beginning of the Christian Church the office and orders of bishop and presbyter were one and the same, has been little perturbed by the objections and taunts of the Catholic Church and has not envied the Swedish and English Churches their so-called advantage that their bishops, through Laurentius Petri and Matthew Parker, have retained the true episcopal succession."[4]

[1] W. Stubbs, *Visitation Charges*, p. 191.

[2] *The National Church of Sweden*, p. 196.

[3] Kidd, *Documents of the Continental Reformation*, p. 234. The Bishops of Skara, Strengnäs and Abö were consecrated January 5, 1528, " without indeed the confirmation of the Pope, but with the ancient rites ".

[4] Münter, *Den Danske Reformationshistorie*, ii, p. 363. " Men den danske Kirke, som stedse har betragtet Ordinationen fra det rigtige Synspunkt, og paastaaet den Saetning, at i Christendommens Begyndelse Biskops- og Presbyter- Embede og Ordination har vaeret een og samme, har lidet bekymret sig om hele den katolske Kirkes Indvendinger og Spot, og har ikke misundent den svenske og engelske Kirke det saakaldte Fortrin, at deres Biskopper igiennem Laurentius Petri og Matthaeus Parker havde den aegte biskoppelige Succession."

5

Another work in which Bugenhagen had a hand was the restoration of the University of Copenhagen.[1] Founded in 1475 under a Bull granted by Sixtus IV to Christian I, it had come into being three years later by the issue of royal letters patent, by which the Bishop, Dean and Provost of Roskilde, with the Dean of Copenhagen, were appointed the governing body. Up to this time Danish students had been accustomed mostly to go abroad for their education, and even after the founding of the national University they continued to go to Germany, France and Italy, and latterly especially to Wittenberg when that University began to grow in fame. Copenhagen never attained eminence among the Universities of Europe, and after the exile of Christian II it entered upon a period of decline. This lack of success has been attributed to a variety of causes. It failed to win royal favour, Frederick I in particular showing little interest in it, and consequently it lacked endowments. The Bishops of Roskilde, who were *ex-officio* its Chancellors, were, with the exception of Lage Urne, not distinguished for love of learning; and among its professors only two, Paul Eliaesen and Cheristen Morsing, attained to any real eminence. Danish students, moreover, attracted to the new learning, would not resort to what they regarded as still a Catholic institution, but preferred to attend the Lutheran colleges at Viborg and Malmø. But the chief reason for its decline was the unrest in the life of the people caused by religious strife, and as this in time developed into civil war, the University after 1530 in effect ceased to be. Its refounding[2] as a Protestant institution was an essential part of Christian III's reconstitution of the Danish Church, for one of its main functions was to be the education of the new clergy. Under its new charter, in the drawing up of which Bugenhagen had a share, the first Rector to be appointed was one of the most distinguished of the older men, Cheristen Morsing, who had been a lecturer before the dissolution. The following list of professors with their subjects was announced at the reopening of the University. Theology: Bugenhagen, Tileman von Hussen, Palladius. Law: Laurentius Sibeney. Medicine: Morsing and

[1] See Werlauff, *Kiøbenhavns Universitet fra dets Stiftelse indtil Reformationen;* Rørdam, *Kjøbenhavns Universitets Historie;* Helveg, op. cit., iv, pp. 14, 15, 26-29; Rashdall, *The Universities of Europe*, ed. 1936, ii, p. 299.

[2] A full account of the refounding of the University is given by Rørdam, op. cit., i, pp. 75-115.

Thomas Zeger. Hebrew: Hans Tausen. Greek: Peder Povlsen. Rhetoric: Oluf Chrysostomus. Dialectic: Jens Sinning. Latin: Peder Parvus. For the maintenance of the professors and the assistance of poor students some grants of Church lands and houses were made, and its income was augmented by a subsidy from the customs dues of the Sound. The reopening of the University was celebrated at an inaugural assembly on September 9, 1537, at which the King and Council and city magistrates were present; and its charter was officially approved at the important Herredag at Odense on June 10, 1539, when the *Church Ordinance* was also adopted.

6

The final stage in the Lutheranizing of Denmark consisted in the drawing up of a full constitution for the Danish Church and its publication in the contemporary form as a *Church Ordinance*. For this purpose the King summoned a number of well-known divines, including Tausen, Sadolin, Vormordsen, Laurenssen, and others, together with two representatives from each of the surviving cathedral Chapters, to meet at Odense on the feast of Epiphany 1537, and to commence work on a draft for the proposed new *Ordinance*.[1] After a time the sittings were transferred to Haderslev, where some of the Slesvig clergy joined in the work. The result of these deliberations was a provisional scheme outlining the doctrine, worship and organization of the reformed Church of Denmark. The commission appears to have used both Danish and German sources in their composition of the *Church Ordinance*. Among the Danish works evidently employed were the *Malmø-bog* of 1530 and the *Forty-three Articles* of 1530, and among the German works there are clear traces of the influence of the following: Luther's *Formula Missæ*, the *Saxon Visitation Articles* and the *Church Ordinances* of Brunswick, Hamburg and Lübeck.[2] The draft, having been submitted to the King, was sent to Luther for his approval, and after it had received his favourable verdict it was laid before the Rigsraad. Accepted by them with only one comment, it was presented to the King for his signature on September 2, the

[1] It is supposed that the Commission consisted of twenty-six evangelical clergy with ten representatives of the Chapters—*i.e.*, two from each of the cathedrals of Viborg, Aarhus, Ribe, Roskilde and Lund. See Engelstoft, *Liturgiens eller Alterbogens og Kirkeritualets Historie*, p. 10.

[2] For a discussion of the sources of the *Church Ordinance* see J. Schnell, *Die Dänische Kirchenordnung*, and L. P. Fabricius, *Danmarks Kirkehistorie*, ii, p. 203. The *Church Ordinances* mentioned, with the *Formula Missae*, will be found in Richter, *Die evangelischen Kirchenordnungen*, vol. i.

notable day of the ordination of the seven Superintendents. Yet further amendments having been made, in its final form it was adopted at the Herredag at Odense on June 14, 1539.

In the view of a recent historian, "the Church Ordinance of 1539 is a very remarkable document considered as an ordinance, though it is evident that it was not composed by men of legally trained minds. It is very long and verbose, interlarded with general observations and references to Scripture: suited rather to be the draft of an ordinance than the ordinance itself. . . . It expresses the desire of Johann Bugenhagen and of the most upright and sensible of the Danish theologians for a future Lutheran Church Order in Denmark; but it is also evidence of the uncertainty of the Church's future position in the community. Such uncertainty must naturally prevail at a moment when the Church had recognized its own subordination to the secular State, and could not yet see what the consequences of this new order would be".[1]

When published the *Church Ordinance*[2] formed a book of over 200 pages, with an introduction by the King outlining the reasons why it was necessary to issue such a Church Order. Then follows an enumeration of the six parts into which the *Ordinance* was divided—viz: (*a*) concerning the preaching of the Gospel and the administration of the sacraments; (*b*) concerning schools and the teaching of the young; (*c*) concerning ceremonies, that there may be uniformity of use throughout the Church; (*d*) concerning the maintenance of the ministry and the relief of the poor; (*e*) concerning the duties of Superintendents and Provosts; (*f*) concerning books for the instruction of the clergy. This plan, however, is not strictly adhered to, and at the end of the book there is a long instruction by Bugenhagen on the duties of canons

[1] Arup, *Danmarks Historie*, ii, p. 504. "Kirkeordinansen af 1539 er et højst maerkeligt aktstykke som forordning betragtet, det ses tydeligt nok, at det ikke er juridisk skolede maend, der har affattet den. Den er meget omfangsrig og ordrig, gennemvaevet af almindelige betragtninger og henvisninger til skriftens ord, snarere et forarbejde til en forordning end selv en forordning. . . . Kirkeordinansen er et udtryk for de aerligste og forstandigste danske teologers og Johan Bugenhagens ønsker om en fremtidig luthersk kirkeordning i Danmark; den er et vidnesbyrd omden uklarhed over den kommende kirkes stilling i samfundet, som naturligt maatte vaere fremherskende i et øjeblik, da kirken vel havde erkendt sin underordning under den verdslige stat, men endnu ikke kunde se, hvilke folger denne nyordning vilde faa."

[2] A copy in the London Library has the following title: "Ordinatio Ecclesiastica Regnorum Daniae et Norwegiae et Ducatuum Sleswicensis Holtsatine etcet. Anno Domini M.D.XXXVII." It has been published by H. Knudsen in *Kirkehistoriske Samlinger*, i, pp. 55-116. A good account of the *Ordinance* is given by Münter, *Kirchengeschichte von Dänemark und Norwegen*, pp. 484-499: and a few extracts relating to the ordination of ministers will be found in Kidd, *Documents*, etc., pp. 328-334.

and monks which contains some repetition of what had already been said.

The preaching of the Gospel has priority of place and directions are given as to its manner and method. To avoid discursive and ineffectual preaching a list of subjects is supplied upon which the clergy are to address their people. This list comprises the divine commandments, the Gospel and faith in God, penitence, the Cross, prayer, good works, free-will, Christian liberty, predestination, tradition, the magistracy, matrimony, the saints, fasting, and images. A warning is given to avoid giving offence or causing perplexity to the simple when speaking on some of these topics.

The sacraments instituted by Christ are declared to be two—viz., Baptism and the Lord's Supper—to which penance is added as a third, for the benefit of sinners who are truly penitent and desirous of forgiveness. Then follow directions for these services or rites: the singing and reading of choir boys in church, the Mass, preaching, Baptism, Absolution, Communion, festivals, matrimony, institution of the clergy, excommunication, visitation of the sick and of those under sentence of death, burial of the dead, and prayers for women at child-birth.

A few extracts from the directions concerning Baptism and the Mass will show the nature of the Danish reforms in the administration of the two great sacraments. Private Masses are abolished. Mass is to be said in the presence of communicants and with the accustomed vestments and lights. The *Kyrie Eleison* and *Gloria in excelsis* may be sung in Latin or in Danish, the Gradual or other Psalms in Danish only; the Collect, Epistle, Gospel and Creed also in the vernacular. After the sermon the communicants approach the altar, the men kneeling on the right, the women on the left, and the exhortation is then read to them. After the Lord's Prayer the priest proceeds with the prayer of consecration in Danish, with a simple use of the Elevation (if it is thought convenient and the people have been instructed about it): the people then communicate in silence, since they have already heard Christ's words of institution. After a thanksgiving the congregation is dismissed with the Blessing.

Baptism is to be administered to infants and the service is to be in Danish. The words of exorcism are retained, but care of the child's health is to be shown in the actual sprinkling with water. No reference is made to Confirmation.

Among further directions relating to other rites are the following. Before the Lord's Supper the minister is to be ready to hear the confessions of those who wish to communicate: absolution is to be given with the laying on of hands. Matrimony is the concern of the civil magistrate, but the minister may hold a service of blessing for the married couple. Ordination with the laying on of hands and prayer is conferred by the Superintendent in his cathedral on candidates who have previously been examined and have taken an oath of loyalty to the King. The newly ordained minister is then inducted into his parish by the Provost.

In all these services the *Ordinance* is concerned mainly to give directions, not to provide the Church with a manual of public prayers. Instructions are given for the recital of the Lord's Prayer or the Creed or a particular Collect, or the reading of appropriate passages of Scripture, or the singing of a hymn, such as the *Veni Creator*, but a complete form of service, with the exception of that for the Ordination of Superintendents, is not provided. It is, in fact, a Directory of Worship, not a Book of Common Prayer.[1]

As to education the *Ordinance* directs that Latin schools are to be set up in every town, each with a minimum of two masters. The boys are to be divided into five classes, according to their standard of knowledge. In the first class, having learnt their letters they are to begin to acquire a simple vocabulary and knowledge of grammar with the aid of a *Donat* and *Cato*.[2] In the second class they proceed to Melanchthon's *Grammar*, with *Æsop's Fables* and selected *Colloquies* of Erasmus. The third class continue the use of Melanchthon's *Grammar*, committing to memory passages from Terence and reading also selected *Comedies* of Plautus and *Letters* of Cicero. Terence is to be used both for learning to speak and for writing letters in Latin. The fourth class begin Vergil, attention being paid to his style, and read also Ovid's *Metamorphoses* and Cicero's *De officiis* and *Epistolæ ad Familiares*. In the fifth and highest class the boys who have attained a sufficient knowledge both in reading, writing and speaking Latin may be instructed in the rudiments of Greek, without, however, dropping their Latin studies.

It was declared to be the responsibility of the magistrates to see that common schools for boys and girls not suited for the Latin

[1] On this see Engelstoft, *Liturgiens eller Alterbogens og Kirkeritualets Historie i Danmark*, pp. 1, 2.

[2] See Lupton, *Life of Colet*, p. 21.

schools are set up where they are needed; and in all schools children are to be brought up piously, the Catechism is to be learnt and, in the case of older children, passages from the Psalms and from the New Testament are to be read. The Superintendent of the diocese and the local clergy are to inform the Crown where the accustomed salaries of the masters are not adequate, and when vacancies occur in benefices they are to be filled up by the institution of masters whose existing stipends are insufficient.

For the maintenance of the ministry the payment of the accustomed tithes is to be continued and the clergy are to retain their right to the offerings of the laity at Christmas, Easter and Whitsun. Two wardens are to be elected in each parish for the care of Church moneys and administration of other ecclesiastical business. Magistrates are to nominate two pious and prudent men as overseers of the poor, and they are to be responsible for the proper disbursement of the moneys collected on behalf of the needy. A chest is to be set up in each town for the reception of offerings for this purpose.

A long section then follows on the duties of Superintendents and Provosts. Being married men with families, they are to be provided with a modest establishment of two maids, a secretary, a messenger, a groom and a page-boy. As they were no longer owners of property, like the old bishops, the *Ordinance* specifies certain allowances of rye, oats, hay, straw and malt, with forty lambs and a hundred golden gylden, which the Crown undertakes to pay to each Superintendent yearly. Their duty is the responsible one of preaching and teaching throughout the diocese and supervising the lives and ministry of the clergy under their care. They are not to concern themselves in legal matters unless summoned to give testimony by the King or Council; but in all cases of conscience they are to be ready to give their advice as doctors of Holy Writ. When they visit a town they are to inspect the schools, and in company with the local magistrate see that all is well in regard both to the teaching of the young and the care of the needy. On the death of a Superintendent the clergy of the diocese are to elect four ministers with full powers to elect a successor. After examination by a neighbouring Superintendent the man chosen is to be confirmed in his office by the King and then ordained in his cathedral by one of his fellow Superintendents, with the assistance of the Provost and five or six neighbouring ministers. The order of service to be followed in such cases is set out later in the book and with a fulness of detail lacking in the other forms of service. Provosts serve under the Superintendents, and their duty is to visit each parish in the diocese yearly and to summon the local magistrates to assist them in enquiring into the general state of the church in regard to the preaching of the Gospel, the administration of the sacraments, the teaching of the young, the condition of the cemeteries and church buildings, and the position of church funds.

A brief but interesting section of the *Ordinance* recounts the books which should be in the possession of the country clergy. First comes the Bible; then Luther's *Postils*; the *Apology* and *Loci Communes* of Melanchthon; a book explaining the Catechism and Luther's *Lesser Catechism*; the *Liber informationis Visitationis Saxonicæ*;[1] and the Danish *Church Ordinance*. To this somewhat meagre list is appended the prohibition that no book in Danish, Latin or German, and especially no work of a theological, political or economic character, is to be printed in Denmark unless it has first received the approval of the University and of each of the Superintendents.

The position of the cathedral canons and of monks and nuns is then briefly alluded to. Canons may retain their rank and their stipends, but they are expected to provide a theologian who shall publicly and in Latin deliver lectures on Holy Scripture at stated times, such lectures being arranged so as not to interfere with the ordinary preaching. The canons must give themselves to sacred study and must celebrate the Lord's Supper every Sunday. They may marry, if they so desire. Monks and nuns may leave their convents and are then free to marry; but if they elect to remain they must keep their vows and follow a life of piety and study. The friars may not go about begging, nor may they preach or hear confessions; if aged and infirm, they may remain in their monasteries, but must put off their habit and not deride " the Gospel ".

The remainder of the *Ordinance* is occupied with the *Instruction* of Bugenhagen on the rule of life for canons and monks, in which he sets out with a wealth of Scriptural quotations and in a somewhat contentious spirit the Lutheran faith in many of its affirmations and denials. At the end is appended a list of those who subscribed to the *Ordinance*—canons, preachers, pastors, as they are variously described, thirty-six in all, among them the well-known names of Laurenssen, Tausen, Vormordsen, Chrysostom, Lang and Tast.

[1] See Laurence, *The Visitation of the Saxon Reformed Church*, pp. 21-54.

7

The *Church Ordinance* sanctioned in 1539 was followed by a series of directions issued between 1540 and 1558 developing or amending the earlier provisions. Thus, to avoid contention in the appointment of the parish clergy, the Articles adopted at Ribe in 1542 (forming an appendix to the *Church Ordinance*) directed that on a vacancy occurring in the ministry of a parish the parishioners should choose seven of their oldest and most respected men, and these, with the advice of the Provost, should select a new parish priest. The various directions issued by authority had to be carried into effect in the parishes and dioceses of Denmark; and the reign of Christian III, ecclesiastically regarded, is the story of the endeavour to apply the reformed methods of faith and worship to the life of the Danish people. No attempt will be made in this work to write the history of the Church of Denmark after the Reformation; but a few remarks will be necessary to indicate the lines upon which the Church developed in the early years of the reign of Christian III.

Though the Lutheran Superintendents succeeded the Catholic bishops in their respective dioceses, the Archbishop of Lund had no successor in the primacy; the seven Superintendents ordained by Bugenhagen were of equal standing, except that Palladius, the Bishop of Zealand, had a certain seniority, due partly to his outstanding abilities, and partly to the importance of his see-city, which was removed from Roskilde to Copenhagen. The Bishop of Zealand was normally one of the theological professors at the University, and Palladius has had many distinguished successors in that office, among whom may be mentioned F. Münter, the celebrated historian, and H. L. Martensen, whose *Dogmatics* were known to most English clergy of a generation or so ago.

One of the most important functions of the new order of Danish bishops was that of the visitation of their dioceses, and it happens that Palladius has left behind him a description of the many subjects for enquiry and for admonition which arose in the course of his tours. His *Visitatsbog* is a contemporary document all the more valuable in that it was written without thought of publication and was not indeed published till the nineteenth century.[1] The instructions contained in it cover the whole compass of the local Church's well-being: the condition of the material edifice,

[1] Lis Jacobsen, *Peder Palladius' Visitatsbog.*

its furniture and churchyard; the duties of parishioners and of parish priests and deacons; the obligation of the payment of tithe and other offerings; the observance of Sundays and holy-days, of prayer and fasting and almsgiving; the making of wills and the provision of Church books; regulations about marriage and excommunication and the punishment of evil-doers; with a variety of injunctions to parents, to boys and girls, to midwives and to witches. Palladius is believed to have taken six years to visit the 390 parishes of his diocese:[1] the work of rebuilding Christian communities on an evangelical basis was a slow and laborious task. One of the difficulties was the shortage of suitable clergy, due partly to the suspension of the University's activities from 1530 to 1537, and partly to the general unsettlement of life in a time of civil war and revolutionary change. Some parish churches were demolished or in disrepair; others with no priest were annexed to a neighbouring parish. There was, however, no wholesale dispossession of the clergy from their benefices, for the vast majority of them, though brought up in the old faith, adapted themselves to the new ways, perhaps, as it has been suggested, without feeling particularly strongly that they were new.[2] The reason for the change-over in some cases is put plainly in the following words: "A great number of the old Catholic priests went over to the Reformation and continued at their posts. The adoption of the new ways was easy to them, for they had long been filled with bitterness and indignation against the old Church, and the Gospel came as a deliverance for themselves, their wives and children. Paul Eliaesen declares that none were more zealous than the sons of the clergy of Jutland to join 'the ungodly sect'. They could not have much love for a Church which, by the imposition of the rule of celibacy, dishonoured their homes and their mothers."[3]

Among the multitudes of clergy who thus accepted the new order there must have been some at least who in doing so compounded

[1] *Palladius' Visitatsbog*, p. 1.

[2] Fabricius, *Danmarks Kirkehistorie*, ii, p. 291; Arup, op. cit., p. 508; *cf.* J. O. Andersen: "practically all the old clergymen remained in office because they willingly accepted the reform" (*Survey of the History of the Church in Denmark*, p. 25).

[3] Jørgensen, *Reformationen i Danmark*, p. 112. "En stor Del af de gamle katolske Sognepraester sluttede sig til Reformationen og blev siddende i deres Embeder. Overgangen til det nye er falden dem let; thi de havde allerede laenge vaeret fyldte med Bitterhed og Uvilje mod den gamle Kirke, og Evangeliet kom som en Befrielse for dem selv, deres Hustruer og Børn. Povl Helgesen fortaeller, at ingen var ivrigere end Praestesønnerne i Jylland til at slutte sig til 'den ugudelige Sekt'. De kunde ikke have meget tilovers for en Kirke, der som en Følge af Cølibatsbudet vanaerede deres Hjem og deres Moder."

with their conscience and sought to retain their posts from motives of self-interest.[1] Many of the old clergy married, sometimes going through the marriage ceremony with the woman with whom they had lived for years, in order to regularize their position and make their children legitimate. In time others were ordained who in lay life were already married, and since the clergy were regarded as belonging to the middle class the temptation existed for these men and for their wives to enter the clerical ranks to improve their social position.[2]

Besides the beneficed clergy there existed a class of assistants known as deacons. These were usually young men who had reached the highest form in their Latin school and were employed as deacons in the near-by parishes, to assist the priest and to teach the young. They were of two kinds, resident and non-resident, the former (*saededegne*) living in the parishes where they actually served, the latter (*løbedegne*) travelling out to a country parish, where they acted as deacon while continuing to live in the nearest town as a senior pupil of the Latin school. This latter arrangement was never popular with the country parishes. Many of these deacons hoped to become clergy themselves, and being sometimes better educated than their parish priest and yet in an inferior social position, there was no lack of occasion for friction and jealousy between the two.[3]

8

During these first years of the reformed Church's existence worship acquired its Lutheran character, though the uniformity of later years was not achieved at once. Since the *Ordinance* did not give a complete form for every service, the practice developed of publishing Manuals to supply what was lacking: such were the *Enchiridion* of Palladius (1538) and Vormordsen's *Haandbog* (1539). Palladius' work is a translation of Luther's *Encheiridion* and contains, besides his Catechism, forms for Baptism and Marriage.[4] The *Haandbog* of Vormordsen is a more ambitious attempt to supply the clergy with a complete directory for worship.[5] Other

[1] H. V. T. F. Bang, *Praestegaardsliv i Danmark og Norge*, p. 13.

[2] Bang, op. cit., pp. 17, 18.

[3] Bang, op. cit., pp. 228, 229.

[4] It is printed facsimile with the accompanying woodcuts in Palladius' *Danske Skrifter*, i, pp. 63 ff.

[5] Its title runs: "Een gantske nyttleig oc alle Sogneprester oc predicantere nødtørftelig Handbog Om den rette Euangeliske Messe oc hennis ustraffelige oc gamble seduanlige Ceremonier med Collecter oc Prefationibus Desligest, om Børn at christne. Bruder ath vye. De siuge oc dennem som fengslede ere at søge. Oc om ath Jorde lug.

similar aids to worship continued to appear until a definitive stage was reached in the publication of Palladius' *Alterbogen* in 1556.[1] This became the authoritative Manual and was reprinted, with alterations and additions, several times during the next hundred years. It opens with a form of confession and a prayer before preaching, both in Latin. Then follow the Collects, Epistles and Gospels for the Sundays of the Christian year, including provision for a weekly *Bededag* (day of prayer) on Thursdays (a characteristic observance of the post-Reformation Church). A litany and prayers for various occasions are followed by the Proper Prefaces for Christmas, Easter, Whitsun and Trinity Sunday in Latin and with musical notation. Then comes the Marriage Service containing the questions to the bridegroom and the bride; the joining of hands and giving of the ring (the latter being permissive only); the declaration of marriage by the priest with the words " those whom God hath joined together . . . "; the reading of passages of Scripture bearing on the duties of man and wife; the laying on of the priest's hands on the heads of the married couple; and the recitation of the Lord's Prayer and a final collect. After the Marriage Service comes a short Order for Baptism, much simplified, though still retaining features of the old ritual. First, the priest utters the prayer, " Fly, unclean spirit . . . ", and then signs with the cross the face and breast of the child. Then follow a prayer; the Gospel (Mark 10, 13); the Lord's Prayer; the questions to the godparents; baptism in the Threefold Name; concluding with a prayer and an address to the sponsors. Forms for Baptism at home and for reception into the Church after an emergency Baptism are also provided. The *Alterbog* contains, besides, a brief Catechism in five parts on the Commandments, the Creed, the Lord's Prayer, and the two Sacraments. The edition of 1564 also comprised a number of additional prayers to be used on various occasions and concluded with the story of the Passion compiled from the four Gospels.

Thus under the leadership of Palladius, assisted by the other bishops, by means of liturgical forms such as these, the framework of Christian worship was being built up among the Danish people

---

Flitteligen effter kongelige maistads Ordinantsis indeholdelse: Colligered, ordinered oc somestedis fordansskedt. Anno Domini MDXXXIX." Part of the Handbook (that giving the *Messe*) has been reprinted, with introduction and notes, by H. Kent in *Braendpunkter i Reformationstidens Gudtjeneste-ordning*.

[1] Published in Palladius' *Danske Skrifter*, iii, pp. 339 ff.

upon an evangelical foundation. Yet much to which the clergy and laity were accustomed was retained. In Torslunde church, Zealand, *e.g.*, is a panel bearing the date 1561 depicting an altar with crucifix and two lights, the celebrant wearing alb and chasuble and his assistant a sleeveless surplice. Two other scenes in the same picture represent a priest in sleeveless surplice baptizing an infant at the font and another preaching from the pulpit in the black gown of everyday wear.[1] Facts such as these support the claim that in Denmark " the Reformation by no means meant a rupture with the past but only a cleansing ".[2]

9

" Education," it has been said, " can on the whole be regarded as a plant transferred from Catholic ground to evangelical soil ".[3] When the monasteries were evacuated by their residents the buildings in many cases continued to be used for schools. Here lived the schoolmaster, called sometimes by the high-sounding title of Rector, and with him any assistants he may have had. The Rector was an ecclesiastic who may also have acted as chaplain at the local church; his immediate superior was the parish priest, while bishops and provosts exercised a general supervision over the schools in their diocese.

Before the Reformation changes the younger sons of the nobility often attended the cathedral or monastic schools in the expectation of ecclesiastical preferment. But with the lowering of the social status of the higher clergy this motive ceased to operate, and the nobility preferred to have their children taught at home by the family chaplain or the local priest. The majority of the pupils attending the schools were, therefore, the children of the poor; and the old custom of children begging from door to door for their food and maintenance (which Christian II had endeavoured to stop[4]) was continued into the new times. In pre-Reformation days it had also been usual for boys to sing the daily services in church, and in some places they continued to do this morning and evening, as part of their school training, for many years after the Reformation. Another feature which survived, in spite of changing times, was

[1] See reproduction in Fabricius, *Danmarks Kirkehistorie*, ii, p. 216.

[2] Fabricius, op. cit., p. 297. " Reformationen slet ikke betød et Brud, kun en Udrensing."

[3] H. V. T. F. Bang, *Latinskoleliv og Studenterliv*, p. 109; a useful work, to which some of the information in the text is indebted.

[4] J. O. Andersen, *Overfor Kirkebruddet*, p. 154.

the performance of school plays—a play of Terence, or one of the old Moralities, or a drama based on Biblical scenes. As to the actual lessons, the *Church Ordinance* had drawn up in some detail a sort of curriculum, which perhaps was to be regarded rather as an ideal to be aimed at than as an account of what actually was being taught: the real state of affairs is pungently described in the following words: "Two subjects appear, both before and after the Reformation, to have been the chief factors in education—Latin and flogging; if the Latin did not often succeed in rising above the level of the famous 'monks' Latin', it may nevertheless be granted that, by way of recompense, the other aspect of philosophical instruction—viz., the flogging—was imparted with a faithfulness worthy of a better cause."[1] All the evidence goes to show that both before and after the Reformation school discipline was brutal and barbaric, and that only a few enlightened spirits like Christiern Pedersen realized this and aimed at something better.[2]

The schools which thus carried on into the transition time the old teaching with the old methods were of two grades: Latin schools, in which Latin was the chief subject taught, and writing schools, for boys and girls capable of only the simplest teaching. In all schools instruction in the Christian faith was an essential element, and the responsibility for this lay mainly with the parochial clergy. Besides giving religious instruction in school, the parish priest and deacon were expected after the Sunday morning service to catechize children and young people in church. For this purpose Palladius had issued in 1537 (only a few weeks after his ordination as Superintendent) a fresh translation of Luther's *Little Catechism*.[3] Sadolin had already published a Danish version of it in 1532, and Vormordsen had produced another in 1537: the

[1] Bang, op. cit., p. 69. "To Genstande synes, baade før og efter Reformationen, at have vaeret Hovedfaktorerne i Undervisningen,—Latin og Prygl; men om end Latinen ofte ikke naaede at haeve sig højere end til at blive det berømte 'Klosterlatin', maa man til Gengaeld indrømme, at den anden Side af den videnskabelige Undervisning, nemlig Pryglene, drives med en Standhaftighed, der var en bedre Sag vaerdig."

[2] Christiern Pedersen's *Danske Skrifter*, iv, p. 505. "De fattige børn, peblinge, oc degne laerde en føye ting aff dem i xv eller xvi aar, met saa megen swar daglig hwstrwgelse sorg angst, nød oc drøffuelse, som de lede aff de wbarmhertelige scolemestere. De kunde nw laere meget mere, oc bedre lerdomme udi try eller iiii aar for uden saadanne daglige hwg og slag." ("The poor children, schoolboys and deacons, learn very little from them in fifteen or sixteen years, with so much daily flogging, grief, terror, distress and torment which they experience at the hands of merciless schoolmasters. They could learn much more and get better instruction in three or four years without such daily floggings and blows.")

[3] Palladius' *Danske Skrifter*, i, pp. 12 ff.

translation of Palladius was a revision of these two earlier works and was issued as a school-book to assist the deacons in their task of giving religious instruction. Whatever faults marred the life of the reformed Church in its earliest days, neglect of its duty to the young cannot be laid at its door. The importance of the Christian education thus imparted by the clergy has been recognized today, and the claim that out of this early teaching of the young grew the Danish schools of later centuries is not unwarranted.

10

A peculiarity of the Reformation in Denmark was that monastic life continued within it for some years after the Church had acquired its Lutheran form.[1] A distinction was drawn between the mendicant and the other Orders in the treatment meted out to them. As early as 1522 Christian II's code had forbidden all begging for alms to the monasteries which had property of their own (*Herreklostre*), and allowed it on certain conditions to the four mendicant Orders only (Dominicans, Franciscans, Carmelites and the Order of the Holy Spirit).[2] By the *Church Ordinance* of 1537 the mendicants themselves were forbidden to beg, preach or hear confessions; and as their houses were mostly in the towns the civic authorities took advantage of this and of the friars' unpopularity to seize their property and convert it to other uses.[3] Monks of the other Orders were allowed to leave their monasteries, and if they did so their Superior was expected to give them clothes and money for immediate expenses on their departure. Those who wished to remain in their monastic home were to continue to live their life under rule; and it was desired that they should attend lectures and read the Scriptures, so that they could take charge of a parish. " This happened to no small extent, and not a few of the first evangelical clergy had been monks."[4] Thus many of the monasteries became emptied of their occupants, and when this happened the land and property were taken over by the Crown and leased, sold or given to lay possessors. " By 1540 thirty-seven monasteries were already purely secular holdings, and in 1559 there were only ten still under ecclesiastical rule, of which five were the Cistercian houses which

[1] See Daugaard, *Om de danske Klostre*, pp. 120 ff.
[2] Andersen, *Overfor Kirkebruddet*, p. 154.
[3] Karup, *Geschichte der katholischen Kirche in Dänemark*, appendix, *passim*.
[4] Jørgensen, op. cit., p. 254. " Dette er ogsaa sket i en ikke ringe Grad, og ikke faa a de første evangeliske Praester havde vaeret Munke."

continued under the supreme direction of the abbot of Sorø."[1] This man, by name Henrik Tornekrands, was a highly respected member of the royal Council, and held his position as head of this group of Cistercian communities with the King's consent and on condition that he and his successors did homage to the Crown.[2] The character of these surviving monasteries necessarily changed with the changing circumstances of the time. The monks were now expected to take a more active part in the life of the Church, some assisting as parish priests in neighbouring churches, others helping in the education of the young, and all conducting themselves and their worship in accordance with the tenor of the *Church Ordinance*. But since they no longer dared to take novices their ultimate disappearance was only a matter of time. The Danish monasteries were almost all extinct under Frederick II and their property taken into the possession of the Crown or given to deserving lay officials.[3]

The position of nuns[4] was similar to that of the monks: the *Church Ordinance* permitted them to leave their convents, though added that, if they wished to marry, they should do so with their nearest friend's advice. During Christian III's reign the property of some of the nunneries was leased by the King to noblemen, no doubt because of the decline in numbers of their occupants, the decline being so serious that in the reign of Christian's successor, Frederick II (1559-88), it was expected the nunneries would disappear. It was, however, decided to maintain the convent at Maribo[5] for women who wished to join it without taking the vows. Two convents are known to have continued their existence into Frederick's reign, both of them belonging to the Order of St. Bridget—viz., the convent of Mariager in the diocese of Aarhus and the convent of Maribo in the diocese of Odense, the latter surviving into the seventeenth century.[6]

The conservatism of some of the measures adopted by Christian III and his advisers is seen in the retention of the canonries at-

[1] Arup, op. cit., ii, p. 533. "1540 var allerede 37 Klostre rent verdslige len, og 1559 var kun 10 endnu under gejstlig styrelse, deraf de 5 cistercienserklostre, der stod under Sorøabbedens overbestyrelse."

[2] Helveg, *Den danske Kirkes Historie*, iv, p. 24. The names of the five Cistercian monasteries were Soer and Esrom in Zealand, Herrevad in Skaane, Vidskild and Øm in Jutland.

[3] Münter, *Den Danske Reformationshistorie*, ii, p. 623.

[4] Daugaard, op. cit., pp. 122 ff.

[5] For this convent see Daugaard, op. cit., pp. 321 ff.

[6] Helveg, op. cit., iv, p. 24; Münter, op. cit., ii, p. 624. The Maribo Convent was secularized in 1621 and its property handed over to the new Academy of Sorø.

tached to the cathedrals. The Rigsdag of 1536 had decided that the cathedral Chapters should continue until the King, in consultation with learned men, should make other provision. This other provision, however, was never made, and the property of the Chapters continued to be held for the benfit of the canons. As the old Catholic canons died off, other clergy, of Lutheran views, succeeded to the position and to the property. The surviving Chapters were five in number—viz., those of Lund, Roskilde, Ribe, Aarhus and Viborg.[1] The church of Our Lady at Copenhagen had also a Chapter of two 'prelates' and eight canons, but it had already been decided that the income from these prebends should pass to the University as the present holders died off. The members of the five cathedral Chapters were expected to observe in a modified form the canonical hours; to nominate one of their number as Rector of the cathedral school; to maintain a scholar who should lecture in Latin on the Scriptures to the canons, schoolmasters, intelligent citizens and others who desired to attend; and generally to assist the bishop in his spiritual duties. If it is surprising that so much of the old capitular organization survived, the explanation probably lies in the fact that the King inherited the right of the old bishops to appoint to vacant canonries, and thus by retaining them he acquired considerable Church patronage with which to reward the friends of the Reformation. During these years of transition there was naturally a certain amount of tension between the older and more recently appointed members of these Chapters. The King himself sanctioned and encouraged the holding of formal debates on controverted points between the theological professors at the University and the Chapters of Lund and Roskilde. But on the whole there is a refreshing absence both of actual persecution[2] and of bitterness and violence in controversy in this period of theological change, when the Danish Church was being reconstructed under the firm and zealous rule of Christian III.

[1] Helveg, op. cit., iv, pp. 46 ff.

[2] *Palladius' Visitatsbog* speaks of the expulsion and hanging of Catholic clergy (" nu ere de tiffue uddreffne aff landet och en part ophengde " p. 62): commenting on which the editor, L. Jacobsen, writes: " This is the only evidence of the hanging of Catholic priests during the Reformation; the injunction to expel them was generally interpreted very humanely." He quotes Professor J. Oscar Andersen's opinion that " Palladius may have been referring to the excesses which took place during the Count's war " (L. Jacobsen, *Palladius' Visitatsbog*, p. 177).

PART II

ASPECTS OF THE DANISH REFORMATION

CHAPTER IV

CHRISTIERN PEDERSEN AND THE TRANSLATION OF THE BIBLE

1

IN Denmark, as in other countries, translations of portions of the Scriptures were made in the Middle Ages, and examples of such versions have survived " the immense shipwreck of libraries and literature which happened during the sixteenth and seventeenth centuries ".[1] Thus there is a MS. in the Royal Library at Copenhagen of a Danish translation of the O.T. up to 2 Kings which belongs to the fifteenth century. It is a small folio of 319 pages and is a literal rendering of the Vulgate into the dialect of Jutland. Vernacular versions also of the Psalter survive in the Hour Books which were in use in nunneries and in private houses in the fifteenth and early sixteenth centuries.[2] With the advent of printing a new era in Bible translation began.

The first printing house in Denmark was founded by Gotfred van Ghemen, a Hollander, who, perhaps at the invitation of Dr. Peder Albertsen, Vice-Chancellor of the University, came to Copenhagen in 1489 and set up there a printing and publishing business.[3] His first book was a small Latin grammar for the use of schools in Denmark; his second was an account of Danish history in rhyming verse. The latter was a popular success and reached three editions; it was the first book actually printed in Danish. After bringing out some romances of chivalry, a dictionary, and an account of the Turks' unsuccessful attack on Rhodes (1480), he turned to religious literature and published in 1508-9 a book on the childhood of Christ and a book of prayers. He died in 1510, and the next chapter in the history of Danish literature opens with the life and writings of the scholar and translator, Christiern Pedersen.[4]

2

Both the year and the place of Pedersen's birth are uncertain, but it may be surmised that he was born about 1480 and it is

[1] *Cambridge Modern History*, i, p. 639.
[2] C. J. Brandt, *Danske Bibeloversaettelsers Historie*, pp. 5-8.
[3] E. Arup, *Danmarks Historie*, ii, p. 301.
[4] For Pedersen see C. J. Brandt, *Om Lunde-Kanniken Christiern Pedersen og hans Skrifter;* and Brandt and Fenger, *Christiern Pedersen's Danske Skrifter.*

known that he received his early education at the large and celebrated school of Roskilde. Possibly he went to the University of Copenhagen, but of this there is no direct evidence. He became a canon of the cathedral of Lund in 1505, and in accordance with a common custom went abroad for further study and took up residence at Paris in 1510. Here he devoted himself at first to classical studies, the immediate fruit of which was his publication of a Latin-Danish dictionary (*Vocabularium ad usum Dacorum*, Paris, 1510). Having taken his M.A. at the University in 1511, in the years following he superintended the printing at Paris of a series of service books for the Church in Denmark, a *Diurnale* (1511) for the use of the canons of Roskilde, and a *Missale* (1514) and a *Breviarium* (1517) for the diocese of Lund. Then came a work which brought him fame in a far wider circle. Christiern possessed the historical temper, with a special interest in the early story of his country; and encouraged by his friend, Lage Urne, Bishop of Roskilde, he determined to bring out an edition of the *Gesta Danorum* of Saxo Grammaticus.[1] For this purpose he returned to Denmark to seek for a suitable MS. in the monastic libraries; he met with no success until Archbishop Birgir, the primate of Lund, discovered a MS. and presented it to Christiern. Other highly-placed dignitaries also offered their help, and by the mediation of Erik Valkendorf, Archbishop of Trondhjem, and of Ove Bilde, the royal Chancellor, Pedersen obtained the King's warm approval for its publication. He then returned to France, arranged with Badius Ascensius for the printing, and published the work at Paris in 1514. "Saxo's work at once aroused great admiration. Even the great humanist, Erasmus of Rotterdam, declared, 'I grant him a lively mind and a brilliant talent, with a style which is never loose or heavy, and is moreover surprisingly rich.'"[2]

In the year (1514) he brought out this historic work he also produced two lesser books in Danish, a *Tidebog—i.e.*, an Office book of prayers and psalms—and an instruction on the Mass (*Bog om Messen*).[3] The latter is a devotional work intended to assist the simple layman to follow more intelligently the words and actions

[1] Little is definitely known of the life of this famous Danish chronicler, but it is believed he was a canon of Roskilde who, encouraged by Absalon, Archbishop of Lund, 1182-1201, composed in florid Latin the legendary history of Denmark's early heroes and kings.

[2] Arup, op. cit., p. 303. "Sakses vaerk vakte straks stor beundring. Selv den store humanist Erasmus Rotterodamus siger: 'jeg tilstaar det: en levende aand og et tindrende talent, en stil som aldrig slappers eller sover, dertil en forunderlig fylde af ord.'"

[3] Brandt and Fenger, *Christiern Pedersen's Danske Skrifter*, ii, pp. 415-476.

of the priest. Pedersen goes through the whole service, dividing it into thirty-three sections, which are made to correspond with the thirty-three years of our Lord's life and with the events of His ministry, Passion, Death and Resurrection. Although there is much in this exposition which seems crude and forced, yet each section has a prayer of a simple and devotional character which, if sincerely used as intended, would have enabled the worshipper reverently to participate in the Mass. But Pedersen's teaching on these matters is still that of the Catholic priest of the pre-Reform era, for he promises that those who hear Mass and read the prayers thus printed will merit 137,000 years' Indulgence—a promise, he declares, " confirmed by many Popes ".[1]

In 1515 followed what was his most important contribution to religious knowledge during his stay in Paris—viz., his *Søndags Postillen.*[2] This was a translation into Danish, with exposition, of the Epistles and Gospels of the Sundays and feast-days of the Church's year. The opening words of the Preface run: " To the praise and honour of Almighty God, the Blessed Virgin Mary and all the saints in heaven, the Epistles and Gospels which are read every Sunday are here translated into Danish, with explanation and commentary on each, for the benefit and salvation of all simple Danish people who do not understand Latin; that they who are ignorant of Latin may themselves read in Danish how they should rightly live according to God's commandment."[3] Although he does not appear conscious of any prohibition by the Church of such translations of Scripture, he was aware of the possibility of prejudice existing in some minds, and therefore in his Preface to the *Postillen* he wrote: " If any one of them (the Apostles) had written the Gospels for the people of Denmark he would certainly have written them in good Danish so that all could understand, for each people ought to know them in their own speech. No one can believe that they are holier in one tongue than another: they are as good in Danish and German as they are in Latin, when they are equally well translated; and unreasonable and cantankerous people cannot truly say that it is wrong or unfitting to translate them into Danish when no one can be saved without them and the holy

[1] *Danske Skrifter*, ii, p. 420.

[2] *Ibid.*, i and ii.

[3] *Ibid.*, i, p. xiii. " Den alsommeckiste Gwd Jomfrw Marie og alle gwdz helghen i hiemmerigiss rige till loff oc aere Alle enfoldige Danske folk som icke forstaa latine til nøtte oc salighed Ere alle Epistler och Ewangelia som laesiss alle sondage udsette paa danske met deriss udtydninger oc i Jerteghen til hwert aff dem At de som icke latine forstaa Mue nw selfue laese paa danske hworlediss de rettelige leffue skwlle effter gwdz budord."

faith."[1] The book seems to have been widely read, and another edition was brought out in 1518. It is especially noteworthy as a product of "the Catholic time", before the Reformation in Denmark really began; and noteworthy too because, as a Danish scholar has recently written, "for all his partiality for the legends of the saints it is marked by a deep respect for the Bible and a trust in the significance of Christ's suffering and death".[2]

Christiern produced one more work before he left Paris, an edition of Peder Laale's *Dictionary*. This had already been published by Gotfred van Ghemen in 1506 and 1508, and it is evidence of the popularity of this work that Christiern thought it worth while to bring out in 1515 another edition of this useful compilation of words and phrases.

So far almost all Pedersen's books, with the exception of the *Postillen* and two smaller religious works, had been in Latin. He had produced books of devotion for the devout; he had compiled dictionaries for the student; and he had made Saxo's *Chronicle* available to the scholar. His work in Paris had been that of an Erasmian humanist, employing the new art of printing to spread light and knowledge, and using his own special gifts for the promotion of piety and learning.

3

Christiern Pedersen returned to Denmark in 1515, residing probably at Lund. These were troublous times for the Chapter of which he was a member, for from the death of Archbishop Birgir in December 1519 to the flight of the King in April 1523 no less than five different men possessed or claimed the see.[3] Christiern acted as Chancellor to the last of these Archbishops-elect, the German Johann von Weze, and for a short period he was also secretary to the King. But when the latter fled the country

[1] *Danske Skrifetr*, i, p. xiv. "Sagde noghen aff dem screffuit evangelia till danmarckiss Righe Da hagde han de dem visselighe screffuit paa ret danske saa alle det forstondet hagde thii hwert menniske bør ath kwnde dem paa sit egeth maal Inghen skall tro ath de ere helligere paa eth twngemaall en paa eth andet De ere saa gode paa danske oc tydske som ded ere paa latine (naar de ellerss reth udtydiss) Thii kand inthet ufornymstigt eller awendsfulth menniske rettelige sige ath det ilde giort eller wbequemmeligt At udsette dem paa danske Men ingen kand bliffue salig for uden dem och den hellige tro."

[2] Kornerup, *Hans Tausens Postil*, i, p. 7. "Det ejendommeligste homiletiske vaerk fra den katolsk Tid i Danmark, Christiern Pedersens (Jertegns) Postil, 1515, der med al sin Forkaerlighed for Helgenlegendernes Vildnis dog er baaret af en dyb Respekt for Bibelens Ord og Fortrøstning til Kristi Lidelses og Døds Betydning."

[3] The five were Aage Sparre, Jørgen Skodborg, Cardinal de Ceci, Didrik Slagheck and Johann von Weze.

Pedersen remained at his post, though his position became very difficult. A letter of his to von Weze, written from Lund on September 1, 1524, expresses his hopes for Christian's return and declares that all, except the nobles, equally long for the King's restoration.[1] A rising led by the famous sea-captain, Søren Norby, a supporter of Christian II, was defeated by the forces of Frederick, and when Lund itself was attacked Pedersen fled and was thereupon deprived of his canonry by the Archbishop-elect, Aage Sparre.[2] His movements after this are difficult to trace, but he may have joined the King at Berlin, where he was staying during the summer of 1526 with his sister Isabella, the wife of the Elector of Brandenburg. When Christian established his small court in the Netherlands at the castle of Lier (four miles south-east of Antwerp), Pedersen followed him there and remained a member of his court for the next five years. A surviving list of the exiled King's followers gives about forty names, with the two ex-Archbishops of Lund and Upsala (von Weze and Gustav Trolle) at the head, and occupying the eighth and ninth positions respectively the names of Hans Mikkelsen and Christiern Pedersen.[3]

During his residence in the Netherlands his chief literary work was the translation of the N.T. and the Psalms. When the first Danish version of the N.T. was exhausted the King entrusted to Pedersen the task of a new translation. He was not a Greek scholar, though perhaps not entirely ignorant of that language;[4] so he had to rely mainly on the Vulgate, using as well Erasmus' Latin version, Luther's German and the earlier Danish N.T. of Vinter and Mikkelsen. The book was printed at Antwerp and completed in August 1529; and a second edition was brought out in 1531.[5] As a literary masterpiece the work is judged to be scarcely inferior to Luther's own and surpasses both the earlier and later Danish versions.[6] It is interesting to note that another brilliantly successful translator, William Tyndale (whose N.T. had been printed at Worms in 1526), was in Antwerp during 1529, and though there is no record that he and Pedersen ever met, yet they had a common friend in the printer Johan Hochstraten.[7] The latter had brought out some of Tyndale's other works at Antwerp, one of the great printing centres of Europe, and it is likely enough that he there

[1] C. J. Brandt, op. cit., pp. 413-415.
[2] December 23, 1525. See C. F. Allen, *De tre nordiske Rigers Historie*, v, p. 69.
[3] Brandt, op. cit., p. 183.
[4] *Danske Skrifter*, iii, p. 554; Brandt, op. cit., p. 194.
[5] Ten second edition is published as vol. iii of the *Danske Skrifter*.
[6] Brahdt, op. cit., pp. 294-295.
[7] Mozley, *William Tyndale*, pp. 123-124.

made acquaintance with Pedersen, for three years later they were in Denmark together, busy at their press in Malmø.

Pedersen next turned his attention to the O.T., and in 1531 brought out his Danish version of the Psalms.[1] Lacking a knowledge of Hebrew, he used various Latin translations, including those of Jacques Lefèvre[2] and Luther[3]; a few of the Psalms he tried to render in verse and rhyme, believing they were meant to be sung.[4] A Danish Psalter had already been brought out by Frans Vormordsen in 1528,[5] and Pedersen appears to be referring to this when he declares that of Psalters formerly published in Danish "all complain that they cannot understand them".[6]

In this year (1531) he brought out various other books of a religious character: (*a*) a book on the Passion,[7] illustrated with woodcuts, and based on a work of Luther's; (*b*) a sermon of Luther's on the Passion,[8] which had been previously translated and published by Paul Eliaesen in 1526; (*c*) Luther's *Betbuchlein*,[9] translated in part by Paul Eliaesen and in an enlarged form by Pedersen under the title "the right way to the Kingdom of Heaven" (published also in an English version by John Gau in 1533); (*d*) a translation of an anonymous German work (published in 1524) entitled "on Faith and Love"[10]; (*e*) two sermons of Luther on "how each shall bear his cross" (delivered in Lent 1531)[11] and "on marriage and the rearing of children" (1519)[12]; and (*f*) "on keeping a child at school and study",[13] a free version of a similar work written by Luther in 1524. All these books—the second edition of the N.T., the Psalter, and the seven smaller works—were printed at Antwerp in the fine Gothic type which he later took with him to Denmark; and it has been suggested[14] that since he could hardly have published so many works in Danish without Christian's approval and support, the King may have regarded them as so many spiritual weapons in the enterprise he was to embark upon when he sailed for Denmark in the late autumn of

[1] Published in *Danske Skrifter*, vol. iv.
[2] Lefèvre published in 1509 his *Quincuplex Psalterium*, a work containing five different versions of the Psalms in Latin, printed in parallel columns.
[3] *Danske Skrifter*, iv, p. 575.
[4] *Ibid.*, iv, p. 153.
[5] See Chapter VII, sect. 3, *post.*
[6] *Danske Skrifter*, iv, p. 154.
[7] *Ibid.*, iv, pp. 159-192: "Om vor Heres Død og Pine."
[8] *Ibid.*, iv, pp. 193-210, "Vor Herris dod oc pine."
[9] *Ibid.*, iv, pp. 211-332, "Den rette vey till Hiemmerigis Rige."
[10] *Ibid.*, iv, pp. 333-423, "Om Troen oc Kerlighed."
[11] *Ibid.*, iv, pp. 425-450, "Hvorledis huert Christet menniske skal bere sit Kaarss."
[12] *Ibid.*, iv, pp. 451-465, "Om Ecteskaff oc børn ath opføde."
[13] *Ibid.*, iv, pp. 467-518, "Om børn ath holde till Scole och Studium."
[14] By Helveg, *Den Danske Kirkes Historie*, iii, p. 899.

that year. Certainly they were a greater success than the King's military preparations: the latter resulted in disaster and ultimately in the King's lifelong imprisonment, while Pedersen's books went everywhere in Scandinavia and were read again and again.[1]

4

The fact that nearly all these books were translations or adaptations of various works of Luther is proof that Pedersen had by now become converted to the new faith. Nothing is known as to the precise circumstances which brought about this change in his religious life. He may have visited Wittenberg for a short time in 1526 after leaving Denmark and there gained convincing proof of the power of the new movement; or he may have been influenced by one or other of the ardent Lutherans among Christian II's following; or it may have been the reading of some of Luther's own writings which brought conviction to him. His own love for the Scriptures and his belief that they should be in the hands of every Christian made the transition easy; and in the Preface to the N.T. (1531) he publicly confesses the errors he formerly held when he wrote the *Postillen.* " I confess the great error of which I was guilty when I inserted in those other books published in Paris the stories of the miracles and legends which people had invented and dreamt, implying that we should live like the saints and thereby merit the Kingdom of Heaven by our own good deeds. This, however, is a lie and a delusion, for Christ alone has made satisfaction for our sins and won for us the heavenly Kingdom by His Death and Passion. I pray you all to dismiss these miracles and legends and put no trust in them, but hold entirely fast and true to God's own Word and Gospel, and let no one move you from them by false teaching. God be blessed eternally, Who hath delivered me from my error by His mercy and allowed me by His grace to learn and understand His Word and Gospel better than I once did in my blindness."[2] This has the authentic Lutheran ring, and there is no

[1] *Danske Skrifter*, iv, pp. 586, 602.

[2] *Ibid.*, iii, p. x. " Jeg bekender her oc selff men store vildefarelse som jeg vaar før udi, den tid jeg lod sette de Jertegen oc fabel i de andre bøger i Paris (som menniskene haffue opdictet och drømet) At mand skulle leffue som de helgene giorde, oc der met faartiene Hiemmerige, oc met deris egne gode gerninger, Hwilket dog er løgn oc vildfarelse. Thi at Christus haffuer all ene giort fyllest for vaare synder, oc fortient oss Hiemmerigis Rige met sin død oc pine. Thi beder jeg alle, ath i lade samme Jertegen oc fabel hen fare, och setter ingen tro eller loffue til dem, Men bliffue all eniste stadelige oc fast hoss Gudz egne sande ord oc Evangelia Oc lader ingen drage eder fra dem met andre falske lerdomme. Gud vere benedidet til evig tid som drog mig aff min vildfarelse aff sin miskundhed Oc unte mig sin naade til at laere oc forstaa sine ord oc Evangelia bedre en jeg giorde førre i min blindhed."

doubt that Pedersen became a sincere and devout confessor of the Lutheran faith. Yet it is noteworthy that he scarcely mentions Luther in his books,[1] while he frequently refers to Erasmus;[2] this perhaps was partly because it was safe to praise Erasmus but sometimes dangerous to praise Luther. While in the Netherlands the Danish King's following were watched suspiciously by the Regentess Margaret: once she caused Hans Mikkelsen and his servant Henrik Smith to be arrested on a charge of heresy, though Christian managed to secure their release. Another adherent of Christian's was less fortunate: Willom van Zwoll was burnt at the stake, October 10, 1529.[3] But it was not only fear of consequences which kept Pedersen from expressly mentioning Luther while he frequently published Luther's books: there was besides a difference of temperament and of outlook between them which prevented complete agreement. Pedersen was of a gentler nature, with the temperament of a student, conservative in feeling and respectful towards tradition. He did not like Luther's disparagement of the Epistle of St. James. " I do not understand," he writes, " how some can presume to call St. James's Epistle an epistle of straw, as if it were of no more value. All Christian men know that he was Christ's apostle and spake by the Holy Spirit. But by what spirit or power they speak who say this God knows best, from Whom nothing can be hid, and He shall judge all."[4] Pedersen's view was the older one that all Scripture is inspired of God and is therefore worthy of man's respect. His zeal and love for the Scriptures were indeed pre-Lutheran. Christian II and some of his circle had already manifested their interest in the study of the Bible before Luther's name was on everyone's lips. Pedersen's edition of the *Postillen* (1515) had been adorned with the royal arms, which suggests that the King had given his approval to, and perhaps had even contributed towards the cost of, the publication. Later, Christian II took the initiative in founding the theological lectureship (1518) filled by Paul Eliaesen and in issuing regulations to the clergy and ordinands in regard to the study of Scripture. This interest in the Bible shown by the King and such personal supporters of his as

[1] Helveg, op. cit., iii, p. 828; Brandt, op. cit., p. 195.

[2] *E.g.* in his Preface to N.T., *Danske Skrifter*, iii, p. ix.

[3] Brandt, op. cit., p. 184.

[4] *Danske Skrifter*, iii, p. 491. " Thi forstaar jeg icke hwor faare somme driste dem till ath kalle dette S. Jacobs breff ith straa breff (lige som det vaare icke mere vert) Dog vide alla christne vel ath han vaar Christi apostel oc talede aff dem helligand. Men hvad gejst eller aand de tale aff, som det sige, det ved Gud alder best, som ingen ting kan skiulis faare, Han skall och døme alle."

Pedersen himself and Hans Mikkelsen seems to have been of native growth and not due specially to the influence of Wittenberg.[1]

5

When Christian II made his tragic attempt to recover his kingdom in 1531, Pedersen may have accompanied him; but there is no direct evidence of this, and it is perhaps more likely that he travelled independently of the royal fleet and reached Denmark overland. At any rate he eventually arrived at Malmø, and with him came his printing press, accompanied probably by Johan Hochstraten, his friend and assistant, and here they appear to have received in 1532 a licence to print.[2] While in Malmø Pedersen married the widow of Christopher Madsen, by whom he had a daughter, Anna;[3] he thus became one of the circle of married clergy, which included Laurenssen and Vormorsden, who were making Malmø a centre of reform.

The first book issued from his press after his return to Denmark was a Danish version of Johan Agricola's *Catechism*.[4] Agricola (1492-1566) was a Wittenberg scholar who became parish priest at Eisleben and later acted as chaplain to the Elector Joachim II. He first published his *Catechism* in 1527 under the title, " A Hundred and Thirty Questions for the Children of the Girls' School at Eisleben ", and the questions grew in number as edition after edition came out. When Pedersen published his Danish translation of it in 1533 the questions had increased to 170, and the book was intended as a complete catechism of the Christian faith for both young and old. This was followed in the same year by a medical work, *En nyttelig Laegebog*, a compilation of what might be called household remedies, drawn partly from MS. sources and partly from his own experience and that of others. In the next year he published a book on herbs, with instructions how to prepare herb-water (*Urtevand*). After this excursion into natural history and the medical art he returned to the publication of historical works, producing in 1534 the *Chronicle of Charlemagne* and *King Olger's Chronicle*, both in the Danish language.[5] The last book to be mentioned in this group of publications is a new edition of *Den danske Psalmebog*, which Pedersen brought out in 1533. The one surviving copy (now in the University Library, Oslo) is incomplete

[1] Andersen, *Overfor Kirkebruddet*, pp. 166-167.
[2] *Danske Skrifter*, iv, p. 605.
[3] Brandt, op. cit., p. 247.
[4] *Danske Skrifter*, iv, pp. 519-567.
[5] Published in *Danske Skrifter*, vol. v.

and lacks the author's name; but there is little doubt that it proceeded from Pedersen's press and that he was the editor. It is not likely, however, that he composed any of the hymns in the collection. "Christiern Pedersen's strength lay in his Danish prose . . . he is not among the hymn-writers of Denmark."[1] The book was an improved and enlarged edition of the earlier hymn-book of Mortensen, but it does not appear to have displaced it.[2]

The varied character of these publications shows that Pedersen took no narrow view of the intellectual needs of his countrymen. He was one of the few men of his time with modern ideas of education who realized the folly and cruelty of the savage treatment of children at the hands of schoolmasters. He condemned outright the merciless floggings which children had to endure and which sometimes led promising pupils to run away from school.[3] In other ways, too, he was a man apart: there are signs that some of the Lutheran clergy did not approve of his historical books which described the old "papistical" times. "They cry out and say that such should not be printed", he remarked at the end of *Olger's Danish Chronicle*.[4] But he believed in a culture based on history, the history of his own land and of classical times. "If I had children," he wrote, "and was able to keep them at school and study, they should learn not only Latin but other languages, and also chronicles and histories; and they should not be content with that, but should learn also to sing, to reckon and keep accounts, to measure distances by land and sea, and to understand the course of the heavenly planets. All these arts are none other than youth's delight and pleasure, when young people are properly taught them in their youth—studies which the Greeks in olden time taught their children when they were young."[5] These words,

[1] P. Severinsen, *Danske Salmedigtning i Reformationstiden*. "Christiern Pedersens Styrke var den danske Prosa. . . . Christiern Pedersen ikke er blandt Danmarks Salmedigtere" (pp. 78-80).

[2] C. J. Brandt, *Vore Danske Kirke-Salmebøger*, pp. 5, 6. See also Christiern Bruun, *Psalmebøger fra Reformationstiden*, i, pp. 193-196; ii, pp. 5-8.

[3] *Danske Skrifter*, iv, p. 503.

[4] *Ibid.*, v, p. 313.

[5] *Ibid.*, iv, p. 505. "Jeg sig for mig ath hagde jeg børn oc formaatte at holde dem til scole oc studium Da skulle de icke all eniste laere latine, men och andre twngemaall Och desligest Krønicker och Historier, De skulle icke heller der met lade dem nøge, Men de skulle och laere vel at siwnge, oc ath regne oc legge regenskaff, oc ath maale dybhed oc langhed paa vand oc land, oc forstaa dem paa hiemmelens planeter oc løb. Alle disse Konster ere icke andet en ungdommens velløst oc leeg, naar unge menniske ret oplerdis i dem i deris ungdom I hwilke Grekerne oplaerde deris børn i forme tid men de vaare unge."

with their Renaissance ring, were written while he was still in the Netherlands; but they were also written within a year of the time when Laurenssen and Eliaesen were waging their controversial war over the reforms at Malmø. There was a liberalism in Pedersen's outlook which, sincere Lutheran though he was, kept him apart from the contemporary theological fray.

6

The outbreak of the civil war in 1534 interrupted Pedersen's literary labours. He became secretary to Jørgen Kock, the powerful burgomaster of Malmø, and travelled to Rostock and Lübeck on political business. Kock's ambition was to make Malmø independent, but the mounting power of Christian III caused the peace party in Malmø to prevail, and the city surrendered to the forces of the new King on April 6, 1536. The end of civil strife and the victory of Christian III brought into prominence the men who were known to be convinced Lutherans. Thus at Lund Frans Vormorsden became the first Superintendent, Hans Spandemager (Olufsen) the parish priest of the cathedral, and Peder Laurenssen theological lecturer. At first no place seems to have been found for Christiern Pedersen: either his Catholic past stood in the way of his promotion, or more probably his own quiet contemplative disposition kept him in the background. He may have occupied some minor post as *vicarius* at the cathedral of Lund; and it was probably at this time that he sold his printing press to Hans Vingaard of Copenhagen. But his genuine literary ability could not be hid; and when Christian III authorized the issue of the whole Bible in Danish and made the University responsible for the work, Christiern Pedersen seems to have been selected as the man to shoulder the main task of translation.[1] His fitness for the work was recognized. " He wielded his pen better than any of his contemporaries. What he wrote as translator was read so easily and understood so correctly that, when peace came again after the storm, the choice was soon made of the man to whom should be entrusted the most important task of rendering the whole Bible into the mother tongue, after the manner of the Master's own translation into German. For Pedersen had not only proved his ability in general to write good Danish and to render German books into his mother tongue, but he had also translated the N.T. and a part of the O.T.,

[1] Molbech, *De danske Bibeloversaettelser*, p. 75.

and had thereby publicly announced his design of issuing the whole Bible in Danish."[1]

Pedersen commenced his work in 1536 and it occupied him about seven years; and an almost equal length of time was spent in the task of revision and printing. A Commission for revision was appointed, consisting of Palladius, Bishop of Zealand; Johannes Maccabaeus[2] and Niels Hemmingsen, professors of theology at Copenhagen; Hans Henriksen, afterwards Canon of Roskilde; and Peder Tidemand, who had himself at one time translated portions of the O.T. into Danish.[3] Their work and their reputation have tended to overshadow Pedersen's unique contribution, and his name was not officially mentioned as a collaborator in the translation of the Bible. His task was made more difficult by the King's expressed desire that the translation should adhere as closely as possible to the German of Luther. Yet it is the considered opinion of one of the leading Danish authorities in this matter that " it may be confidently assumed that a large part of the merit attaching to the Bible translation of Christian III, regarded from the standpoint both of the Church and of literature, belongs to Christiern Pedersen ".[4] When the Bible finally came out in the summer of 1550, Pedersen had accomplished his last and greatest work. He was then a man of about seventy, and he lived but four years longer. Some time before his death he had gone to live with a relative who was parish priest at Helsinge (1½ miles N.E. of Hillerød) and there he died on January 16, 1554.

[1] Brandt, op. cit., p. 316. " Han førte en bedre Pen end nogen af hans samtidige. Man laeste saa let og forstod saa godt, hvad hans Pen havde gjort sig till Tolk for, saa, da der var kommen Stille efter Stormen, har Valget vist snart vaeret truffet, hvem det betydningsfulde Arbejde skulde betros: at tilvejebringe en fuldstaendig Bibel paa Modersmaalet, selvfølgelig efter Mesterens egen Oversaettelse paa tysk. Thi Christiern Pedersen havde jo ikke blot i Almindelighed godtgjort sin Dygtighed i at skrive Modersmaalet og fordanske tyske Arbejder, men han havde allerede selv oversat baade det ny Testamente og en del af det gamle, og havde derhos offentlig erklaeret, at det var hans Agt at udsaette den hele Bibel paa dansk."

[2] Otherwise John Macalpine, a Scottish cleric who had left his native land to reside first in England (as Canon of Salisbury) and then at Wittenberg, where he was made Doctor in Theology (1542). From there he was sent by Melanchthon to Denmark, to be chaplain to Christian III and Professor of Theology in the University of Copenhagen. See *The Richt Vay to the Kingdom of Heuine*, by John Gau, ed. by A. F. Mitchell, Scottish Text Society 1886-87, pp. xii, xiii.

[3] Molbech, op. cit., pp. 70, 71.

[4] Brandt, op. cit., p. 333. " Tør det vel trostig antages, at en Hoveddel af den kirkelige og sproglige Fortjeneste, der maa tillaeges Christian III's Bibel-Oversaettelse, tilhører Christiern Pedersen."

7

The Bible of 1550 was not only the crown of Pedersen's career, but also marked the completion of the Reformation in Denmark. Compared with the somewhat intricate story of the English Bible the stages of the translation of the Scriptures into Danish are few and simple.[1] The first Danish N.T. was that of Mikkelsen and Vinter, published at Leipsig in 1524 on the initiative of Christian II, who possibly had conceived the plan before his exile from Denmark. It was not a literary success and Paul Eliaesen was perhaps justified in his criticism that Mikkelsen's version was " neither Danish nor German " and that " from good metal he had made a bad coinage ".[2] The next Danish version of the N.T. was, like the first, due to Christian II's encouragement and was the work of one of his exiled followers. While living in the Netherlands the King persuaded Pedersen to bring out a revised translation, which was published at Antwerp in 1529 and was reprinted two years later. Though based chiefly on the Vulgate and Erasmus' Latin version, it was written in clear and idiomatic Danish and was a marked literary achievement.

The first portion of the O.T. to be translated in the Reformation period was the *Psalter*. Frederick I gave his sanction to the Danish version of the Psalms which Frans Vormordsen, assisted by Paul Eliaesen, had printed at Rostock in 1528. Three years later, Christiern Pedersen, dissatisfied with Vormordsen's attempt, published a better translation of the Psalms at Antwerp (1531). This was followed by the more ambitious attempt of Hans Tausen to translate the whole of the O.T. into Danish; but he got no farther than the five books of Moses, published at Magdeburg in 1535. It was, however, well received and a second and third edition was brought out in 1536 and 1537. A Danish priest, Peder Tidemand, then brought out a translation of three more O.T. books: the *Book of Judges* in 1539, and the *Wisdom of Solomon* and *Ecclesiasticus* in 1541. These all followed Luther's text and were printed at Magdeburg. The final step was the production in the way described of the entire Scriptures, known as the Bible of Christian III, and printed by Ludovich Dietz at Copenhagen in 1550. With the exception of Tausen's translation of the Pentateuch, which appears to have been made from the Hebrew,[3] none of these Danish

[1] See Molbech, *De danske Bibeloversaettelser*, pp. 26-77.
[2] Secher, *Povel Eliesens Danske Skrifter*, p. 91.
[3] Rørdam, *Kjøbenhavns Universitets Historie*, i, p. 474.

versions were based on the original languages. The first Danish Bible to be translated direct from the Hebrew and Greek was that of H. P. Resen, who almost single-handed and after years of labour produced a new translation in 1607, four years before the appearance of the English Authorized Version.[1]

8

Christiern Pedersen has been called the first Danish writer of importance.[2] He was not an original thinker or an independent author; in all his works he either edited or translated or interpreted the work of others. But he possessed a clear and easy style and was a man of versatile mind and wide interests; and next to the advancement of the Gospel his chief desire was to increase his countrymen's knowledge of the early glories of their fatherland. He was a patriotic Dane, loyal to the Scandinavian union, and had no love for Germans: this, with his genuine affection for Christian II, accounts for the cloud under which he lived in some of his later years. His life opened with brilliant promise. As the editor of Saxo's *Chronicle* he won fame for himself and the support and patronage of Christian II and the primates of Lund and Trondhjem. When the King fell on troublous times Pedersen shared his exile, but contributed to the Lutheran movement by his published works. On his return to Denmark he lived a retired life at Malmø, occupied in literary employments, until he emerged again into the daylight of fame and honour as the chief translator of the first Danish Bible.

He is the earliest representative of that characteristically Danish type of mind which conceives the true national life of Denmark to lie in the union of Christianity, popular education and a knowledge of Danish history.[3] Like Paul Eliaesen, he was a conservative reformer, but, unlike him, he was not a controversialist. Eliaesen remained a Catholic, though a liberal and reforming one, to the end of his days; while Pedersen, beginning as a Catholic, became a Lutheran, yet clung to the culture of the past, and, like the scribe of the Gospels, brought out of his treasure " things new and old ". Two tributes from his countrymen unite to stress this, his essential, characteristic. " He was sufficiently open-eyed and warm-hearted to welcome the Reformation with joy; yet he was perhaps of too historical a temper entirely to approve a revolution which took so

[1] Helveg, *Den Danske Kirkes Historie*, iv, p. 233.
[2] Brandt, op. cit., p. 389. [3] Arup, *Danmarks Historie*, ii, p. 303.

little care to preserve that which was good in the old and which might have been made to serve as a link with the past."[1] "What especially distinguishes Christiern Pedersen, what constitutes his intellectual characteristic, is the natural way his love for the past and his desire for the spread of its culture among the people mingled with a sincere acceptance of the pure Gospel. While most reforming preachers, in order to combat Papistry thoroughly, studied only too often how to suppress everything which, as inherited from the past, was the people's spiritual possession, he, on the other hand, knew how to purify without rejecting, and thereby to maintain his love for tradition and history, for proverb and ballad. But he stood alone in his age, and only from ancient records has an industrious student been able to collect these otherwise unknown and rare notices of his last days."[2]

[1] Brandt, op. cit., p. 5. " Var han end klarøjet og varmt følende nok at hilse Reformationen med Glaede, saa var han maaske dog en for historisk Natur, till uden videre at billige en Omvaeltning, der tog saa lidet Hensyn til at bevare, hvad der var godt i det gamle og kunde været tjenligt til at danne Bindeledet med Fortiden."

[2] Helveg, op. cit., iv, p. 98. " Hvad der saerlig udmaerker Christen Pedersen, hvad der udgjør hans aandelige Eiendommelighed, er den naturlige Maade, hvorpaa Kjaerlighed til Fortiden og til dens folkelige Udvikling sammensmaeltede med en oprigtig Tilegnelse af det rensede Evangelium. Medens den reformatoriske Praediken saedvanlig, for ret grundgt at bekjaempe Papisteriet, ikkun altfor meget lagde an paa at nedbryde Alt, hvad der som Fortidens Arv var Folkets aandelige Eiendom, saa vidste han at luttre uden at vrage, og derved at bevare sin Kjaerlighed til Sagn og Historie, til Ordsprog og Folkeviser. Men han stod ene i sin Tid—og kun af gamle Thingbøger har en flittig Gransker kunnet meddele disse forhen ubekjendte, sparsomme Efterretninger om hans sidste Levedage."

CHAPTER V

HANS TAUSEN AND THE ADVANCE OF LUTHERANISM

1

THE career of Hans Tausen,[1] though by no means uneventful, showed less vicissitude than that of Christiern Pedersen and was marked by a greater success than that of Paul Eliaesen. Bred a monk and a scholar, he became Denmark's leading reformer, and died a Lutheran bishop. Born in 1494 of gentle parentage, he went to school at Odense in his native Funen. In 1515, at the age of twenty-one, he entered the Johannite monastery at Antvorskov, where he took the vows. Eskild Tomesen, the abbot, was a man of distinction and a member of the Danish Rigsraad[2]; recognizing the young monk's abilities, he sent him to study at the University of Rostock, and here Tausen took his master's degree in 1519. In the autumn of 1521 he went to Copenhagen for further study at the University, but soon went abroad again, this time to the Universities of Lyons and Cologne; and from there he proceeded to Wittenberg in the summer of 1523, where he was won over to the Lutheran movement. He was recalled to Antvorskov in 1524, but openly confessed his new convictions, and was thereupon sent to the Johannite community at Viborg, the prior of which, Peder Jensen, as a man of learning, was entrusted with the task of reclaiming Tausen to the Catholic faith. Tausen, no longer a young monk, but a mature man of thirty-one and a travelled scholar, was not to be easily turned. How he was allowed to preach in the monastery church, and how he there attracted hearers from the town, has already been related.[3] The year after his coming to Viborg he left the monastery and renounced his vows. To avert the punishment which might have ensued the King was asked to intervene, and Frederick issued his letter of protection, October 23, 1526,

[1] The chief authorities for Hans Tausen are: H. F. Rørdam, *Smaaskrifter af Hans Tausen*, and the same writer's *Kjøbenhavns Universitets Historie*; B. Kornerup, *Hans Tausens Postil*; L. Schmitt, *Johann Tausen;* and H. Knudsen, *Bidrag til Oplysning af den Danske Reformationshistorie.*

[2] The prior of Antvorskov had the spiritual oversight of all the communities in the north belonging to the Order of St. John of Jerusalem. See Heise, *Skibykrøniken*, p. 132, note.

[3] Chapter II, sect. 3.

appointing Tausen his chaplain, and allowing him " to preach the holy Gospel " in Viborg. This act of the King was to cause him constant trouble with the bishops, who regarded it as an infringement of his electoral charter as well as an encouragement of heresy.

Tausen's first foothold as a free Evangelical preacher in Viborg was the small church of St. John, lent him by the parish priest, Jakob Skjønning, a man of liberal views; when this could not contain the numbers of those who desired to hear him he preached in the churchyard, and finally his supporters one day gained forcible possession of the large church of the Greyfriars, which had been locked against Tausen, and here he began to hold a regular Sunday afternoon service, while the brethren continued their daily Offices and Masses as heretofore. This arrangement went on uneasily until 1529, when the friars were deprived of their church and held their services for a time in a small chapel nearby; but in the year following the community came to an end with the expulsion of the brethren by order of the King.

While living at Viborg as an Evangelical preacher under the King's protection Tausen produced three literary works. (*a*) The first was a free rendering of Luther's *Himmelbrief*, published at Wittenberg in 1524, which Tausen brought out under the title, *A Pitiful Complaint and a Friendly Offer*.[1] It was a hortatory discourse, purporting to be spoken by our Lord and addressed to His followers complaining of their failures in discipleship and inviting them to a purer and more sincere way of life. Tausen's version was printed by Hans Vingaard at Viborg and brought out in 1528.

(*b*) The Bishop of Viborg at this time was Jørgen Friis, admitted by even Roman Catholic authorities[2] to have been a man of worldly and unchaste life. Feeling perhaps his incompetence to deal with the growth of Lutheranism in his see-city, he allowed his colleague, Jens Andersen, Bishop of Odense, an able though by no means spiritually-minded prelate, to address a letter to the citizens of Viborg and Aalborg warning them against heresy. Hans Tausen answered this letter, and though the bishop's pastoral is not extant much of it is quoted by Tausen point by point in his reply.[3] It was published at Viborg by Hans Vingaard in 1529 and is strongly controversial in character. Quoting the bishop's claim to be Bishop of Odense, Tausen proceeds to expose the abuses of the contem-

[1] Rørdam, *Smaaskrifter*, pp. 1-22. *Et ynkeligt Klagemaal og et venligt Tilbud.*
[2] *E.g.* by L. Schmitt, S.J., *Paulus Heliä*, p. 67.
[3] Rørdam, op. cit., pp. 23-94. *Edt kort anstvor til bispenss sendhaebreff aff Othense.*

porary episcopate and declares that "Christ did not appoint us apostles and bishops to rule lands and kingdoms, to plague and harm poor people, to gather such riches for the Church as they do, but only to preach the holy Gospel by word and good Christian example."[1] Christ and His apostles, Tausen affirms, saw in preaching by word of mouth their most important task, and if learned and able men had only imitated them in this, things would be better for mankind today. We should then have escaped the fate of having the clergy of the Catholic Church arrogating to themselves the right of interpreting Scripture and mixing it with their own human views and opinions.[2] When the bishop speaks of apostate monks who preach Luther's heresy to the citizens of Viborg, Tausen retorts that it is no heresy which they preach, but the true Gospel, which a large part of the people of Viborg have accepted. He repudiates the term "apostate monk", and declares that the vows that he took at Baptism are the ones he desires to keep, because they were made to God; the monkish vows taken by himself at the monastery of Antvorskov were human impositions, drawing the obedience he owes to God away from God to human authorities. So far from being an apostate, he claims he is a banished and exiled man.[3]

(*c*) Tausen's third work was a form of baptism of infants in Danish, based on the Roman Office (*En ret Fadzon at christne Børn med paa Danske*). In order not to break with the old ways too abruptly, he retained the ceremonies of signing the cross and the use of oil, salt and lights; but those who used the service were at liberty to observe or to omit such usages, as they wished. "No one shall be constrained or forced to use this form, but every man is free to use or to omit therein, as time, place and people's convenience direct. For the signing with the cross and the use of oil and lights are not meant just to terrify the devil, but these and various other signs are inserted in the holy sacrament merely to give it enrichment and dignity. . . . They are outward signs and nothing more, and Baptism is quite complete without them: they are not essential to the service, unless as a concession to the simple. Nothing is demanded in this sacrament as essential except a strong Christian

[1] Rørdam, op. cit., p. 29. "Christus haffver icke indskicket oss apostler och bisper till ath raadhae oc regerae land och righae, till ath plaggae och skadthae fattigh almow, till ath samblae sodant Kirckenss ligindhefae ssom i giørae, Men aldeenestae till ath predickae thet helighe Evangelium met oerd och godhae christelighae exempler."

[2] Rørdam, op. cit., pp. 82-84.

[3] Rørdam, op. cit., pp. 41-44.

prayer for the child to God and water as a true attestation to men."[1] His belief was that much of the irreligion of the time was due to the people's ignorance both of the words of the baptismal Office and of its essential meaning: his publication of the service in Danish was intended to remedy this.

During his years of ministry at the Greyfriars' church at Viborg (1526-29) Tausen, in spite of his seeming conservatism, took three decisive steps which involved a complete breach with traditional order. (*a*) He introduced Evangelical methods of worship, with hymn-singing in Danish, and celebrated both Baptism and the Supper " in the Evangelical way ".[2] One of the features of the new worship was the greater prominence given to preaching. Although sermons were plentiful enough in the late Middle Ages, inevitably they took on a greater importance when they became the vehicle of the new message. " It was not the spokesmen of the Lutheran reform who are to be credited with having introduced the liturgical sermon, yet it lay in the nature of things that in a very different manner than formerly preaching was to attain honour and dignity through their labours, and that both in form, content and purpose the sermon became completely changed. It was through the proclamation of the Word that Tausen and his companions won a hearing for the new message among the great majority of the people; they liked to style themselves, as Frans Vormordsen says, ' we evangelical preachers ' (as we are now called and indeed are.)"[3] Similar changes were attempted in the cathedral at Viborg, where three of the canons—Christen Stub, Jakob Hansen and Jens Hansen—favoured reform. Supported by the burgomaster and Council, and apparently with the tacit

[1] Engelstoft, *Liturgiens eller Alterbogens og Kirkeritualets Historie i Danmark*, pp. 180-181. " Ingen skal vaere nødt eller tvunget (til at bruge denne Form), men hver Mand fri at gjøre og lade herudi, som Tiden, Stedet og Personernes Leilighed giver sig. Thi Djaevelen lader sig ikke forfaerde med Kors, Olie eller Lys, men disse og andre flere Tegn ere indskikkede dette Hellige Sacrament ikkun til en Prydelse og Herlighed. . . . Udvortes Tegn ere de og intet Andet, uden kvilke Daaben kan vel fuldkommes og eiere nødtørstelige dertil, uden hvis man vil spare og skaane de Enfoldige. Her aeskes intet nødtørsteligt til dette Sacrament uden en kraftig christelig Bøn til Gud for Barnet og Vand til en sandt Vidnesbyrd hos Menneskene."

[2] Rørdam, *Kjøbenhavns Universitets Historie*, i, p. 455. " En ordnet Gudstjeneste indrettedes med danske Psalmesang, med Daab og Nadvere efter evangelisk Vis."

[3] Kornerup, *Hans Tausens Postil*, i, p. 7. " Var det saaledes ikke den lutherske Reformationsbevaegelses Talsmaend, der har Fortjenesten af at have indført Praediket-jenesten, men det laa in Forholdenes Natur, at den paa en ganske anden Maade end før maatte blive bragt til Aere og Vaerdighed ved deres Virksomhed, og at Praediken baade i Form, Inhold og Maal nu blev fuldstaendigt aendret. Det var gennem Ordets Forkyndelse, at Tausen og hans Faeller hos Folkets store Maengde vandt Ørenlyd for det nye Budskab; selv yndede—som Frants Vormordsen siger—at benaevne sig oss (som nw kalles oc vdi sandhedt ere) ewangeliske praedickere."

approval of the King, they introduced a Communion Service, with sermon and hymns, in Danish. The other canons on the Chapter continued the old services and opposed the innovation, with the result that scenes of violence occurred, in one of which Tausen is reported to have figured. A priest, known for his loud voice as Claus Raaber ("the Trumpet"), was about to say Mass in the cathedral when, in the presence of a large number of citizens, the canon, Christen Stub, ran up and snatched the chalice from the priest's hand and threw it on the ground; an uproar ensued, the priest was hustled out of the cathedral, and Tausen, so it is said, mounted the pulpit and preached a sermon on the text "Fallen, fallen is Babylon the great". Other accounts do not mention Tausen's name, and the occurrence may have happened after his departure from Viborg. But the Evangelical services were maintained and the cathedral remained in the control of the reform party.[1]

(*b*) After the destruction of most of the churches in Viborg there remained in the possession of the reformers, besides the cathedral, the two large churches of the Greyfriars and the Blackfriars. These became parish churches, and Tausen was placed in charge of the Greyfriars and Sadolin established at the Blackfriars. Jørgen Sadolin had studied at Wittenberg and came to Viborg in 1526. A royal letter of protection[2] permitted him to open a school for students unable to go to Copenhagen, and this became a training-ground for some of the future Lutheran clergy. Tausen's second decisive step in the breach with traditional order was his ordination of Sadolin as an Evangelical minister, a step which naturally shocked the bishops. At the Herredag at Copenhagen in 1530 one of the complaints brought against the reformers by the bishops was that Tausen had usurped episcopal powers in ordaining men to the ministry.[3] Tausen's reply was "that he had not ordained priests, for that belonged to God alone. But he had presented to the laity capable, learned and honest persons, and by the common people's will and desire he and other Christian men, with public prayer and laying-on of hands, had authorized them to preach the Gospel and to serve the holy Church with sacraments and other proper rites. They claimed to have done this with Scriptural warrant, according to the apostles' teaching and ex-

[1] Helveg, *Den Danske Kirkes Historie*, iii, pp. 802-804.
[2] A transcript of the original is printed in Kornerup, *Reformationen i Danmark*, p. 1.
[3] See Article 26 in the *Twenty-seven Articles*, apud Schmitt, *Paulus Heliä*, p. 83.

ample, and with so much the greater reason in that they whose duty it was to do this had neglected it ".[1]

(*c*) In this setting aside of episcopal ordination Luther had led the way. In his address to the Bohemian Utraquists (*De instituendis ministris*)[2] of November 1523 he had advised them not to insist on ordination by bishops, but to choose and ordain their own ministers. As Lutheran communities came into being in the towns and cities of Germany, Luther's comparative indifference to questions of organization resulted in the ignoring of the bishops' authority and the ordination of new ministers by the leaders of the local Lutheran Churches. Thus Tausen was but following the example and precept of the great German reformer in this question of ordination, as also in the third decisive step which he took in these days—viz., his marriage. Luther had married Catherine von Bora in June 1525; Tausen's marriage followed about a year later. His wife is said to have been Dorothea, the sister of his friend and colleague, Sadolin, though there is some doubt on that point. Paul Eliaesen sharply accuses Tausen of being the first Danish priest to marry[3]; whether he was actually the first is not certain, but he was undoubtedly among the first of the many Danish clergy who abandoned celibacy. When at the Herredag of Odense in 1527 the question of clerical marriage was raised, it was not formally legalized; but the matter was left in the position that the clergy who preached the Gospel and who entered on matrimony could count on royal protection. Tausen in this, as in other matters, was a leader among his brethren: " he was of a vehement nature and opposition only goaded him on ".[4]

2

The death of Lage Urne, Bishop of Roskilde, in the spring of 1529 removed the strongest barrier against Lutheran influences invading the capital. At the suggestion of some of the citizens of

[1] J. S. B. Suhr, *Tausens Levnet*, p. xix. " At hand icke haffwer Viid Praester, thi det hør Gud allene til. Men duelige, laerde oc skickelige Personer, haffwer hand vel forklerit for Almuen, ic aff Menige Folckis vilge oc begjere, haffwer hand oc andre Christne Maend, med almindelig Bøn til Gud og Haenders paalegelse, samtøcht dennem til at praedicke Evangelium, oc at tienne den Hellige Kircke, med Sacramenter oc anden vedbørlig tienniste, oc det Kjende de sig at haffwe gjort med skriftelig skiel efter Apostlenis Laerdom og Exempel, oc med saa megit dis større skiel, at de som det skulde gjøre, ere der forsommelige udi."

[2] *Luthers Werke* (Weimar), xii, pp. 160 ff.; and Kidd, *Documents of the Continental Reformation*, p. 124.

[3] Heise, *Skibykrøniken*, p. 112.

[4] Rørdam, *Kjøbenhavns Universitets Historie*, i, p. 455.

Copenhagen the King called Tausen to take up work in the city, and in the autumn of 1529 he was installed as Evangelical preacher in the church of St. Nicholas. Here, with one or two interruptions, he remained until his appointment as Lutheran Bishop of Ribe in 1541. At the services in St. Nicholas he introduced Mortensen's hymn-book and celebrated the Lord's Supper in Danish, retaining, as he himself reminded his opponents, some of the old ceremonial, such as the use of vestments, and lights, and the Elevation of the Sacrament.[1]

Within a year of his coming to Copenhagen there assembled in the capital the Herredag which was to settle, if possible, the religious problem, and in the discussions and negotiations of this national conference Tausen played a prominent part. The course of the proceedings having been recounted in an earlier chapter it is only necessary to allude to one matter relating to Tausen's personal participation in it—viz., whether he was the author of the Forty-three Articles, later known as the *Copenhagen Confession*. Whereas it was formerly assumed that, as he was the natural leader of the Evangelical preachers present at the Herredag, he was most likely to have been the chief, if not the sole, author of the document, more recently it has been suggested with some probability that in view of the similarity between the tone of the *Articles* and that of the *Malmøbogen* it was Peder Laurenssen who composed them both.[2] If, however, Tausen may no longer be regarded as the actual author of the *Copenhagen Confession*, he was undoubtedly the author of another work of considerable importance in the history of the Reformation in Denmark. In 1531 Paul Eliaesen wrote his *Short Instruction on the Holy Mass* (*En kort Undervisning om den hellige Messe*), which is now lost; Tausen composed a reply to this which was published at Malmø by Oluf Ulriksen in 1531.[3] It illustrates both Tausen's general attitude as a reformer and also his doctrinal position in regard to the sacrament in particular.

(*a*) On the profoundly important question as to the sacrificial character of the Mass, Tausen writes that Eliaesen may deny that he has made the Mass a sacrifice, but in this he lies. " You say that you have not made the Mass a new offering for the living and the

[1] Rørdam, *Smaaskrifter*, p. 161. " Haffuer ieg end nu her til daggs holdet aller vanlige ceremonier y messen, oc inted formandledh enten y messeklaeder, lyusstendning eller sacramentens opløftelse."

[2] Schnell, *Die Danische Kirchenordnung*, p. 36.

[3] Rørdam, *Smaaskrifter*, pp. 94-163: *Svar til den falske og unkristelige Undervisning som Lector Povel skrev. Cf.* Rørdam's comment in the preface, p. xviii: " er det et for vor Reformationshistorie saerdeles vigtigt Skrift."

dead and for the forgiveness of sins? Would God that that were so, that you were innocent of that . . . but unfortunately it is only too true that you have."[1] "The Mass," Tausen declares, "is no memorial sacrifice, as you (Eliaesen) call it, but a new testament, as Christ Himself calls it, with which He assures us of the forgiveness of all sins for the sake of His precious blood and innocent death."[2] On the other hand, Tausen denies that he regards the sacrament as a bare sign. "I hold not the sacrament for a mere naked sign and nothing else, but for such a sign . . . that under the visible bread and wine the true body and blood of Jesus Christ is received."[3]

(*b*) Tausen discusses the invocation of saints, and expresses his opinion clearly. "How fares it with the departed saints and friends of God, whether they pray for us, is known to God, Who knows all; but well I know that we have no command from God in Holy Writ to call upon them for any help or intercession. Rather indeed God firmly commands us to let those who are departed rest as they are and not concern ourselves about them."[4] Quoting our Lord's words, "Come unto Me", etc., he concludes his argument by triumphantly adding, "now all pious and good Christians, who do not think it better to hear and obey these words, which are our Lord Jesus Christ's own words, than the misleading and deceiving words of Lector Paul, who says, 'No, no; go not to Jesus Christ, but to others, such as St. Nicholas for a safe voyage, St. Gertrude for a good inn' etc.?"[5]

(*c*) On the question of solitary Masses Tausen has no difficulty in showing that it is contrary to God's ordering and to Christ's institution that priests should receive the sacrament alone, and by

[1] Rørdam, op. cit., p. 98. "Siger thu att the haffue icke giort Messen til ett nyt offer for leffuendis oc døde til syndz forladelse? O Gud giffue thet saa wore, at the vore vskyldige ther vdi. . . . Men thess waer thet er altomegett sant."

[2] Rørdam, op. cit., p. 113. "Saa er nu thenne messe inthet amindeligt offer, som thu kaller thet, men eet nyt testamente, som Christus selff kalder hende, met huilket han beskeder oss alle synders forladelse, formiddelss sitt dyre blod oc uskyldige død."

[3] Rørdam, op. cit., p. 161. "Ieg holder icke sacramentet for ett blott oc bart taegn allene oc indtiid andett, men for saadantt ett taegn . . . att wnder thet siunlige brød oc win anammiss Jesu Christi sande legomme oc blod."

[4] Rørdam, op. cit., p. 120. "Huorledes fadt er mett the hellige affgangne Gudz venner, om the bede for oss, thet weed Gud, som allting veed, thet veed ieg weel att wy haffue ingen befalning aff Gud y then hellige scrifft, att paakalle thennom om nogen hielp eller forbeed, men fast mere befaler Gud oss, att wy skulle lade thennom betemme som ere borte oc affdøde, oc intet bekømre oss ther mett."

[5] Rørdam, op. cit., p. 129. "Nw alle fromme gode christne . . . huad tyckiss eder monne thet waere bedre att høre oc lyde thesse ordt, som ere vor herris Jesu Christi egne ordt, End then forlederis oc bedrageris ord Lector Pouels, som siger. ney, ney gaar icke til Jesum Christum, men til andre som er St. Nicolaus for haffzens fare, St. Gertrud for eet got herbergh, etc."

N.T. examples he demonstrates that the presence of Christian people at the service is in accordance with the Divine will.

(*d*) Further questions raised are whether the sacrament is to be immediately received after Consecration, or may be worshipped without reception; whether the words of Consecration should be spoken or whispered; and whether prayers at Mass may be said for farm animals, horses, cattle, swine, etc. The last point is in allusion to the medieval practice of asking for a Mass to be said at the occurrence of some personal or domestic difficulty. " People have used the Mass for every kind of harm which may have happened to their cattle or other property. If something is lost, then a Mass is said that it may be found again. If there is delay in the birth of a calf or a foal, a Mass must be said: and whatsoever may be lacking, all shall be made good with Masses."[1] On all such points Tausen adopts the reformed position, and though his language is sometimes regrettably violent and his attacks on his opponent remorseless, yet the lack of restraint in controversy, which both sides manifested, was in some measure due to the acuteness with which they felt the points in debate; and that these matters were of more than ephemeral interest is shown by the fact that some of them are still being debated today.

About a year after this work on the Mass Tausen translated a book of Luther's which had been published at Wittenberg in 1531 under the title, *Auff das Vermeint Keiserlich Edict, Ausgangen jm 1531 jare, nach dem Reichs tage des* 1530 *jars.*[2] The Edict referred to was the Recess of the famous Diet of Augsburg (1530) which " declared the Confession of the Protestants confuted, allowed them till April 15, 1531, to conform, forbade innovations till then, and committed the enforcement of its terms to the Imperial Chamber ".[3] Although an appeal to force had been postponed for a time it was felt by the Protestants that coercion, and perhaps war, were not far off; and the Lutherans of Denmark were the more anxious that their King should come out boldly on the side of the new faith. Tausen therefore translated Luther's work, which was a strongly controversial product, not uncongenial to the Danish reformer, dealing with the Mass, free-will, faith and works, etc. He

[1] Rørdam, op. cit., p. 155. " At mand haffuer bruget hende for alle honde skade, som er skeet paa queg eller andet gotz, hagde mandt tafft noget, tha skulle ther sigis een messe fore at thet motte findis igen, kunde een kalff eller eet føl icke saa snart fødis tha motte ther sigis een messe fore, oc huadsomhelst ther fattedis, tha sculle thet alt forhuerfinns met messer."

[2] *Luthers Werke* (Weimar), xxx, iii, pp. 331 ff.

[3] Kidd, *The Continental Reformation*, p. 56.

prefaced it with an exhortation to King Frederick not to follow the example of Emperor and Pope in their Edict of 1530 threatening to hinder and suppress the Gospel; but to follow the example of O.T. kings like Asa, Hezekiah and Josiah in suppressing heathenism and idolatry, in abolishing error and superstition, and in encouraging the progress of true religion. The work remained in MS. till printed in the nineteenth century.[1] The death of Frederick in the spring of 1533 may have been the reason why the work was not published at the time.

3

The King's death left the Catholic majority of the Rigsraad in control of the government and deprived Tausen of his chief protector. The consequences were soon visible in the behaviour of the Herredag which met in Copenhagen in June of that year.[2] Besides the members of the Rigsraad attending the Herredag, some of the lesser nobility and the burgomasters and representatives of the two chief cities, Copenhagen and Malmø, were consulted, although they received no official invitation to be present at the proceedings. On July 3 they issued a Recess[3] which declared that " each bishop and prelate shall conduct himself according to his episcopal office . . . and in his diocese shall alone have complete authority to ordain priests and preachers who shall say Mass and the divine office according to Christian custom and teach their parishioners to live in accordance with the holy Gospel. . . . If any shall presume to ordain parish priests or preachers otherwise than with the bishop's will and consent, he shall be prosecuted in court and punished according to the rigour of the law ". It was further enacted that all the property and goods for which churches, monasteries or the spiritual estate were the trustees should be retained by them; that all cathedrals, monasteries, convents and parish churches should continue with their rights; and that, lastly, for the good of religion a university should be maintained in the kingdom where men from every diocese could be taught and

[1] Rørdam, op. cit., pp. 164-236: *Et tilborligt, straengt svar af Doctor Morten Luther paa det Mandat . . . ,"* etc.

[2] Full account in Heise, *Herredagen in Kjøbenhavn* 1533 (*Historisk Tidsskrift*, series 4, vol. 3).

[3] Heise, op. cit., pp. 489-490. " Att huer biskop oc prelathe skall skucke oc haffue seg effter siitt biscopelig embett . . . oc wdj siit stifft schall alene haffue fuldt magt tull att skiicke presther oc predickere, som schulle uphollde meszer oc gudtz tienniste effther christelig skiick, oc lerae theris sognefolck att leffue effther thet hellige euangelium. . . . Velder oc seg noghen till at skucke sogne prester eller predickaerae anderledeis endt mett bispens wulliig oe samtyckae, tha skall hand ther fore forfølligis tiil tyngge oc straffis for woldt effther loghenn."

educated, in addition to the local cathedral schools, which should continue as heretofore. Here was the beginning of a Catholic reaction which threatened with disaster the whole movement of reform. Tausen was the first to experience its effects.[1] He was summoned to appear before the Herredag on July 14 and accused of using scandalous language of the bishops; of intruding himself into the churches of Copenhagen; and of heretical teaching on the Lord's Supper. Paul Eliaesen was the spokesman for the bishops, and Tausen's book in reply to Eliaesen's work on the Mass was the evidence adduced for his heretical sacramental teaching. The trial caused great excitement in the city; crowds of people assembled outside the Council house demanding Tausen's release; and a party of soldiery was sent by Wullenwever, who was on board a ship in the harbour, to support the citizens. Intimidated by the popular clamour, the bishops yielded to the intercessions made on Tausen's behalf by some of the Herredag, and the sentence imposed was that after a month's grace he was to leave Zealand and Scaania, and that he was not to write any book, or preach, or execute any spiritual function without the permission of the bishop in whose diocese he was residing. Tausen therefore left the Council a free man, and before the month's respite was up the High Steward, Mogens Gjø, had intervened and arranged a compromise with Rønnov, the Bishop of Roskilde. Tausen promised to refrain from all abuse of the bishops and clergy, to be obedient and loyal to the bishop, and to further the good of the spiritual estate: and Rønnov having agreed to these terms, Tausen was at liberty to resume his ministry. But he seems to have lost some of his popularity among the common people by this concession, and perhaps to have lost also some of the influence which hitherto he had possessed as the chief leader of reform.

It was probably at this time that Tausen began his translation of the Bible.[2] He got as far as the five Books of Moses which were published at Magdeburg in 1535, the choice of a German rather than a Danish printer being dictated by the circumstances of the time. Civil war had broken out in Denmark in the early summer of 1534 and for a year Copenhagen had to endure the rigour of a severe siege. Count Christopher, Albert, Duke of Mecklenburg, Jørgen Kock and Ambrosius Bogbinder were the leaders of resistance, but the peace party finally prevailed and Copenhagen surrendered to Duke Christian on July 19, 1536. During these

[1] Heise, op. cit., pp. 436-466. [2] Molbech, *De danske Bibeloversaettelser*, pp. 63 ff.

tumultuous years Tausen continued his ministry at St. Nicholas, Copenhagen. One of the conditions imposed at the surrender of the capital was that Tausen with the other principal insurgents who had been pardoned should form up in line and supplicate for a royal letter of protection. Through the mediation of Christian's chaplain, Johann Albretsen, Tausen obtained this and was restored to his post at St. Nicholas.[1] He was one of the Lutheran divines who, with representatives of the cathedral clergy, were summoned early in 1537 to prepare a draft for the forthcoming *Church Ordinance*; but although occupying an important post in the capital and in spite of his record as one of the leading reformers, he was passed over in the appointment and ordination of the seven Lutheran bishops at the memorable ceremony in the church of Our Lady on September 2 in the same year. The reason for this is not known, whether it was his democratic sympathies which stood in his way, or whether the King had already decided to give him the difficult but important post of lecturer at Roskilde, still something of a Catholic stronghold.[2] But before he went to Roskilde he was appointed lecturer in Hebrew at the University, a significant step in the quickening of intellectual life which marked the refounding of the University. "He had recently evinced striking evidence of his knowledge of Hebrew—a knowledge very rare in contemporary Denmark—by his translation of the five Books of Moses from the original. This was the first time that the elements of this language —still quite unknown at that time to the majority of scholars— were the subject of lectures at the University of Copenhagen."[3] He did not, however, continue long at this work, for in February 1538 he became lecturer in Scripture at the cathedral of Roskilde, and here he remained till he was appointed Bishop of Ribe in 1541. His hearers at Roskilde would be partly the older clergy bred up in Roman Catholic ways whom he would seek to instruct in the reformed faith; and partly the students, unable to proceed to Copenhagen, whom he prepared for ordination. That Tausen did not neglect his own studies is shown by the fact that in July 1538 he proceeded to the degree of Bachelor in Holy Scripture at the University.

[1] Schmitt, *Hans Tausen*, p. 62.
[2] Schmitt, op. cit., p. 63, *note*.
[3] Rørdam, *Kjøbenhavns Universitets Historie*, i, p. 474. "Om sin for den Tid og isaer for vort Land sjeldne Kundskab i det hebraiske Sprog havde han nys aflagt et talende Vidnesbyrd i sin efter Grundtexten udarbejdede Oversaettelse af de fem Mosebøger. Og det var første Gang, at Elementerne af dette for de fleste studerede Folk dengang endnu ganske ubekjendte Sprog bleve foredragne ved Kjøbenhavns Universitet."

Tausen's chief literary work in these years, apart from his translation of the Mosaic books, was the production of his *Postils* which were published by Hans Walther at Magdeburg in 1539. The fact that its dedication to Christian III is dated from Copenhagen 1536 shows that he had been occupied with this work for at least three years. The book, issued in two parts, a winter and a summer part, consists of the Epistles and Gospels for the Sundays and Holy-days of the year, translated into Danish. With each Epistle follows a brief explanation of its meaning, and a longer exposition sets out the lessons of each Gospel. The form was not original, for Luther had brought out his *Adventspostille* at Wittenberg in 1522,[1] Olaus Petri, the Swedish reformer, had published his *Postilla* in 1530,[2] and Christiern Pedersen had produced his *Postils* at Paris as early as 1515. Tausen's object is stated in the Preface. " This work is not written for those who are great and profound scholars, well versed in the Scriptures, which indeed intelligent people can easily understand; it is written for those who have not studied seriously and have never really heard of the interpretation of Holy Writ. It is specially intended for those who are appointed to teach others, who would willingly give of their best, but lack the ability. . . . I have in these *Postils* not made it my goal or my desire to please the high-brows, but only to meet the needs of simple people and particularly to help and serve the parish clergy who have need of plain and simple instruction. . . . My object has been to promote a twofold good—viz., that the ordinary clergy of good-will may improve in their ministry and that the unlearned laity may become instructed and zealous. For I have indeed learnt the lesson in the course of the twelve or thirteen years during which I have preached the Gospel that many are standing still and in learning remain as they were, not through any ill-will or through dislike of the Word or of Evangelical teaching, but through ignorance, of which they themselves are conscious, with the result that they do not believe themselves capable of satisfying their people in the way they give their teaching."[3] His aim was thus to awaken and instruct the parish

[1] *Luthers Werke* (Weimar), x, pt. i.

[2] C. A. Cornelius, *Svenska Kyrkans Historia*, p. 139.

[3] Kornerup, *Hans Tausens Postil*: Preface. " Dette arbeyd go de wenner er berammed, icke for deres skyld som noget høylig oc grundelig ere boglaerde, oc ij scriften synderlig ofuede oc wel forfarne, huilket forstandigt folk wel kan lettelig besinde. Men for dennom som icke haffue saare studeret, oc ey meget haffue hørd aff den hellige scrifftes wdlegning, synderlig dennom huilke dog ere beskickede till att laere andre, oc wilde wel gierne giøre det beste, men hafuet wdi formuen. . . . Ieg haffuer med denne Postill icke seet høyt op, oc ey tenekt til her med att fornøye de wyse aande, men allerneste at rame enfoldige folkes tarff oc synderlig de Sognpresters gafn oc nytte, som en groff oc

clergy and through them the common people. " It was with Tausen as with Luther that in the pulpit it was not Papistry which was the worst enemy he had to contend with, but rather he was faced with the task of overcoming the gross materialism and indifference which despised everything spiritual and of dispersing the deep fog of ignorance in which the truths of the Gospel were enwrapped."[1]

4

On the death of Hans Vandal, the Lutheran Bishop of Ribe, Tausen was elected by the canons and clergy to succeed him, and his appointment was confirmed by Christian III in a decree of October 21, 1541. He was ordained as Superintendent by Bugenhagen in Ribe cathedral on April 30, 1542, in the presence of the King and Council and of the six other Danish Superintendents. The fact that his predecessor was a German who did not speak Danish may have had some bearing on the unsatisfactory condition in which Tausen found the diocese. There survives a pastoral letter of his, bearing no date, addressed to the clergy of Ribe,[2] in which he sternly condemns the superstitious beliefs and practices which he evidently found existing as he made his visitations of the parishes under his care. The preaching of the Gospel had not eradicated the abuses of the time. " Now that we," he declares, " in these latter days have by God's grace been vouchsafed afresh pure doctrine and true worship, yet the old Serpent has not failed to raise up varied hindrances and obstacles to the work of the Lord Christ and of holy Church in the shape of Anabaptists and impugners of the sacrament, of sorcery and witchcraft, and still to this day labours to draw the simple away from the pure Word and

---

enfoldig undervisning haffue behoff, till att affwerrie thoo skader, oc forfremme ett dubbet gaffn, att enfoldige willige prestmend bode motte bliffue wed deres tienste, oc vlaerd almow kunde worde laerd oc vforsømet. Thii ieg haffuer y sandhed for nommed oc forfaret ij desse xii eller xiii aar, ieg haffue predicket Euangelium att mange haffue standet y stampe, oc ere ij laerdom bleffue de samme de wore, icke aff nogen ond willie eller had til ondet oc den Euangeliske laerdom, men aff en wanwittighed de fornomme oc følde ij seg sielff, att de trøstede seg icke till att fornøye oc giøre sine folk fylleste wdi de maade om de hadde taget wed den laerdom."

[1] Helveg, *Den Danske Kirkes Historie*, iv, p. 42. " Det gik Tausen som Luther, at naar han kom paa Praedikestolen, saa var Papisteriet ikke den vaerste Fjende, han havde at bekjaempe, men det gjaldt saavel om at overvinde den raadende Kjødelighed og Ligegyldighed, der ringeagtede alt aanderligt, som at sprede den tykke Uvidenheds Mulm, hvori de evangeliske Sandheden vare indhyllede."

[2] Rørdam, *Hans Tausens Smaaskrifter*, pp. 239-261: *Sendebrev til aller Provster og Sognepraester i Ribe Stift.*

the true Christ."[1] He quotes passages from Scripture which condemn idolatry and witchcraft and urges the clergy earnestly to instruct their people in better ways. The letter abounds in homely common sense. If one is wronged, he says, then turn to the proper authorities for help and protection; if one is sick, then resort to the doctor for healing; but do not, he pleads, fly to sorcery or fortune-telling. He combines simplicity of teaching with genuine piety and manly sense. " There is therefore no better counsel than diligently to put before your people the Divine intention of the first commandment, with simple and clear exposition which the truly pious can understand—viz., that He alone will be God, not only in the creation and governing of His creatures, but still more in our minds and hearts, in our conduct and opinions, in our faith and worship; and that His will and commandment are not fulfilled by our not speaking about idols, or by our not outwardly offering worship to idols, or by our having no actual image of an idol to fall down to. But let us," he adds, " have crucifixes and other similar pictures and symbols which express to us God's goodness."[2] More than most of his writings this letter exhibits his zeal for the truth, his scorn of superstition, his reliance on Scripture and his pastoral spirit. As an aid to worship he brought out in 1544 a new edition of the *Danske Psalmebog*. No copy of it survives, but many successive editions of the *Psalmebog* continued to come out, based on Tausen's book, which contained for the first time translations of some Latin hymns used in medieval times.[3] But the record of his life as a Lutheran bishop cannot be followed here: for his Superintendency lasted nearly twenty years, and he lived on into the reign of Frederick II, dying on November 11, 1561.

[1] Rørdam, op. cit., p. 242. " Siden wij ere nu aff Gudz naade i desse siste dage paa ny besøgte med den reene lerdom oc rette Gudz dyrckelse, da haffuer den gamle Slange dog icke forsømet sig, at gøre den Herre Christo oc den hellige Kircke adskillig hinder oc gensigelse, med gendøbere oc sacramentskendere, med spaadom oc troldom, oc endnu paa denne dag arbeyder i derpaa, at drage eenfoldige hierten fra det reene ord oc then rette Christo."

[2] Rørdam, op. cit., p. 258. " Derfor er her ingen bedre raad, end at i flittelig legge eders almu det første Gudz bud for, med eenfoldig oc klar udleggelse, at de rett grondelig konde forstaa, huad Gud meen der med, at hand allene wil were Gud, icke alleneste udi creaturers skaffning oc regering, men ald mest i wor hu oc tancke, act oc mening, troo oc tilfluct, oc at Gudz willig oc befalling fuldgøres icke der med, at wij tale om ingen affgud, udvortes tilbede ingen affgud, haffue ingen affgudebillede at faldne neder for. Men haffue crucifix oc andre sodane billeder oc formalinge, som betegne oss Gudz welgerning."

[3] C. J. Brandt, *Vore Danske Kirke-Salmebøger*, pp. 7, 8.

5

The Jesuit author of a comprehensive survey of Tausen's life concludes his study with the assertion that the only real service the reformer did his country was his contribution to the improvement of the Danish language.[1] The inequity of this judgment is matched by the bitterness of Eliaesen's diatribes against the reformer, for whom " the most obstinate of all heretics " is his mildest description. Cooler judgments today will assess Tausen's contribution to the cause of religion more generously.

(I) For the seven years 1526-33 he was undoubtedly the leading figure in the proclamation of the Lutheran faith in Denmark. Protected by royal favour and supported by faithful laity, both at Viborg and Copenhagen, he established a strong centre of Lutheran worship and of Evangelical preaching. To the ministry of the Word he added the service of his pen, and in writings such as his *Reply* to Eliaesen's *Instruction on the Mass* he proved himself to be a redoubtable opponent of what he conceived to be the errors and abuses of the Roman faith. But though the leading reformer in those first years of religious change, he was only *primus inter pares*: other men of almost equal stature stood beside him and laboured in the same cause. Sadolin, first at Viborg and afterwards at Odense, Laurenssen and Vormordsen at Malmø, and Christiern Pedersen at Malmø and Lund, were all of them distinguished men and powerfully contributed to the furtherance of the reformed faith. To call Tausen, as has been frequently done,[2] " the Danish Luther " is a misnomer: neither the work he accomplished nor the stature of the man himself warrants putting him in the same class with the great German. The Danish Reformation was the work, not of one man, nor even of a group of men, but, like the Reformation in other lands, a complex product of factors, personal and economic, political and religious.

(II) Among these factors were the influence of German thought and the example of the Saxon reformers: the natural tendency during the religious changes had been to look to Wittenberg for guidance and inspiration. His (Tausen's) " interpretation was a faithful though markedly personal reproduction of the Lutheran

[1] Schmitt, *Hans Tausen*, p. 113. " Soll nun etwa Tausen gar keine Verdienste um sein Vaterland haben? Wir finden nur das eine, dass er zur Ausbildung der dänischen Sprache mitgeholfen und eine grosse Redegewandtheit besessen hat."

[2] *E.g.*, by J. S. B. Suhr in *Tausens Levnet*, p. lvi, " Danmarks herlige Luther "; *cf. Camb. Mod. Hist.* ii, p. 609.

message of sin and grace based on Holy Scripture. His being charged with Zwinglianism was an error, due to the fact that he abided simply by Luther's original, practical, religious conception of the Supper (as the Lord's testament of the forgiveness of sins, with the Body and Blood of Christ in the Elements as the seal); Luther's change of front with its sharper emphasis on the Real Presence he did not participate in, and in Denmark it had no significance, since here there were no sacramentarians ".[1] In fact, Tausen, though he had drawn his inspiration from Wittenberg and had become a follower of Luther during his stay in the Elector's University, did not remain an exact exponent of Lutheranism. In liturgical matters he was loyal enough to the conservative tradition of the Saxon school. In both the Gospel sacraments he retained some of the Catholic ceremonies: in Baptism, the use of oil, salt and tapers, and the signing of the cross; in Communion, the use of the vestments and lights, and the Elevation; and he did not advocate the expulsion of crucifixes and pictures from the churches. But in his doctrine of the Lord's Supper he diverged from Luther's view of the Real Presence, with the result he was accused of Zwinglianism. But his own teaching is contained in an important passage in his *Reply* to Eliaesen's *Instruction on the Mass.* " Because I call the sacrament a sign Lector Paul declares that I hold it to be nothing more than a sacramental sign. I have, however, given him many times formerly my clear and candid opinion—*e.g.*, in my answer to his first chapter, in the simple and plain statement that Christ ' gives us in the sacrament His sacred Body and Blood, not to offer up but to eat '. With this and many such similar expressions I have sufficiently made it evident that I do not hold the sacrament for a bare and naked sign and nothing else, but for such a sign as carries with it, as it were, that which it signifies—viz., that under the visible bread and wine is received by the innocent and righteous the true Body and Blood of Jesus Christ by means of faith in that Word with which Christ has bequeathed us the sacrament. In order that there may be no

[1] *Ekklesia*, ii, p. 28. " Seine Auffassung wurde eine treue, aber persönlich geprägte Wiedergabe der lutherischen Botschaft von Sünde und Gnade auf Grund der Heiligen Schrift. Wenn er des Zwinglianismus bezichtigt wurde, war das ein Irrtum, dadurch hervorgerufen, dass er einfach bei der ursprünglichen, praktisch-religiösen Auffassung Luthers vom Abendmahl blieb (als dem Testament des Herrn von der Sündenvergebung, mit Leib und Blut Christi in dem Elementen als Siegel); die Frontveränderung Luthers mit der schärferen Betonung der Realpräsenz hatte er nicht mit erlebt, und sie war in Dänemark gegenstandslos, weil es hier keine Sakramentierer gab."

misconception by anyone of my view—since Lector Paul makes this imputation—I have to this day retained all the customary ceremonies in the Mass, and made no change in the vestments, or lights, or elevation of the sacrament."[1] Thus Tausen appears to have taught in Denmark the view which Cranmer and Ridley later were to maintain in England.

Though not the Danish Luther, Tausen, by reason of the vigour of his personality and the independence of his views, was, as Eliaesen declares, " the standard-bearer of all Lutherans in Denmark ".[2] To him and to his colleagues, both in their reaffirmation of the faith of the Gospel and in their retention of traditional ceremonies, the reformed Church of Denmark today looks back as to its true progenitors. Lutherans though they became, they were first and foremost Danes, who bequeathed to posterity a form of Christianity acceptable to their countrymen, and a Church liberal, evangelical and national.

[1] Rørdam, op. cit., pp. 160-161. "Forthy ieg kaller sacramentet ett tegn, tha sigher L. Pouel meg thet paa, att ieg holder thet icke andet att waere, end ett sacramenteligt taegn, Ther som ieg haffuer dog giffuet hannom min blotte oc bare mening tilkende godt tiidt tilforn, y mitt suar til thet første capitell met tesse blotte oc bare ord (oc ther til met giffuer han oss sitt hellige legomme oc blod y sacramentet, icke offre men att aede etc.) mett the ord oc andre sodanne flere giffwer ieg eoch nog tilkende at ieg holder icke sacramentet for ett blott oc bart tegn allene oc indtiid andett, men for saandatt ett taegn, som fører mett sig liige thet samme som thett betegner, att wnder thet siunlige brød oc win anammiss Jesu Christi sande legomme oc blod, met uskylldighed oc retfefdighed, formiddelss troen til thet ordt som Christus haffuer hoss thet samme sacramente bestillet, Oc paa thet ieg ville aldeliss waere aff huer mand wmistenckt, I thet L. Pouel mig y thenne maade tilleger, tha haffuer ieg end nu her til daggs holdet alle vanlige ceremonier y messen, oc inted foruandledh enten y messeklaeder, lyusstendning eller sacramentens opløfftelse."

[2] Heise, *Skibykrøniken*, p. 131.

CHAPTER VI

PEDER LAURENSSEN AND THE DEFENCE OF REFORM

1

THE Carmelite Order was pre-eminently the learned Order in the Denmark of the early sixteenth century[1] and contributed more to the Reformation movement in that country than any other community. Paul Eliaesen mentions seven of the Order by name who became Lutherans: Peder Laurenssen, Frans Vormordsen, Anders Liung, Movrids Samsing, Mogens Sten, Ole Pind and Markus Pedersen.[2] Of these, the first two were distinguished men, Vormordsen becoming the first Lutheran Bishop of Lund, and Laurenssen, the subject of this chapter, a leading scholar and writer on the side of reform. He was born at Naestved in Zealand in 1490 or earlier. A fellow-townsman, Morten Pedersen, was prior of the Carmelite house at Landskrona and may have influenced Laurenssen's choice of the Order, for in due course he became a Carmelite friar, though nothing is known as to when or where he took the vows. His education appears to have had a humanist trend, for he quotes Cato and Horace and has some knowledge of Greek.[3] The first certain information about him is that he became a lecturer at the Carmelite College during the time Paul Eliaesen was principal (1519-22). When Eliaesen had to leave his post Laurenssen may have retired to the Carmelite house at Assens in Funen; at any rate he is known to have been a member of that community before he finally abandoned the Order to become a Lutheran. This happened in 1527, and in less than two years he moved to Malmø, where he entered on what may be called his life-work as a leading Lutheran teacher and scholar in that city.

Frederick I, in a letter of June 5, 1529,[4] had sanctioned the founding of an Evangelical clergy school at Malmø, and to this Laurenssen was appointed as *in sacris literis lector*. He was also

[1] H. F. Rørdam, *Malmøbogen af Peder Laurenssen*, p. ii; this, with the same author's edition of Laurenssen's *En stakket Undervisning*, Heise's edition of Eliaesen's *Skibykrøniken* and *En Kristelig Undervisning*, ed. by C. J. Brandt, are the chief authorities for Peder Laurenssen.

[2] *Skibykrøniken, p.* 63.

[3] Rørdam, *Malmøbogen*, p. ii.

[4] Published in H. Knudsen, *Bidrag til Oplysning af den Danske Reformationshistorie*, p. 158.

engaged in much literary activity and became, in Eliaesen's words, " the town's accredited writer ".[1] The same year he married Anne, the sister of Klavs Mortensen, the author of the earliest Danish hymnary. The Malmø reformers were, indeed, a group of men linked together by ties of natural or spiritual kinship; and with Laurenssen and Vormordsen (ex-colleagues at the Carmelite College), Klavs Mortensen and Hans Spandemager, both natives of Malmø, and Oluf Gyldenmund, the humanist, there co-operated also Oluf Ulricksen, formerly a Swedish priest, and now in charge of a printing press in the town. From this press twenty-seven works are known to have been issued in these years, among them a *Psalmebog*, often reprinted, and a *Messebog*, both in Danish, and most of Laurenssen's own writings.[2] His first known work was *A Short Answer to the Pastoral of the Archbishop of Lund*, which appeared in 1529, but is now lost.[3] The following year he brought out his most important surviving work, the so-called *Malmø-Bog*, of which an account will be given.

2

Among the twenty-one Evangelical clergy who assembled at the Herredag in Copenhagen in July 1530 were five from Malmø, the two parish clergy, Mortensen and Spandemager, and the three lecturers, Laurenssen, Vormordsen and Gyldenmund. Laurenssen had a chief hand in the composition of the *Forty-three Articles* which were issued as the Evangelical Confession, and he may also have been responsible for an anonymous account of the proceedings of the Herredag which was printed at Malmø in the autumn of that year.[4] The Catholic reaction following the death of Frederick I and the resort to force which ensued involved Laurenssen in the turmoil of civil and ecclesiastical strife. Torben Bilde, the Archbishop of Lund, released by the death of the King from his promise not to oppose Lutheran preaching, proceeded with the concurrence of the Chapter of Lund—" quite the most conservative Chapter in Denmark "[5]—to take measures against the new faith. The parish priests of Helsingborg, Landskrona and Traelleborg were dismissed from their parishes and banished from the diocese. Laurenssen took up their cause and addressed two letters to the Chapter defending the action the three clergy had taken: they

[1] *Skibykrøniken*, p. 125. [2] Brandt, *En Kristelig Undervisning*, p. 3.
[3] Rørdam, op. cit., p. v. *Eet kortt svar paa thet sendhebreff, som werdighe Fadher Archielectus till Lund* . . . etc.
[4] Rørdam, op. cit., p. xxi.
[5] H. Heden, *Studier till Danmarks Reformations Historia*, p. 17.

were punished for attempting to change the Mass into Communion, granting the Cup to the laity, and themselves entering on matrimony. In his *Expostulatio . . . ad Canonicos Lundenses* published at Malmø he justified these practices as based on Scripture and primitive custom.[1] The reformers at Malmø were soon after declared outlawed at the Landsting of Skaane; and the city authorities retaliated by seizing and partly demolishing the castle, making hostages of certain nobles, and joining in close alliance with Lübeck. In June 1534 Count Christopher arrived in the Sound with a fleet supplied by Lübeck to lead the campaign for the reinstatement of Christian II and the protection of the Lutheran faith. Laurenssen issued at this time a Danish translation of a letter which Christian II had written from Flanders in 1526 to Johann Wendlandt, the burgomaster of Dantzig: it was republished now in the vernacular with the object of aiding the King's cause, since in it he admitted his former errors and declared his adhesion to God's Word and the Gospel.[2] This was scarcely ingenuous on the part of Laurenssen, since four years subsequent to that letter Christian had renounced Lutheranism, and in his present expectation of recovering his freedom and his throne declarations of his religious views were not above suspicion. Jørgen Kock and the civic authorities of Malmø had by this time got complete control of the city, and as the price of their support of Count Christopher's cause they demanded freedom for Lutheran preaching and the confirmation of the liberties of their town, demands which the Count was ready enough to concede.

The double victory in the summer of 1535 of the forces of Duke Christian changed the face of affairs, and by the following spring a considerable party in Malmø were ready to surrender. In the absence of Jørgen Kock, who had gone to Copenhagen, the burgomasters Jep Nielsen and Jens Klavsen Fynbo, backed by the Lutheran clergy, came to terms with Christian and on April 6, 1536, yielded up the city. Freedom for Lutheran preaching was promised and many of its civic privileges granted. Laurenssen, with the other Malmø clergy, was thus assured of protection in his ministry, and a few months later received from the Crown the presentation of the parish of Oxie in the neighbourhood of Malmø. Early in the following year he, with many of the prominent clergy, were summoned to meet at Odense to prepare a draft of a *Church Ordinance* which, after further revision, became the foundation of

[1] Rørdam, op. cit., p. xlvii. [2] Rørdam, op. cit., p. lx.

the new ecclesiastical system in Denmark. The reconstruction of the University as a Lutheran institution meant that the clergy school at Malmø was no longer needed, and Laurenssen in consequence became lecturer in theology at the cathedral of Lund. His former colleagues at Malmø were also given different posts: Frans Vormordsen rose to the dignity of Superintendent of the diocese of Lund; Hans Spandemager became parish priest of that cathedral city; and Oluf Gyldenmund was called to be parish priest of the church of Our Lady at Copenhagen, later becoming professor of rhetoric at the University. Of Laurenssen no further record survives. He died in 1552.

3

In January 1530 Ulricksen published at his press at Malmø Laurenssen's most important work under the title, *The Occasion and true Explanation of the new Reform . . . begun and carried out in the Christian town of Malmø.*[1] After an introductory allusion to the darkness and ignorance of past times, Laurenssen announces that the burgomasters, council, preachers and teachers in Malmø have carried through a reform of Christian worship. He then plunges into the heart of his subject and discloses the true secret of the Reformation changes in worship—viz., the displacement of external and human ordinances by a worship inward and spiritual. "In our blindness we have so obstinately introduced our self-invented and outward worship and ordinances and established them by written law and statutes, and for many centuries have so bound the consciences of poor people to maintain this worship as a uniform custom that they have held more firmly to these human laws and commandments than to the Word and Law of Christ. But the true Christian practice is that of charity which we ought to observe towards one another, and in this law and commandment of charity we are alone recognized by God to be His disciples. True Christian people are known, not by their clothing or its colour, not by much reading or singing, not by eating one food one day and another food another day, not by going to church and kneeling behind a priest or monk who stands in front of an altar and cries out his wares and has a Mass ready for what any imbecile person may desire: long masses, golden masses, silent masses, read masses,

[1] *Orsagen oc een rett forclaring paa then ny Reformats, ordinering og skick om messzen, predicken oc anden rett Gudts tienneste oc christelig dyrckelse som begyndt och giort er udi then Christelige Stadt Malmo* A.D. 1529. See ed. by H. F. Rørdam, Copenhagen, 1868.

sung masses, masses for pestilence, for good luck, for riches, for victory over one's enemies, for headache, toothache, backache, for colds, masses for horses, for geese, for swine . . . it is not possible briefly to enumerate all the huckstering and traffic which is used in the name of the Mass."[1] "For four or five hundred years now we have had so many different monasteries, monastic rules, ceremonies, outward works, various services in churches, etc., and by these every man has desired to be justified and saved. We have all the time been taught that God is to be thanked by this or that work, this or that rule or ceremony, and we have never been able to come to that knowledge of the truth and of divine worship of which St. Paul speaks. The truth is belief in Jesus Christ and in forgiveness through Him, His Works and His Righteousness; and such faith alone calms, satisfies and saves, and makes our consciences at peace with God, however great our sins be (2 Tim. 3, Rom. 5)."[2]

Having thus declared his belief in the true significance of the changes in worship made at Malmø, Laurenssen takes in order the main topics of Christian faith and practice, and expounds in detail the Lutheran view. The following passages illustrate his teaching on *the Mass:*

"According to Christ's institution and example, recorded in Matt. 26, Mark 14, Luke 22 and in St. Paul's teaching in 1 Cor. 11, we have arranged that the Testament of Christ, or the Mass, shall

[1] Rørdam, op. cit. "I wor forblindelse, haffue wi saa haardelige indførte thenne wor selffdictede wdvortis gudts tienneste oc budet oc mett schreffwen louff oc statuter hende befestedt oc i mange hwndrede aar saa beplicted fattige menneskes conscientier, tilatt opholde thenne tienneste aff een sedvane, att fattige menneske acthe fast mere menneskens schrifft oc bud end Christi ord oc lowff, oc then rett christen skick oc kierlighed som oss bør att holde emmellom hwer anden, i huilken kierlighets louff oc bud wi alleneste kiendis aff gwd, att waere hans discipeler rette christen menneske icke aff kleder eller farffwe, icke aff møgen lessning eller sang, icke aff enehonde mad een dag att aedhe, oc een anden een anden dag, icke aff thet wi gaa til kircke oc ligge bag een prest eller mwnck som staar for ett altere oc slar wd sin kram, oc haffver messe fall, ehwad slauff mand vil haffue thenom aff—Lange messer, eller forgylte messer, thiende messer, lessne messer, siungne messer, messer pestilentie, for god lycke, rigdom, att offweruinde fiende, messer for hoffwed werck, tende werck, ryg werck, for kollde siwge, messer for hesthe, for gess, for swin. . . . Thet er icke mweligt at wi kwnde korteligen wpregne all then kram oc kiøffmanskaff aff som ther brwgis wnder messens naffn" (folio 6).

[2] Rørdam, op. cit. "Her aff ere nw fire eller fem hwndrett aar optenckt saa mangle attskillige Closter, Mwncke regle, ceremonier, wdvortis gierninger, attskillige tienester i templer o.s.v. Aff huilcke hwer wille bliffwe retuisse oc salige, altid laerendis att teckis gwd mett then eller then gierningh, the eller the regle oc ceremonier, och dog aldrig kwnde komme till then rette sandhets oc gwdts dyrckelses kendelse, som St. Powel siger Hwilcken sandhet er iesu christi thro oc forladelse paa hannom, hans gierningher oc retuiset Oc thenne thro aleneste stiller, rolig tryg oc fredsommelig giør wore conscientier hoss gwdh, e hwor store synder we haffwe" (folio 8).

take place in the presence of the congregation when they are assembled to hear God's Word. Whosoever desires to receive the Body and Blood of Christ shall in the presence of the congregation go in Christian faith and with true intention to receive the blessed Sacrament, the Body in the bread, and Christ's Blood in the wine, in both kinds, in memory of the Death of Jesus Christ and of the shedding of His Blood and as a certain guarantee and true confirmation given us, by means of His Passion and Death, of the forgiveness of our sins and an assurance to our conscience of God's friendship."[1] "Our priests say the Mass openly in the presence of the congregation and in our own Danish tongue and administer it in church reverently and in a Christian and becoming manner, so that the people can understand and be aroused to the remembrance of His Passion, Death and holy Life, and stirred to praise and thanksgiving in accordance with the tenor of Scripture. Thus they will themselves be able to pray and sing God's praise fittingly, and answer with 'Amen' to the prayers, as St. Paul enjoins (1 Cor. xiv)."[2]

"The Mass in itself is nothing other than a present memorial of what He once said, and begins, 'our Lord Jesus Christ in the night in which He was betrayed,' etc. . . . In some churches whole psalms are sung by the people, in others one verse by the clergy. In the Greek church the people also sing together the *Kyrie eleison* and other common hymns. In the Latin Mass the clerks sing."[3]

"We are first and foremost entirely content with that one

[1] Rørdam, op. cit. "Haffwe the skicket effter christi indset oc exempel Mat. 26, Mar. 14, Luce 22 oc St. Pauli lerdom 1 Cor. 11 att christi testamente eller messen skal waeri i menig almuis neruaerelse, nar the forsamlis att høre gudts ord Oc huilken ther haffver attraa oc begering til christi legomme oc blod han skal i forsamlingens asiun gaa i een christelig thro oc rett mening att anamme thet verdige Sacramente, legom wdi brød, oc christi blod i win i twenne parte, legommet serdelis oc blodet serdelis, i iesu christi dødts oc blodts udgiiffuelses hukommelse, til een wished pant oc sand stadfestning, oss giort er formedelst hans pine oc dødt Oc thette Sacramente paa wor synders forladelse, oc en tryghet i vore conscientier paa guds wenscab" (folio 20, 21).

[2] Rørdam, op. cit. "Thenne forneffnde messe, then siger oc tracterir wore prester obenbarlige for menig forsamlingh paa wort eghet danske tungemaal erlige christelige oc tilbørlige i kircken, saa att almuen maa oc kand thet forstaa, och paamindis oc opweckis til hans pines døds oc welgierningers hukommelse til loff oc tacksigelse effter scriftens lydelse, saa att the kunde selff bede oc siwnge skickelige guds loff, oc sware amen til anders bønner, som St. Powel bescriffuer" (folio 21).

[3] Rørdam, op. cit. "Messen i seg selff, er inthet andett end then hukommelse som nu til forn om er taled, oc begyndis hwn ther Vor herre Jesus Christus i then nat ther han bleff forraad o.s.v. . . . Wdi somme kircker siwnges heele psalmer aff almwen, i some ett werss aff klerckeriid. Then Grescke kircke oc menighet siwnger almindelige kyrieeleyson oc anden almindelig sang. Udi then latiniske messe siwngher klerckene" (folio 24).

perfect sacrifice which Christ made when He offered Himself on the cross for us and the sins of the whole world: and for this we thank Him with heart and mouth. Our faith and open confession is that Christ's Body and Blood were once offered unto death, and can never be offered or slain again, and can certainly not be offered again for the living or the dead (as the Papists say)."[1]

From these passages it will be seen that a wide cleavage in doctrine separated the reformed service from its late medieval counterpart: yet the Danish reformers were conservative in their retention of the main structure of the old service. In the *Malmø Mass* of 1529 the order is: Confession, Absolution, Introit, Kyrie eleison, Gloria in excelsis, Collect, Epistle and Gospel, Creed, Hymn, Sermon, Psalm, Exposition of the Lord's Prayer, Sanctus, Consecration, Agnus Dei, Communion, Hymn and Blessing. At the Consecration the priest recites the words of Institution and is directed to elevate the sacramental Bread and Wine; and at the Communion he is to administer with the words, " the reception of the body of Jesus Christ strengthen you unto everlasting life "; " the participation in the blood of Jesus Christ be your help and comfort ". While most of the old liturgy was thus retained, following the example of Luther's *German Mass* the medieval Canon was set aside, and the concluding portion consisted of an Exhortation to communicants, the Lord's Prayer, the words of Institution with the Elevation, and the Communion and Blessing. The service was in Danish, but the Introit, Gloria in excelsis and Creed might be sung or said in Danish or in Latin.[2]

This union of the old and new in Lutheran worship is seen also in the service of *Baptism.* " This is the first outward sign of God's goodwill and grace towards us, that through water and baptism we are assured that we are His friends and children in the true Christian faith."[3] " To be baptized in water, or sprinkled therewith, is the outward sign denoting the inward cleansing which the

[1] Rørdam, op. cit. " Først oc fremmest ere wi aldelis wel til fredts met thet ene fuldkommelige offer ther christus offrede seg selff paa korsed for oss oc all werdsens synder Oc ther faare tacke wy hannom aff hierte oc mund thette her troendis oc obenbare sigendis, att christi legomme oc blod er en gang offred oc dødet, oc kand aldrig offris eller dødis mere Oc kand thett ingelunde offris mere for leffuendis eller døde (som papister sige) " (folio 25).

[2] See C. R. Martin, *Sveriges Første Svenska Massa*, pp. 35-63, where the Malmø-Mass is conveniently set out with the Nurnberg Mass of 1525, Luther's German Mass of 1526 and the Swedish Mass of 1531 in parallel columns.

[3] Rørdam, op. cit. " Thet er thet første gwdts veluilligheds oc naadis wdvortis tegen emodt oss, att wi formedelst vand oc døbelse, bliffue wiss paa at wi ere hans wenner oc børn i then sande christi thro " (folio 30).

Holy Ghost brings about in heart and soul."[1] "We administer baptism in Danish, the language the people understand, with a few of the ceremonies, including the presence of godparents and sponsors, which have been customary before. In order that many of those that hear it may be admonished and edified thereby, we administer it immediately after the sermon when people are gathered together. For the sacraments ought to be administered in the presence of the people and to the benefit and instruction of many."[2]

In both sacraments the emphasis was laid on the use of the vernacular, the presence of the laity and the Scriptural warrant: given these, there was no effort made to banish ceremonies of long standing or which could be helpfully retained. The greatest break with tradition had been made by Luther when in his treatise *On the Babylonish Captivity* he denied that there were seven sacraments and admitted, provisionally, only three: "baptism, penance and the bread".[3] This, or a modification of it, was the view adopted by all the reformed Churches, and Laurenssen expresses the teaching which prevailed in Denmark when he declares: "the outward sacraments or signs of the New Testament, instituted by Christ, are no more than two, baptism and participation in Christ's table".[4] Apart from this revolutionary change, the break with medieval tradition was made as little violent as possible, although the positive aims of the reformers—to make the services intelligible and congregational, as well as Scriptural—involved the use of the vernacular and a greater emphasis on preaching.

As with Baptism and the Communion, so also with *Marriage*, the service was translated into Danish. "This ceremony, or the Wedding Service, we hold in Danish for the many good and instructive passages which it contains. It has been published a short time ago for the benefit and enlightenment of the laity, that Christian readers may themselves read and discover how much Scripture has to say

[1] Rørdam, op. cit. "Att døbis y wandett eller ther met offverstenkis, thet er wdvortis tegn bemerckendis then indvortis reenlighet, huilken then Helligand giør i siel oc hierte" (folio 31).

[2] Rørdam, op. cit. "Tha handle oc tractere wi samme dob paa danske, thet maal almuen kand forstaa, met nogle faa ceremonier met faddere oc forloffwere, som en part seduan haffwer waeret tilforn Oc paa thet flere kand thet høre paamindis oc forbedris ther af, tha holde wi thenne dob nest effther predicken i menighedts forsammling Thi att Sacramente bør att brwgis i almwis nerwaerelse mange til gaffn oc paamindelse" (folio 31, 32).

[3] *Luthers Werke* (Weimar), vi, p. 501.

[4] Rørdam, op. cit. "Thet ny testamentis wdvortis sacramente eller tegn som a Christo ere skickede oc indsette, the ere icke wden tw, som er dob oc christi bords deelactighet" (folio 30).

in honour of matrimony: for Scripture is our guide to salvation and our true monitor unto the kingdom of heaven."[1] But the major part of what Laurenssen has to say under this heading is concerned with clerical marriage, for the celibacy of the clergy and the sacrificial character of the Mass were the two nodal points in the controversies of the Reformation. " The state of matrimony is for all (whether clergy or laity) who are not gifted with the grace of chastity in heart and mind, as a remedy against the sin of unchastity which brings God's wrath on people who are given over to adultery, fornication and the unclean living which we now unfortunately see only too commonly. The wrath of God indeed rests grievously upon us who are called Christian people, as well—and indeed more—on ecclesiastics as on those whom we call the laity; and this Divine vengeance hangs over us because we do not reverence God's Word, but basely, under the pretence of a false chastity, disdain matrimony, that wholesome remedy and the commandment of the Holy Spirit."[2] It seems at first sight strange that clerical marriage, which might be regarded simply as a matter of ecclesiastical discipline, should become one of the burning questions of the day. But Laurenssen and the reformers saw that in it were involved three important issues. (*a*) The permission of the clergy to marry meant the denial of the view, prevalent through the Middle Ages, that celibacy was the " higher " life; if the clergy married, then marriage was holy, and home life and family life (just as much as the monastic life) were a religious vocation. Christian marriage for all who are called to it, whether clergy or laity—that was the reformers' message, and one of their best contributions to the elevation of human society. (*b*) Compulsory celibacy inevitably put a strain on human nature, greater than some of " the religious " could sustain, with the result that misconduct was by no means uncommon, as Paul Eliaesen

[1] Rørdam, op. cit. " Thenne Ceremonie eller brudwielse holle wi oc paa danske for mange gode artickel oc lerdom skyld, som hwn indeholder, huilken oc nw kortt tiidt tilforn er wdgangen oc prenthet menig mand til gaffn oc forbedring, Som thw christne laesere, maa selff laese oc offwerfare, hvor thw findes møghet gott oc erligt om egteskaff wddraget aff schrifften Huilket som er allis wore saligheds regel oc sand wnderuiissning til himmerige " (folio 34).

[2] Rørdam, op. cit. " Then egteskaffs stadt er alle (ingen wndertagen geystlige eller verdslige) thennom som icke ere begaffwen met kyskheds naade i hw och hierte till ett raad oc legdom emodt wkyskheds synd oc gwds fortørnelse som menneske er ganske møget tilbøyget i hoor skiørleffnet oc anden wreenhet som wy maa thess waer nw almindelige see, att gwd fortørnes mett swarlige yblandt oss som kallis christne menneske, saa well (oc end ydermere) kirkens personer som andre ther wi kalle almuis folk Oc er thet een sand guds heffn offwer oss, forthi att vi icke acte gwds ordt Oc i øgenskalckhed wnder ett falsk kyskhedts skin forsmaa we thet gode raad, oc then helligandz bwd som er egteskaff " (folio 32).

reluctantly but candidly admits.[1] The reformers believed that clerical marriage would lead to a cleansing of the common life. (*c*) The appeal to Scripture which was characteristic of the reformers, though not confined to them, seemed to warrant the clergy marrying, and the claim of St. Paul, that it would be right for him "to lead about a wife, a sister", is frequently quoted. Thus Scripture appeared to confirm what marriage itself and common experience alike taught, that the clergy should be free to enter on matrimony and that celibacy should not be imposed on them.

On the subject of *Confession* Laurenssen appears at first to take a negative view, which afterwards broadens out into a recognition of its value. "That we should confess in a priest's ear or in a monk's lap we have no command from God; neither has any priest or bishop received command to search out people's hearts for their secret sins."[2] While he thus appears to reject the confessional outright, he then proceeds to outline a modification of it which he claims gives it spiritual value. "It is, however, good to confess (as we do here in Malmø) before priests, wise and learned in the Scriptures, or before other sensible men, when our failings in knowledge or in good morals are disturbing our spiritual state. When we are in grief, sorrow, despair, despondency or any other sinful temptation, it is good to go to such wise and worthy priests or laymen, as one who is sick or is hurt goes to an experienced physician, and asks counsel and help from their teaching and consolation. They will give us advice and declare unto us God's grace and forgiveness, and they will pray with us and we with them for God's presence and help, as Christ has promised us. Thus we shall be led to confession and our conscience thereby become quiet, contented and at peace."[3] It may be noted that this is the view of Confession which Luther himself took in his earlier days, for in *The Babylonish Captivity* he writes: "The secret

[1] *E.g.*, *Danske Skrifter*, pp. 421, 433.

[2] Rørdam, op. cit. "Att wi skwlle giøre schrifftemaal i nogen prestis øre eller i nogen munkis kwell eller skødt, this haffwe wi ingen befalning wppaa aff gwd Icke haffwe heller prester eller bisper ther befalning paa, att the skulle the lønlige synder wdgranske aff folckis hierter" (folio 37).

[3] Rørdam, op. cit. "Tha er dog gott (som we oc her i Malmø giøre) att wi bekende oss for viise oc kloge prester i scriften, eller andre forstandige mend, nar oss feyler paa nogen lerdom eller goder seder som wor siel er anrørendis, Eller oc nar wi ere i bedrøffwellse, sorg, fortwil mistrøst, eller anden synds frestelse, att wi gaa til samme forstandige gode prester eller mend, liige som een siwg eller saard, til en god wel forfaren laege, oc bedis raadt oc hielp aff hannom lerdom oc trøst, oc han siger oss raadt oc forkynder oss gwds naade oc affløsning offwer oss oc beder mett oss oc wi mett hannom om gwds nerwaerelse oc naade som christus haffwer oss loffwet, oc ther faare skwlle wi drages til schrifftemaal oc ther bliffwer wor conscientz rolig, tryg oc fredsommelig" (folio 37).

confession, however, which is now practised, though it cannot be proved from Scripture, is in my opinion highly satisfactory, and useful or even necessary. I could not wish it did not exist; nay, I rejoice that it does exist in the Church of Christ, for it is the one great remedy for afflicted consciences; when, after laying open our conscience to a brother, and unveiling all the evil which lay hid there, we receive from the mouth of that brother the word of consolation sent forth from God, receiving which by faith we find peace in a sense of the mercy of God."[1] Once again this illustrates the essential conservatism of the Lutheran position in matters which were arousing acute controversy.

In the latter part of his book Laurenssen writes about the organization and institutional life of the Church. He asserts that it is the duty of the laity to maintain the clergy who adopt the Evangelical faith; but the tithe on corn, according to the Malmø reforms, is to be given, not to the clergy, but to a hospital for the sick and needy. The burgomaster and council are to appoint physicians to look after the sick poor, who, if found incurable, are to be put into this hospital. Begging is not to be allowed; alms previously given to the mendicant friars are to be given to the really needy; a chest for the reception of these alms is to be placed in each church; and in every parish two or three responsible men are to be appointed as overseers of the poor.

The attitude of the authorities at Malmø towards *Monasticism*, as depicted by Laurenssen, appears for that age to have been tolerant and reasonable. Laurenssen gives his own opinion that monasticism, being a human and not a Divine institution, is fundamentally a mistake. " In short, the monastic life, with all its vows and present usages, though agreeable enough, it may be, to the individual, is no real piety or Divine service pleasing to God, for it is a mere human invention and commandment, by which God is served in vain."[2] He then proceeds to state the policy which the city authorities adopted towards the religious Orders; and as he seems to have acted as their secretary he would have had full information of their plans. " The burgomasters, council and people here in Malmø forbid monks under vows to beg, or to preach their fables and dreams, or to celebrate the errors of their Masses in the

[1] Wace and Buchheim, *Luther's Primary Works* (1883), p. 209.

[2] Rørdam, op. cit. " Summa summarum paa closter leffned oc muncke leffnet med alle siine løffte oc skick som nu er Thet er wel att skick oc leffned for seg selff, men thet er ingen gudelighed eller gwds thienneste, huilcken Gud er behaffwelig Forthi att thet er menneskens paafund oc bwdt, i huilket gud forgeffwes thiennes " (folio 45).

presence of the people."[1] But the measures adopted were not simply negative, nor was the complete abolition of the monastic life the aim of the Malmø reformers. Laurenssen outlines in the following passage a policy at once tolerant and constructive. "The burgomasters and council, with forty citizens, direct that the brethren who are willing honestly to conform themselves according to God's Word and true Christian teaching, as is fitting, and to lay aside all wrong preaching, false indulgences and deceit, giving no further cause for disturbances or quarrels, but sincerely preaching the pure and true Word of God, and serving under their own rule and charter, helping the sick and the poor (as they in any case ought to do by God's law)—such brethren shall be maintained honourably in food and clothing. But if they will not do this and will not minister to the poor and sick, they may yet remain in their monastery and be provided with food and clothing, on the condition, however, that they shall not resist, secretly or openly, the progress of God's Word, and that, moreover, they shall thereafter conduct themselves as Christian men ought to do."[2] How far the civic authorities were sincere in this policy of apparent tolerance and goodwill may perhaps be open to doubt. From other sources it is known that pressure was put on the Greyfriars to vacate their house in order that it might be reconstituted as a hospital, and sporadic acts of violence undoubtedly occurred.[3] However, both the prior and sub-prior of the Franciscans became reconciled to the new order, the former becoming warden of the new hospital and the latter reverting to lay life; and the brethren who wished to keep their vows removed themselves to the Greyfriars' house at Lund. The attitude adopted by the Malmø reformers anticipated in some degree the policy of the *Church Ordinance* of 1537 which forbade monks to beg, preach or hear confessions, allowed them to leave their houses if they so wished,

[1] Rärdam, op. cit. " Ther faare haffuer Borgemester, Raad oc menig almwe her i Mallmø forbudet forschreffne muncke, att trygle eller predicke theris fabel oc drøme, att holde theris messis misbrugelse obenbare for almwen " (folio 48).

[2] Rørdam, op. cit. " Indginge Borgemester oc Raadt met xl borgere . . . att the brødre, ther waere inde wille redelige skicke seg effter guds ordt oc rett christen lerdom som tilbørligt wore, oc afflegge all wrang predicken falst aflad oc bedregerii, giiffwe ingen ydermere orsage till opløff oc trette. Men reenlige predicke then pwre och sande gwdts ordt, oc effther theris egen regel oc fundats thienne oc behelpe the siwge oc arme som thenonm bwrde dog alligeuel att giøre effter guds louff, oc ther farre skulle the haffue erlig klede oc føde. Men wille the icke end thet giore, att the icke wille thienne the arme oc siuge, tha motte the end dog met vilkaar, at the skulle icke staa emodt gudts ordts fremgang lønlige eller obenbarlige, oc ther til att the skulle ther effter skicke seg som christne men bwrde att giøre " (folio 48, 49).

[3] See Chapter II, sect. 6, *ante*.

and endeavoured to reform the lives of those who desired to remain.

The reformers at Malmø had educational plans which Laurenssen describes in his book. The clergy school had been founded by royal permission in 1529. "The honourable burgomasters and council in Malmø have, with the approval and consent of our most gracious lord, His Majesty the King, founded and erected a school and place of study to which they have called and appointed some wise men, learned both in Scripture and in polite letters and scholarship, to teach and instruct poor clerks and other persons desirous of attending. They are to give lectures, freely and without cost, on subjects useful and advantageous both to themselves and to others whom they may in the future be able further to help and instruct."[1] The school was to be a theological college rather than a university: the main subject was knowledge of the Bible, and Greek and Latin were taught as helpful to that end. "We have not called our school a university, or, in imitation of others, a *studium generale*, in which the degrees of master and doctor are bought and sold at great cost . . . but we desire, according to our ability, to help poor clerks to graduate without expense in order that they may understand the Bible and its value."[2] No doubt the school served a useful purpose until, as has been noted, the reconstitution of the University at Copenhagen rendered the Malmø college unnecessary.

The desirability of children receiving a proper education is emphasized in Laurenssen's book, and parents are expected to send their children to school that they may learn to read and write, to acquire the elements of Latin, and to be able to express themselves both in Latin and in their own tongue when they read or sing. New schools have been opened in the city, and the burgomasters and council are willing that children attending such should beg for their dinners, if they need to. "Formerly children

[1] Rørdam, op. cit. "Tha haffwe Erlige mend Borgemeste oc Raadt her wdi Mallmø, mett wor kiereste Naadigste Herris Kongelige Maiestatis willis oc samtycke, skicket oc opreyst en Scole oc studium Oc ther til kallet oc indseet nogle lerde oc wiise mend, baade y then hellige schrifft oc anden bogelig konst oc lerdom, som skulle laere och wnderuiise fattige klercke oc personer huilke hiid wille komme, saa att the skulle forgeffuis oc for wden penningis wdgiiffuelse faa leytzer oc lerdom som thennom nyttelige oc bequemme kand waere, baade thennom selff oc andre som the kwnde i framtiiden ther met framdelis behelpe oc laere" (folio 50).

[2] Rørdam, op. cit. "Icke haffue we heller kallet wor scole eller studium noget vniuersitet effter andres seed noget almindelidt studium, ther som købis och sellies store titell, Mesters och Doctores naffn, met stor omkaastning. . . . Men wi wille aff vor formue promouere oc behelpe wden guld oc penninge, fattige klercke at the sculle aa wnderstand i schrifften oc gaffn" (folio 51).

were sent to school with a view to advancement in the Church and in the hope, perhaps, of obtaining a good parish, or even a canonry or a bishopric; now we shall see whether people will send them in order to learn the Christian faith. Such Christian education will not advantage us from a wordly standpoint, but it will bring us spiritual honour and the true riches."[1]

The last section of the book is concerned with the question of pictures in churches, and in this matter Laurenssen expresses what may be called the general Protestant view. Pictures are in themselves harmless, but may be abused, and if a cause of superstition are better away; in any case gifts bestowed on such things are better devoted to God's living pictures, to men and women in need. " Christian men are free either to have or not to have pictures in churches, as in any other outward usage or ceremony." " We will not reject or despise images or pictures, where they are used in a Christian manner; but we will certainly not honour them with genuflexions or with unprofitable expenditure on candles, clothes, or money offerings. The latter we ought to bestow on God's living images, our poor brothers and sisters, for we have God's command to give food and clothing to them, but not to stocks and stones and dead images, the work of men's hands."[2]

4

Laurenssen's book was answered in 1530 by Paul Eliaesen, whose work *Against the Malmø Book* presents the Roman Catholic side in the contemporary controversies. His book, however, remained in MS. until published in the nineteenth century in the volume of his collected writings.[3] On most of the points discussed —faith and works, sacraments and the Mass, clerical marriage, the monastic life, penance, requiems, tithes—he takes the orthodox Roman Catholic view. He is quick to detect the inconsistencies of his opponents. Speaking of Luther's sacramental teaching, *e.g.*, he declares Luther asserts first that the sacraments are seven, then

[1] Rørdam, op. cit., folio 52.

[2] Rørdam, op. cit. " Att haffue billede i kircker eller icke haffwe thennom thet er christne menneske friit liige som anden wdvortis skick eller ceremonier " (folio 53). " Icke wille wi heller bortkaste eller foracte billede eller taffler, hwor mandt icke anderledis thennom brwger end christelige som nw sagdt er Men dog ville wi icke heller aere thennom mett knaefald eller wnytteligh omkostning mett liwss, klaeder, offer, gwld, sølff oc penninge Men thette bør oss oc wille wi kaaste paa guds leffwende billede, wore fattige met brødre oc met søstre, om huilke wi haffwe gwds bwdt oc befalning, at offre, giffwe klaede oc føde thennom oc icke om stock, steen oc døde billede, som er menneskens handwerck och gerning " (folio 55).

[3] *Povel Eliaesen's Danske Skrifter*, ed. C. G. Secher.

three, then two, finally one; and he adds, "Would he not be wiser and safer to join with the old Christian Church and say with her: 'the Church's sacraments are seven, but three—baptism, the sacrament of the altar and penance—are universally necessary, while the other four—confirmation, orders, unction and marriage—are not universally necessary'?"[1] He finds, too, that Laurenssen's teaching on the sacraments is different from Luther's. "When he [Laurenssen] declares that the sacraments are not effectual actions conveying grace, but are merely signs which declare grace and produce no other special power or effect, he says what is not only contrary to the faith and teaching of Christendom, but is also against his own master, Martin Luther, who in this article of faith has now reached a different view."[2]

Concerning the Mass itself, Eliaesen defends most of the practices which were the subject of the reformers' strictures—the service in Latin, Communion in one kind and the system of private Masses; but while his arguments on these points are of the usual cast, he makes two interesting and important admissions which to a large degree justify the cry for reform. "I find," he says, "that two things have brought the Mass into ruin and contempt: first, the great number of priests who are found all over the world ordained to their holy office indiscriminately; secondly, the avarice, not of those who say Mass, but of those who draw the income and who ought themselves to be saying Mass. . . . Since custom impels them to maintain the service for the sake of the income and the benefits which they get from it, they go preferably to priests who are poor and make the best bargain they can. So through their greed and the poor priests' need and poverty the Mass is abused, since what is given the latter for the daily Mass does not pay for their food, let alone their clothing and other regular requirements. For the great owners of the Church's riches the Mass is the poorest job for keeping body and soul together. He who waits at their table, makes their bed and runs their errands has both food, clothing and wages . . . but the poor chaplain, who

[1] Secher, op. cit., p. 410. "Mwnne thet icke fordi waere wisse oc tryggere att tale mett then gamble christen kircke oc saa siige mett henne: kirckins sacramentt ere siw, men the try ere wdaff nød som ere dob, alterins sacrament oc wederkiendilse, ov the andre fijre som ere faermilse, wijelse, chrijsme oc aechtestatt, ere icke wdaff nød."

[2] Secher, op. cit., p. 410. "Men att hwn siiger sacramentene inthet wijrcke mett noghen krafftt, men aldene att waere eett teghen ther mercker naade oc wircker dog inghen anden synderlig krafftt eller naade, thet siiger hwn icke alsomeniste emod christendoms tro oc laerdom men oc saa emod theris eghen mestere Morten Luther, ther wdi thet støcke mening haffuer nw fangett eett endett sind."

ministers in God's service, does so for his bare maintenance, and when he has not enough is compelled to use the Mass as a means of begging, and so longs and prays and seeks for Mass-farthings that he may satisfy his lord."[1] In this admission Eliaesen goes some way towards conceding the reformers' case, but in the equally controverted question of clerical marriage he is less accommodating. While admitting frankly the prevalent evils of profligacy he sees the remedy to lie, not in the clergy and monks abandoning their celibacy, but in all, married and celibates, laity and clergy, alike keeping to their vows. Where evils exist they are to be found neither in marriage nor in celibacy, but in the men and women who misuse either estate. In the first days of the relaxation of clerical and monastic celibacy it is probable that some clergy married ill-advisedly, and there was, to say the least, something unseemly in the sight of monks and nuns deserting their spiritual homes and rushing into matrimony. Eliaesen, therefore, had some justification for his strictures; but his attitude was not merely critical, for he made the interesting suggestion that clergy should not be allowed to marry without their bishop's consent. " Readers will now know what my opinion is of this new matrimony entered into by priests and monks in these days on the plea that profligacy, adultery and unchastity should no longer prevail among Christian people. If such marriages would banish profligacy, adultery and unchastity, would God that all unmarried folk of whatever kind were truly married this day. But now we find many wise and sagacious men who think that this new matrimony, in the conditions in which it is entered on today, is not much more chaste than foul adultery and lewd living. If obedient and well-brought-up children may not wed with persons who are entirely unobjectionable, unless their parents have given their consent, then neither

[1] Secher, op. cit., p. 395. " Ieg befinder att twenne sager haffue kommett messen wdi fald oc foragtt, først thet store tall prester som findis offuer all werden wiigde till thet hellige embede wden altt forskiell, ther nest gijrighed, icke theris som siige messe, men theris som renthen haffue oc burde selffue att siige messe. . . . Oc nar the schule tha for seedijn skyld oppeholde tieniste for rente oc welfaerd som the haffue, tha gaa the ij wall mett fattige prester oc kiøbe thet nøijeste the kwnne. Saa komme bode theris gijrighed oc fattige presters tarff oc armod messen wdi mijsbrug, nar thet thenom giffuis for daglig messe kand icke betale theris kaaste end sije kleder oc andett som hør till daglig taering oc behoff. Hoss thenom som ere store herrer aff kirckins rente er messen thet armiste huerff som brugis kand till liffs biaering. Then som tien for theris bord, reeder theris seng oc riider theris aerinde haffuer bode kaast, kleder oc løn . . . men then arme capellan som scall giøre tieniste wdi Gudz handell giffuer bode penninge oc giør tieniste for then blotte kaast. Oc nar hand haffuer thenom icke naermer, tha scall hand nødis till att bruge messen for eett trøglerij oc ther fore lengis, biide oc søge effter messe penninge, att hand kand giøre sijn herre fyldist."

should ecclesiastics, who are forbidden the married state by their special character and obligation, enter it without the permission and approval of their bishop and ecclesiastical superiors, who are their spiritual parents."[1]

Eliaesen's attitude to these questions of the day was not, as can be seen from the above, precisely that of the usual Roman Catholic controversialist, yet on the whole he takes the orthodox standpoint. The two *apologias* are, in fact, opposed in principle and in detail. The above-quoted extracts from the *Malmø Book* and its Roman Catholic reply convey, it is hoped, a picture of what the changes in religion meant to the people of Malmø in the decade 1527-37. The sharp, controversial exchanges in either book have, indeed, been omitted, and the picture needs supplementing by such a record of dispossession and of violence as is given in the account of the expulsion of the Greyfriars from the town.[2] But the two books, written by brother Carmelites, who had been fellow-lecturers together at the college at Copenhagen, disclose the cleavage which can arise between men diversely affected by the ferment of religious change.

5

In 1531 there appeared from the Malmø press a little work entitled *A Christian Instruction on Confession and the Sacrament.*[3] The name of the author is not disclosed, but it may have been from the pen of Peder Laurenssen, since the teaching is in harmony with

[1] Secher, op. cit., p. 498. "Saa kand thu fromme laesere fraemdelis besinde aff mange wilkaar huad mening ieg haffuer om desse ny aechteschaff ther brugis aff prester oc mwncke ij thenne tiid, wnderthet skijn att skiørleffnett, hoor oc anden wreenhed, schule icke lenger regneere blantt christett folck. Kwnne sliige giifftermaall formeene skiørleffnett, hoor oc anden wreenhed, giiffue Gud att alle wgiiffte folck ij huad slag the wdaff ere wdaff wore well giiffte paa thenne dag. Men nw findis mange aff the wiise oc kloge som mene, att desse ny giifftermaall wnder thr wilkaar the nw brwgis, ere icke møgett reenere end wreentt hoor oc skiørleffnett. Maa icke lydige oc gode børn giiffte seg mett the personer som ere aldelis wbehindrede, theris foraeldre wberaadde oc watsporde, tha maa icke heller geestlige folck som iw behindede fra aechteschaffs wilkaar mett synderlig iett oc forplictilse, heller thet giøre wden kirckens prelaters oc forstanderis samtøcke oc tilladilse, som ere theris aandlige foreldre."

[2] See Chapter II, sect. 6, *ante*.

[3] C. J. Brandt, *En kristelig Undervisning om Skriftemaal og Sakramentet.* The original of the two questions and answers quoted in the text is as follows: "Huadt tror tw eller huad bekender tw att waere y thett Sacramente? Gensuar. Under brød oc viin er Christi sande legomme oc blod, oc thet er icke nog at ieg thet ved Men ieg maa oc tro at myn herre Christus haffuer giffuit meg thette testamente til een wiss forseiling oc pantt. Huarfore tager tw thet tegn Er icke troen teg nog? Gensuar. Thettet egn tager ieg ther fore at ieg scal sterke myn tro ther met, icke saa at ieg twiler paa myn tro, Men forti gud haffver giffuit meg thette tegn lige som ordenne aff sin milde naade oc barmhiaertighed at bruge, tha vil ieg icke for acte thet."

that of the *Malmø Book*. The tractate is in two parts. (*a*) An instruction on how to confess, in which it is said that confession is to be made to " the priest or any other learned man ". This agrees with what Laurenssen says in the *Malmø Book* that suitable laymen as well as the clergy may hear the confessions of the penitent; and it may be noted that the penitent addresses the confessor as " dear brother " and not " reverend father ". In the form of absolution both the *Malmø Book* and the tractate quote our Lord's words to the sick of the palsy (Matt. 9), " Son, thy sins be forgiven thee ". (*b*) The second part consists of four questions and answers on the subject of the sacrament, the second and fourth in particular showing the type of sacramental teaching now issuing from Malmø. " What do you believe and confess to be in this sacrament?" (Answer): " Under the bread and wine is Christ's true Body and Blood, and it is not enough that I know this, but I must also believe that my Lord Jesus Christ has given me this testament as a certain surety and pledge." " Why do you take this sign? Is not faith enough ?" (Answer): " I take this sign to strengthen my faith therewith, not as doubting my faith; but since God has given me this sign to use in accordance with His words of tender grace and mercy I will not scorn it."

Although Laurenssen may have been the actual author of this little book, its issue anonymously may be taken to imply that it presents the common view of the Malmø reformers on two questions of prime importance for the religious life of the people—viz., whether confession was to be continued, and, if so, under what form; and what was to be the belief of the ordinary man as to the meaning and purpose of the sacrament.

Two years later Laurenssen brought out another work, the occasion of which appears to have been the publication by Styge Krumpen, Bishop of Børglum, of some statutes which Laurenssen felt compelled to answer. The result was his *Short Instruction*, written while he was lecturer at the college at Malmø, and published in 1533 by Johan Hochstraten from his press in that city. It is a scholarly little work, with many references to Scripture, to the Fathers and to Canon law, traversing the whole field of contemporary controversy, yet with an admirable brevity. It will be sufficient to quote his views on the place of the ministry in the Church. " True Christian priesthood—in spirit and in truth—consists in the inner anointing of the Holy Spirit, His virtues and gifts, experience, wisdom, understanding and judgment, and in the abolition of the deceitfulness of sin and of all uncleanness and of the desires of the flesh, together with the cleansing by faith in Christ Jesus. In Him all true Christians are priests and are ordained by Him through the Holy Spirit, to make known the mighty benefits of Him who called them from sin and darkness to His Divine understanding and experience. . . . This is the true and proper Christian priesthood in the Church of Christ. A second and exterior priesthood is to be found in the particular calling and election by the Christian laity, under the direction of Christian bishops, or of ministers of the Church, and with the laying on of their hands, of suitable persons to preach the holy Gospel and the pure and sacred Scriptures, without human invention and device."[1]

In this passage Laurenssen asserts two principles which are involved in the Protestant position—viz., the priesthood of the Christian laity and the functional character of the ministry. Within the Christian Church today these two principles are still debated; and the antinomy between Catholic and Protestant, between Rome and the Reformation turns in some degree upon the opposed answers to the questions whether the laity are subordinate to the clergy or their ecclesiastical equals, and whether the ministry is one of Orders or of Office.[2] Laurenssen and Eliaesen answered these questions differently, and the variance between them was symptomatic of the cleavage between the Catholic and the Protestant which originated in the sixteenth century and is still unbridged.

[1] Rørdam, *Peder Laurenssens En stakket Undervisning*, pp. 68. 69. "Ret Christet prestedømme er i aand oc sandhed i induertis smørgelsse som er den helligandz dygder oc gaffuer, opliuselsse, wisdom, forstand oc dom, oc i syndzens oc al vrenhedz aff regilsse oc kødzens begaerings affkraffuelse oc renselsse wed troen i Christo Jesu, I huilcken alla rette Christne ere prester, oc ere skickede aff hannem wed den hellige aand, at kundgøre hans krafftige welgerninger, som kallede dem fra synd oc morckhed till sin guddommelig forstand oc opliuselsse. . . . Oc dette er det sande oc rette Christne prestedømme i den Christne kircke. En andet vduertis prestedømme er i besynderligt kald oc udkaaring aff Christen almwe, mett Christne Bispers eller kirckens tieneris befalling oc henders paaleggelse paa bequemme personer till at predick det hellige Euangelium oc den hellige rene scrifft, vden menniskens dicth oc paafund."

[2] See C.S.S.S. *Leaflet* for April 1934, notes on Holy Orders, by B. J. Kidd, p. 11.

CHAPTER VII

PAUL ELIAESEN AND THE FAILURE OF CONSERVATIVE REFORM

1

PAUL ELIAESEN (Povl Helgesen)[1] was one of a number of Erasmian reformers who in the early Reformation period were to be found in most European countries. Egidius of Viterbo in Italy, Alfonso de Valdes in Spain, Lefèvre in France, Pirckheimer in Germany, Colet in England and Hector Boece in Scotland differed in various ways, but were all agreed as to the necessity of reform being undertaken by the Church itself: they wished, that is to say, for a reform which should be authoritative and conservative. Paul Eliaesen's attitude was similar, though he had his own distinctive approach to this fundamental question of the time.

He was born about 1480[2] at Varberg, a town on the Swedish coast which was then in the Danish province of Halland. His father is said to have been a Dane, his mother a Swede, but nothing is otherwise known of them or of their home circumstances. From the fact that Eliaesen mentions a certain " Master Svend of Skara " as his teacher[3] it may be inferred that he received his education at Skara, the seat of a Swedish bishopric in West Gøtland. Nothing more is known of his early life until he is met with at the Carmelite monastery of Helsingør (Elsinore) in 1517. The Carmelites, or White Friars, first came to Denmark in 1410, and the province of the Order to which Denmark belonged had its centre at the Helsingør monastery, for there the Provincial prior resided. When Eliaesen entered this community this office was held by a man of some note, Dr. Anders Kristiernsen, professor of theology at the University of Copenhagen, and sometimes employed on royal embassies. Eliaesen remained a member of this monastery for the rest of his life, and succeeded Kristiernsen as Provincial prior, retaining this office in all probability till his death.

The foundation of the Carmelite college at Copenhagen and the appointment of Eliaesen as its first principal[4] brought him into

[1] The chief sources for Paul Eliaesen are: Heise, *Skibykrøniken*; Secher, *Povel Eliesens Danske Skrifter*; Engelstoft, *Paulus Eliae;* Schmitt, *Paulus Heliä*; Andersen, *Paulus Helie*.

[2] Professor J. O. Andersen, however, puts the year of his birth not before 1485: *Paulus Helie*, p. 8.

[3] Secher, *Povel Eliaesens Danske Skrifter*, p. 299.

[4] See Chapter I, sect. 4.

prominence. Christian II requested him to translate a Latin book, possibly *The Prince* of Machiavelli, but Eliaesen soon abandoned the task when he realized the character of the work. He translated instead the *Institutio principis Christiani* which Erasmus had brought out in 1516 with a dedicatory epistle to King Charles I of Spain: the fame of Erasmus and the excellence of the instructions conveyed in his book inspired Eliaesen with the hope that his own King would benefit from its persual. But the King was alienated by the frank speaking of Eliaesen's dedication and by the unpalatable fact that it was dated January 24, 1522, the very day when the King's Machiavellian counsellor, Didrik Slagheck, was burnt at the stake in the market-place of Copenhagen. Eliaesen's relations with the King were further worsened by a sermon he preached in the royal chapel at which the King took deep offence; the result was the abrupt termination of his work at Copenhagen and his flight to Aarhus, where he took refuge with the bishop, Ove Bilde.

Eliaesen's three years' residence at the Carmelite College (1519-22) was probably the most fruitful period of his life, though perhaps this was not his own view of the matter. Writing later of those days in his *Skibykrøniken*, he declared that " the brethren of both Orders (Carmelites and Cistercians) whom he had advanced by his commendations, instructed in knowledge and helped to honours and reputation, had all been changed wellnigh to wolves, and had fallen away, not only from him, but from the obedience they owed the Church ";[1] and he attributed this to the disastrous influence of Lutheranism. But among his students were men like Laurenssen and Vormordsen, who later rose to eminence in the reformed Church, and Eliaesen himself could not but be aware of the good work that he had accomplished and of the good relations that had existed between the students and himself. In a letter to Peder Iversen, Canon of Lund, written in 1524 when insinuations against his orthodoxy were being made, he declared with evident satisfaction: " I have young men who value me highly; they will not allow even my clothing to be harmed, much less my reputation or my name."[2]

The falling away, as he regarded it, of many of his best students

[1] *Skibykrøniken*, p. 63. " De Brødre af begge Ordnerne, som han havde forfremmet ved sine Anbefalinger, oplaert i Videnskaberne og skaffet Haeder og Anseelse, alle de forvandledes naesten til Ulve og faldt ikke blot fra ham, men fra den Lydighed, de skyldte Kirken."

[2] *Skibykrøniken*, p. 206. " Jeg har unge Mennesker, der saette stor Pris paa mig; de ville ikke taale, at min Klaedning uden videre sønderrives, endsige da mit Rygte eller mit Navn."

to Lutheranism, though a source of deep disappointment to Eliaesen himself, may have been due more to his influence than he realized. His teaching during these early years at the Carmelite College and in the University seems to have been in accord with the new learning, and perhaps was somewhat similar in method to that which John Colet had earlier used at Oxford.[1] "His lectures were almost certainly expositions of the writings of the New Testament, or, as he himself usually called them, 'the serious studies'; and quite certainly he went to work in a way which contrasted strongly with the old scholastic method, so that his lectures, while they attracted the young, aroused ill-will and scandal among the old. . . . There is no doubt that Eliaesen's appearance in these years roused an unusual stir, and that in his lectures he developed views and opinions which struck like lightning, with the result that his hearers never forgot them all their lives. We may therefore surely call these years, not only the happiest in his life, but also those which have given him his importance in the history of the Church."[2] Yet in these days when the new learning was contending with the old, an Erasmian scholar like Eliaesen was bound to find his path difficult. In the above-quoted letter to Iversen he writes: "There are some who wish nothing more than to abolish entirely all serious studies, of which their view is that by my midnight watches and my efforts they have been of service in some of the schools of Denmark, though in this they are wrong. I have tried according to my ability, but little have I accomplished, partly because of my own weak powers, but chiefly because of the folly of some old men who unceasingly cry out against the patrons of learning . . . and who would rather barbarism should prevail everlastingly than that they who were once held as rabbis and teachers should lose ever so little of their

[1] Andersen, *Paulus Helie*, p. 46. "At P.H. i hvert Fald nu har opfattet sin Undervisning i Skriften i bibelhumanistisk Aand, kan ikke betvivles, da han (1524) karakteriserer den som Fortolkning af Kristus, Peter og Paulus." C. T. Engelstoft discusses in his *Paulus Eliae*, pp. 26 ff., the character of the teaching given at the University of Copenhagen at this time.

[2] Helveg, *Den Danske Kirkes Historie*, iii, p. 544. "Hvad han foredrog, har sikkert naermest vaeret Fortolkning af det N.T.'s Skrifter, eller, som han selv gjerne betegner det, 'de alvorligere Studier', og ganske vist gjorde han det paa en Maade, som maatte skikke staerkt af mod den gamle skolastiske Methode, hvorfor hans Forelaesninger, idet de drog de Unge til sig, vakte Uvillie og Forargelse blandt de Gamle. . . . Utvivlsomt er det, at Povel Eliesens Optraeden i disse Aar vakte et overordentligt Røre, at han i sine Forelaesninger udviklede Tanker og Anskuelser, der slog ned som Lyn og gjorde den Virkning, at hans Tilhørere aldrig i deres Liv glemte dem, hvorfor vi sikkert kunne naevne disse Aar ikke blot som de lykkeligste i hans Liv, men som dem, der have givet hans Liv Betydning i Kirkens Historie."

honour. They do not see that this is evidence, not of piety, but of envy, that they are hating the knowledge which they do not understand. . . . They proclaim as heretics those who in the schools interpret Christ or Paul or Peter."[1]

2

After abandoning perforce his work at the Carmelite College, Eliaesen became involved in the growing movement of opposition to Christian II. In his letter to Peder Iversen already quoted he claims to have done more than anyone in opposing the King's actions. "Name me," he writes, "if you can, among all those who with braggart words boast of having done everything, even one who by speech and by pen has opposed the King's violence with such outspokenness as I have done."[2] In the same letter he declares that after the King's flight he (Eliaesen) was invited to draw up a statement of the reasons for the King's abdication; and a considerable section of the *Skibykrøniken* is taken up with a list of grievances against Christian II, which he elaborates with much severity.[3] It is evident that a complete change in his attitude to the King had occurred. In the earlier years of the reign the King's zeal for learning and his sympathies with the common people had stirred a chord in the heart of the Carmelite, who was devoted to scholarship and was himself sprung from the people. But the bloody deeds done in Sweden, the legislation adversely affecting the Church's inherited constitution, and the preaching of new doctrines by foreign scholars introduced by the King convinced Eliaesen that Christian II was becoming a tyrant and a heretic whom it was his duty to oppose.

Meanwhile a change was going on in Eliaesen's own mind and heart. While at the University his teaching appears to have been

[1] *Skibykrøniken*, p. 204. "Der er dem, som intet andet ønske, end at de grundigere Studier rent maatte udslukkes, om hvilke de tro, at de ved min Nattevaagen og ved mine Bestraebelser ere blevne fremhjulpne i nogle af Danmarks Skoler, skønt de dog heri tage fejl. Forsøgt det har jeg vel efter Evne, men kun lidet har jeg kunnet udrette saa vel paa Grund af mine egne svage Kraefter som fornemmelig for nogle taabelige Oldinges Skyld, som uafladelig raabe mod Videnskabens Maecener . . . at de hellere ville, at Barbariet skal herske til evig Tid, end at de selv, som fordum ere holdte fra Rabbinere og Laerere, skulle miste endog nok saa lidt af deres Anseelse. De indsee ikke, at det vidner om Misundelse og ikke om Gudfrygtighed, at hade de Videnskaber, de ikke kende . . . udraabe de den for Kaetter, som i Skoler fortolker enten Kristus eller Paulus eller Petrus."

[2] *Skibykrøniken*, p. 200. "Naevn mig, om du kan, blandt alle dem, der i højtravende Talemaader skryde af, at de have udrettet det hele, blot en eneste, der i Tale som i Skrift med saa stor Frimodighed har modsat sig hans Voldsfaerd, som jeg har gjort."

[3] *Skibykrøniken*, pp. 73-91.

based on Scripture and humane learning, and his contemptuous reference to the upholders of the old theology who " proclaim as heretics those who in the schools interpret Christ or Paul or Peter " puts him on the liberal side of the dividing line between the old and the new learning. In 1524 he translated into Danish Luther's *Betbuchlein*,[1] though the work was not published till two years later; believing, as he says in the preface, that Luther's teaching contained both truth and falsehood, his object was " to separate the good from the evil, the wheat from the tares, and to issue the result in Danish ".[2] But this translation of a work of Luther's, together with his attitude to the supporters of the old learning, made him suspected of Lutheranism; and in the dedication of the *Bedebog* to the councillor Oluf Rosenkrantz he alludes to this. " I may well ask, my dear friend, why you should complain that at one time I preached differently from what I now do; that is, that then I preached with Luther and now against him." He then proceeds to explain his attitude to Luther. " If I at any time had been of Luther's opinion, I would thank God that He had delivered me out of the devil's snare which has caught for a time some who are wiser than I have ever been. I do not acknowledge, however, having at any time belonged to Luther or to any of his followers. So far as I have ever recognized, or still recognize, the power of Luther's books, I do so, not because Luther has written such things, but because I have read them in the books of Jerome and Bernard and in the *Revelation* of St. Bridget. There one reads of the avarice, pride, unchastity and other great and gross sins which for many years have been shamelessly committed both among clergy and laity. That much sin exists is unfortunately only too true; but there are no greater lies than those which Luther has spoken and written against the Church's sacrament."[3] It may be surmised

[1] Published in Secher, *Povel Eliesens Danske Skrifter*, pp. 1-53.

[2] Secher, op. cit., p. 1.

[3] Secher, op. cit., p. 2. " Jegh haffuer well spurdt, kiaere her Oluff, at ieg er forklaget hoss edher, at ieg skulde eth stund anderledis predicke en iegh nw giør, thet er, at ieg tha predickedt med Luther, oc nw y mod. Men ther som ieg haffde noghen tijdt waerid aff Luthers meningh, tha wilde iegh tacke gud, at hand haffde migh forløst aff then dieffuels snare, ther haffuer tha hegtet till een tijdt thennom, som ere wijsere en iegh noghen tijdt bliffuer. Dog ieg icke kendis meg nogen tijdt waere besooren anthen medt Luther eller nogher aff hans tilhengere. Saa møget som ieg nogen tijd gaff macht aff Luthers bøger, Thet giffuer ieg en nw macht, icke forthi at Luther saa schriffuer, men ath ieg less thet samme wdtij Hieronimi oc Bernhardi bøger Oc y Sancte Birgitte obenbarelsse, som er om gerighedt, hoffmod oc wkysckhedt Oc andhre store oc groffne syndher, ther y mange aar wbluelige driffwis bode blandt then geestlige oc then verdslige stath, at møgen syndt er till thet er (dess waer waer) for møget sandt. Men ther findis tha ingen støre løghen en then som Luther haffuer taldt oc screffuedt mod kirckens Sacrament."

that what attracted Eliaesen in Luther's earliest books was their Scriptural basis and their attack on the moral evils of the time, but that his sense of loyalty to the Church was shocked by Luther's criticisms of the Church's sacramental system. He had probably read Luther's *Babylonian Captivity* (published in Latin in October 1520) for he alludes to it in terms which imply that he both knew and strongly disapproved of its contents.[1] His attitude to Lutheranism, in fact, hardened: in this he resembled Erasmus and other humanists. Luther's behaviour at Worms in challenging the inerrancy of Pope and Councils, his violence, and the radicalism of some of his followers disgusted Erasmus, who in September 1524 issued his *De libero Arbitrio* which criticised one of Luther's main positions. The following year Luther replied in his *De servo Arbitrio*, and the breach, which had been widening, became unbridgeable. " Thoughtful men sided with Erasmus, who, followed by Willibald Pirckheimer, Crotus Rubianus, and the Humanists generally, abandoned the Reformation."[2] Amongst them must be reckoned Paul Eliaesen, who after 1524 stiffened in his resistance to reform and became increasingly recognized as the literary champion of the Catholic Church in Denmark. Yet he never became obscurantist or the blind upholder of the existing state of affairs. To the end of his life he hoped for religious revival and was ready to make concessions to the reforming spirit of the age, so long as the unity of the Church and its authoritative teaching were maintained.

3

With the accession of Frederick I Eliaesen appears to have regained his position as lecturer at the University: little, however, is known of his activities in the next two or three years. By 1526 copies of the Danish *New Testament*, sponsored by Christian II and prefaced by a contentious epistle of Hans Mikkelsen, were percolating into the country. Eliaesen felt the time had come for him to act. He had translated Luther's *Betbuchlein* in 1524, but left it in MS. He now determined to publish it so that " the people might lay aside the German books which they so eagerly read ". It was printed by the Brethren of the Common Life at Rostock and came out in 1526.[3] It is a work of plain instruction on the Ten

[1] Secher, op. cit., p. 81.
[2] Kidd, *The Continental Reformation*, p. 37.
[3] Secher, op. cit., pp. 1-53. *Een cristelig vnderwissningh paa the thij Gudz budord, then menige Cristen kirkis tro ock loffue. Wor herris bønn Pater noster, oc huore Jesus Christi død oc pijne schalle rettelige begaas oc tracteris.*

Commandments, the Creed and the Lord's Prayer, with a meditation on the passion of Jesus Christ, and is an earnest plea for sincerity in religion. The following year he brought out the first of his surviving works of controversy: his *Answer* to Hans Mikkelsen's Preface to the Danish *New Testament.*[1] At the close of the work it is stated that it was written (or perhaps finished) at Odense in Advent 1526, and was printed at Rostock by the Brethren of St. Michael's Monastery in April 1527. Evidently, therefore, Eliaesen was present at Odense during the sitting of the Herredag in December 1526; his work may have been read in MS. by some of the bishops and its publication advocated as a means of strengthening the Catholic cause.

Shortly before the Herredag reassembled at Odense in August 1527 the Swedish King, Gustav Vasa, summoned a Riksdag to meet at Vesterås. This marked an important advance of the Reformation movement in the neighbouring country. Previous to the meeting Gustav Vasa had circulated a dozen questions to the Swedish clergy on the doctrine and government of the Church: a copy of these came into Eliaesen's hands, and after some delay he published his second considerable work, *Some Christian Answers to the Questions which King Gustav of Sweden has addressed to all his Clergy.*[2] It was published at Copenhagen in 1528 and was therefore too late to affect the course of events in Sweden: probably he had Denmark rather than Sweden in his mind. It covers most of the points under debate and is written in the contemporary manner of controversy. This holds good of another of his major works which has already been mentioned, his *Reply* to the *Malmø Book* of Peder Laurenssen.[3] But two lesser books written by him in 1528 have a different character.

One of them was published under the title, *How sick, infirm, wounded, poor and needy people should be looked after and cared for: a short Instruction by Brother Paul Helie.*[4] It is addressed to Niels Stemp, burgomaster of Copenhagen, and was written as a result of a consultation the two had had concerning the foundation of a

[1] Secher, op. cit., pp. 55-142. *Till thet ketterlige, wcristelige och wbesindige breff, som then wbesckemmede kettere Hans Mikkelssen aff Malmø lod wdgaa met thet ny Testamente, ther koningh Cristiern lod ynckellige och wtilbørlige forwandle paa sith tijrannischke wildt, oc icke Gudt till loff, eet kort och tilbørligt swar.*

[2] Secher, op. cit., pp. 167-326. *Nogre Christelige Suar till the spørsmaall som Koning Gøstaff till Swerigis Rijge lodt wdgaa till sith gantsche Klerckerij, berammede aff Broder Paulo Helie.*

[3] Secher, op. cit., pp. 341-509. *Imod Malmø-Bogen.*

[4] Secher, op. cit., pp. 143-166. *Huore krancke, mijslige sarre, arme oc fattige menniskir schule tracteris oc besørgis, een kort vnderwijsning aff broder Paulo Helie.*

hospital for the sick and afflicted people of the city. Eliaesen declares that if he had been rich he would gladly have helped in this cause, but as he was not—and he was quite content to be poor—he would try what he could do with pen and paper. He laments that among the many great sins now prevailing, one of the worst is the unmerciful harshness of the treatment given to those who are already in a sad plight through sickness or poverty. After enumerating the manifold occasions and mischances which bring men to misfortune, he explains that the increase of disease demands the institution of a new hospital in Copenhagen. He discusses the difficulties of such an undertaking and illustrates them from the experience of the past. Where hospitals have been endowed such provision has frequently been abused by princes and lords, who have intruded their servants and dependents into them, and thus robbed the poor of their rights. Though he recognizes the advantage of an endowment, he shows that such benefactions are a temptation to the covetousness of the powerful. It would be well, he suggests, if an assessment from taxes and dues could be made for the benefit of hospitals, for by that means the money which comes from the common man would return to him again. The appointment of able and trustworthy men in charge of the hospitals' resources is commended, and the habit of giving to those already rich lavish presents at weddings and christenings is deprecated: such gifts might better go to the sick poor. He strongly disapproves of the custom of men begging on behalf of hospitals, for it leads to many ill practices. He ends his plea by reminding his readers that the sick and the needy are not the only deserving recipients of charity, nor is the founding of hospitals the only way of helping them. There are the children to be considered. Whoever takes the child of a poor man into his home and cares for him as his own builds a hospital. Whoever provides for the honourable maintenance of poor girls builds a hospital. Whoever loves his wife and children and protects his home from the contamination of the world's evils builds a hospital. Such in brief outline is Eliaesen's contribution to one of the urgent problems of his day. It depicts a somewhat stern ascetic in a new light, as a man of kindly human feeling, with a deep sympathy for the common people and a chivalrous desire to help them in their troubles.

The other small work produced at this time was a piece of Biblical scholarship. His friend and former colleague, Frans Vormordsen, brought out in 1528 a Danish translation of the

Psalms in which he had received assistance from Eliaesen; and the latter had made a further contribution to the work by translating part of St. Athanasius' *Letter to Marcellinus on the Interpretation of the Psalms*, adding it as an appendix under the title *On the Power of the Psalter*.[1] In the dedication Vormordsen expresses his indebtedness to his old colleague. " The good father, Lector Paul, has followed the great Athanasius, a holy Archbishop of Alexandria, who among other works in his time composed a small book on the power of the holy Psalter, which has been translated from Greek into Latin by Angelo Politian and then some years ago by Johannes Reuchlin. This book Lector Paul has now translated into Danish and allowed it to appear with this Psalter. . . . He has earned no small thanks in doing what will add much value to this work."[2] Eliaesen made his translation most probably from one of the Latin versions, for it is unlikely that he was in any true sense a Greek scholar,[3] although it is possible he may have acquired, or endeavoured to acquire, some slight knowledge of Greek, somewhat like the efforts of Dean Colet and Bishop Fisher to learn the language in their mature years. His translation, however made, is of special interest as being probably the first translation into Danish of a work of a Church Father[4] and also as illustrating his willingness to encourage a vernacular version of the Psalms for the use of ordinary people. In acknowledging the help he had received Vormordsen pays this further tribute to his friend: " At my request he [Eliaesen] has done this more readily than would be credited by his opponents, who decry him as the enemy of the holy Gospel. He has approved and furthered a work which gives the true meaning of Scripture in the common tongue. He is convinced that this would be of great advantage, not only for all Danes, but also for Swedes and Norwegians and others who share a common tongue with the Danes."[5] Unfortunately the good relations existing between the two men did not last. In 1529 Vormordsen went to Malmø, became one of the Lutheran clergy of that city and later married. A complete breach followed, and each in subsequent works referred to the other in terms of bitter recrimination.

[1] The original is in Migne, vol. 27, pp. 11ff.; and Eliaesen's translation is in Secher, op. cit., pp. 327-340.

[2] Engelstoft, *Paulus Eliae*, p. 440, *note* 33.

[3] Andersen, *Paulus Helie*, p. 58. " Om han ovorhovedet har laert noget Graesk, er højst tivivlsomt."

[4] Engelstoft, op. cit., p. 439.

[5] Schmitt, *Paulus Helia*, p. 53.

4

Very little is known of the last years of Paul Eliaesen. The advance of Lutheranism in Copenhagen after the Herredag of 1530 led to a suspension of the activities of the University, and Eliaesen no longer dared to reside there; Helsingør and Roskilde were his two homes in these closing years. His days were saddened by the decline of his own Order in Denmark: one by one the Carmelite houses ceased to be. During the troubled years 1533 and 1534 he lived at Roskilde: here he resumed his Bible lectures and held the position of Lector on the cathedral Chapter. Here, too, he published his last works. In his earlier years he had translated the *Institutio principis Christiani* of Erasmus for the benefit of Christian II, but this had remained in MS.; now he brought it out in a revised form with a view to it being read, perhaps, by the new King, when he should be chosen. The outbreak of civil war disappointed his hopes and rendered the work nugatory.

The collection of historical notes, known as the *Skibykrøniken*,[1] was put together by Eliaesen over a period of years and was never published by him. The MS. was discovered in 1650 in the church of Skiby in Zealand, hidden in the wall behind the altar; and although the work is anonymous there is little doubt that it is from his pen. The book begins with a kind of genealogy showing how the royal family of Scandinavia traces back to Svend Estridsen in the eleventh century; it then proceeds to give historical notes upon the Oldenborg line of Kings from Christian I to Frederick I. The last recorded events belong to the autumn of 1534, and the work ends abruptly in the middle of a sentence. In the earlier parts the notes are sparse and occasional in character; as the author reaches his own times they become fuller, and relate to persons and events connected with the places where he himself had lived, such as Copenhagen, Roskilde and Aarhus. His judgments on character and conduct are decided and often severe: he seeks to show that evil-doing brings its own punishment. In spite of the bias imparted by the author's strong views his book remains a valuable source for the history of the Reformation in Denmark and a very interesting literary document.

Eliaesen's last work, published at Roskilde in 1534, was perhaps his most important: its title ran, "*A Short Instruction on Christian Union and Concord against the Disunion and Dissensions*

[1] See the edition by A. Heise, with valuable notes.

which at the present time have disturbed the united Fellowship of the Universal Church to the great harm of Christendom."[1] The earlier part of this work consists of a translation of a portion of a work of Erasmus, the *De amabili ecclesiæ concordia.*[2] While in form a commentary on Psalm 84, it is in substance a moving appeal for " Christian Union and Concord " which gathers up the thoughts of Erasmus in these years of increasing conflict. Here is a brief summary of his plea for Church unity:

Whatever has come down from our forefathers and received the sanction of general approval should be retained; nor should novelties be introduced unless necessity or obvious advantage warrants them. Doctrines like the freedom of the will are difficult subjects to discuss and should be left to the handling of theologians. But we can all agree that we can do nothing of ourselves and are entirely dependent on divine grace; and we can also agree that faith is of the greatest importance and is the gift of the Holy Spirit. With regard to prayers for the dead, it is a pious opinion to believe that such are of advantage to the departed, but money spent on funeral processions and on Masses founded out of personal vainglory is money wasted. Those who do not practise prayer for the dead must not mock at the simplicity of those who do. It is a pious belief, too, that saints are able to afford us help, but those who do not believe this should address their prayers directly to God and not disturb those who sincerely invoke the help of the saints. Though there may be much superstition in such a practice which deserves exposure, yet simple piety should be borne with, even when mingled with a little error. It is not to be wondered at that images of the saints have been destroyed, for idolatry is a fearful sin. But statuary and pictures were formerly valued as a kind of poetry, and it would be a good thing if the walls of every home had fitting pictures of the life of Jesus Christ. Churches should only contain pictures of which the subjects are Scriptural. Those to whom the images of the saints do not appeal are welcome to their

[1] *Een kort vnderwiisning til een Christelig foreening och forligilse, emod huess wchristelige twyst oc twedrackt som nw haffuer i wor tiid skiørdet then menige Christen kirckis eendregtige samflnd, Christendommen till eet stortt affbreck.* For this work see C. T. Engelstoft, *Paulus Eliae* pp. 510-527.

[2] See Erasmus' *Works*, Leyden edition, vol. v, 498 B-506. P. S. Allen has a paper on this tractate of Erasmus in his volume of lectures entitled *Erasmus* (Oxford 1934). Referring to the many editions and translations of this book, Allen mentions a translation into Danish, which is no doubt Eliaesen's, though he does not mention Eliaesen's name. For the summary in the text the writer has been helped by Allen's translation (the first one to be made in English) of the latter part of this treatise of Erasmus.

opinion, but they should not mock at those who venerate them as an aid to devotion. The same applies to the veneration of relics of the saints: St. Paul would have allowed each man to have his own opinion. Without question the best way to venerate the saints is to imitate their lives. Some do not believe that sacramental confession was instituted by Christ; but they should grant that it has beneficial uses and is sanctioned by long practice. Abuses have, of course, cropped up: people, *e.g.*, leave one confessor to try another, or they make meticulous recitals of their sins. The chief thing is so to order one's life that we do not fall into any great sin; he who does that is free of the burden of confession. Those who believe that it was Christ Himself who instituted it should all the more carefully comply with it, allowing others who think differently to hold their own view until a Church Council has given a clear judgment on the matter. As to the Mass, it is true that abuses have crept in and they should be remedied. Such faults as walking about while Mass is going on, or saying Mass for a trivial intention, or leaving the church before the service is finished are clearly wrong; but there is no reason to decry the service itself. Some wish for Communion at Mass: that, no doubt, was Christ's intention and was the practice in the early days. But the laity have grown indifferent: it would not be right to offer heavenly food to those unwilling. Others raise objections about adoration. If Christ Himself is there He is to be adored. But the sacrament of bread and wine is there for deepest devotion and not for display. Those who have confused themselves with the many opinions about the sacrament would be well advised to adhere to the belief which the Church has handed down to us—viz., that the true Body and Blood of the Lord is there in reality. Fasting is inculcated by the Church as a matter of health, both of body and mind: those who are not benefited by the practice are under no obligation; yet to refuse the rule because the Church imposes it is simply contumacy. Error has carried some unhappy men into Anabaptism. The baptism practised in the Church for fourteen hundred years does not satisfy them; they ignore the precept of the Church about rendering " to Cæsar the things that are Cæsar's "; and they forget that community of goods was only practised when the Church was in its infancy, and even then not among all Christians. But nowadays the minds of many people are shaken, and any new opinion, however absurd, finds followers. However, if by counsels of moderation and measures of prudence we take thought for the problem of Church unity we may yet with one heart address one another, and say, "How amiable are thy tabernacles, O Lord of Hosts."

To this transcription of Erasmus' thoughts on unity Eliaesen adds a second part as his own contribution to this composite work. In this he deals with certain subjects which, he says, Erasmus had passed over. Time—or the advance of Lutheranism—seems to have brought him a mellowing of temper and a willingness to make concessions. "He goes farthest in concession in regard to clerical marriage, provided only the permission is given in a lawful manner; he even speaks derisively of those who hesitate when such permission has been given when he says: 'it must be a convenient piety' which can endure a priest who is a fornicator or an adulterer, and reject another who is married yet otherwise an honourable man."[1] In regard to the Mass he held firmly that the dignity of the sacrament demanded the Latin tongue, and believed its retention would aid in maintaining a knowledge of the language; but he was willing that a hymn before and after Mass should be sung in Danish, if sung by men who were fitted by voice and training. He adhered, on the whole, to the custom of administering the Communion in one kind, but was willing that the Cup should be granted to those who humbly desired it, but should be refused to those who condemned the old Catholic ways.[2] Concessions such as these have caused him to be charged[3] with adopting a mediating attitude and a kind of cryptocatholicism: but broadly it may be said that in these years of increasing conflict, with Protestantism advancing both in Scandinavia and Germany, Eliaesen was at one with Erasmus. Both were nearing the close of their lives, and both dreaded, as Luther himself did, the outbreak of hostilities between the two religious parties. They asked, therefore, that if concessions were granted to the Lutherans they should be granted also to the Catholics; they pleaded with the extremists of both wings for mutual forbearance; and they pinned their hopes of a

[1] Helveg, *Den Danske Kirkes Historie*, iii, p. 984. "Videst gaaer han i Indrommelser med Hensyn til Praesters Aegteskab, naar Tilladsen kun blev givet ad lovlig Vei, ja spotter endog med dem, der have Betaenkelighed ved at en saadan Tilladelse blev givet, naar han siger, 'det maatte vaere en behaendig Gudelighed' at kunne fordrage en Praest der er Skjørlevner og Hoerkarl, og vrage en anden, som vel er gift, men ellers en aerlig Mand." *Cf.* Schmitt, *Paulus Heliä*, p. 118.

[2] Helveg, op. cit., p. 984. The late Bishop W. E. Collins (*vide Camb. Mod. Hist.*, ii, p. 609) went too far when he wrote: "His [Eliaesen's] last effort at peace-making, his *Christian Reconciliation and Accord*, written about 1534, is an earnest plea for peace on the basis of the historic system of the Church, with the services in Danish, communion in both kinds, marriage of the clergy and the like."

[3] By Schmitt, op. cit., p. 155.

settlement to the holding of a Church Council which by its authoritative decisions should bring peace and unity to Christendom.

5

With the publication of this characteristic plea Paul Eliaesen disappears from history. Legend has given to him the opprobrious nickname of " Paul Turncoat ", made him interpreter for Martin Reinhard, and asserted that he deserted Lutheranism when bribed by the bishops with a canonry at Roskilde. But Paul was never a Lutheran, though he was a reformer; the harsh nickname hardly fits a sincere and lifelong Catholic; and the story of his interpreting for Reinhard appears to be simply a mistake. The measure of truth in these stories is that he did accept a Roskilde canonry, though when he did so is unknown; and that he reacted to the convulsions of the time by shifting his position, sometimes to the right, sometimes to the left, but always keeping his place as a central, conservative and reforming Catholic.

One slight trace of him in his last days is provided by an inscription on an old door of the church at Skiby;[1] the door was destroyed when the church was restored in 1854, but the architect, Professor Storck, has recorded that he remembers distinctly that the door bore the inscription, " da Paulus Eliae var Kirkevaerge " (" when Paul Eliaesen was churchwarden "). Though this has been doubted, the subsequent finding of the *Skibykrøniken* MS. at Skiby supports the view that he had some connexion with this church. The abrupt ending of the MS. in the middle of a sentence has led to the surmise either that he was suddenly overtaken by death or that his writing was interrupted by an incursion of his enemies. The boldness of his condemnation of Christian II and Frederick I would have made it advisable to hide the MS. while Christian III lived, and so it remained hidden until discovered more than a century later. Strangely enough, nothing is known of the time or place of Eliaesen's death. The usual conjecture is that he passed away at Roskilde in 1535 or 1536. His sudden disappearance is hard to account for unless he fell a victim to some deed of violence, and the authorities had the affair hushed up. However that may be, neither friend nor foe has left the world any news of his final end.

[1] Heise, *Skibykrøniken*, p. 10.

6

In his *Reply* to the *Malmø Book* Eliaesen describes the three parties which had risen from the religious upheaval. " Some are so fallen away to the new learning that they will tread under foot the holiness of Christendom, and so change everything that they will give the old Church no reverence or honour, as if she had been so blinded and hardened in mind and soul, in creed and doctrine, that she had never done or managed anything by God's grace or according to God's will. . . . Others, on the other hand, are so unfriendly to the new learning and so dependent on the old that they will defend alike evil and good, vice and virtue, and will acknowledge no sin, fault, abuse or error, which, in fact, have long existed, but follow at all costs the old learning they have been accustomed to. . . . But besides these two parties there is a third, consisting of some honest and sensible men who do not give their entire adhesion to either side, but desire that what is Christian and right may be established and confirmed and prevail, and that what is unchristian and wrong, the result of greed, ill-management or abuse, may be either abolished or improved and reformed."[1] To this middle party Eliaesen claimed to belong. " During the crisis of the Reformation he became the principal leader of an intermediate party, which on material points agreed with Luther but which was absolutely against a breach in the church."[2]

It is clear that in his attempt to follow a policy of conservative reform he failed, and the failure may be attributed in the main to the revolutionary forces accompanying the Reformation. The bishops, as the official leaders of the Church, were given the opportunity of concurring in, or even of initiating, some measures

[1] Secher, op. cit., p. 346. " Somme ere saa faldne wdi then ny handell att the all christendoms hellighed wele platt traede wnder føder oc saa alting forwandle, att the wele then gamble christne kircke inghen agtt eller aere offuergiffue, liigerwiiss som hwn waerett haffde saa forblindett oc forstockett fra sind oc skiell, fra scrifftt oc lerdom, att hwn aldrig noghett schaffede eller skickede aff Gudz raad eller effter Gudz willie. . . . Somme twertt emod ere saa thenne ny handell wbewaarede oc then gamble anhengindis att the wele forsuare bode ontt oc gott, bode synd oc dygd, oc fordi wele inthet lade affalde wdaff huess synd, brøst, mijsbrug eller wildfarilse som ij lang tiid waerett haffuer, men ij alle maade forfolge huess gammill handell the lenge brugett haffue. . . . Men forwden desse twenne slag findis oc saa thet tredie oc the ere nogre gode retsindige mend, ther saa ere begge slag mettfaeldige att the paa inghen siide then gantsche handell magtt, oc ere fordi begaerindis att thet som er christeligtt oc redeligt maa stadfestis, bliffue bestandigtt oc haffue magtt, men thet som er wchristeligtt oc wredeligtt aff gijrighed, mijshandell oc mijsbrug forwandlett eller forbijstrett, maa aenthen affleggis eller oc forbaedris oc reformeeris."

[2] J. O. Andersen, *Survey of the History of the Church in Denmark*, p. 16.

of reform which might have appeased the growing discontent. In worship, a partial use of the vernacular and the granting of the Cup to the laity; in discipline, the limitation of the number of priests and of mendicants, and permission for the marriage of the parochial clergy; in organization, the transfer of some of the wealth of the Church to schools, colleges and hospitals, and the abolition of such abuses as indulgences and papal provisions—measures such as these would have satisfied the longing of the better minds for new life within the Church, and would have left the historic system of the Church of Denmark intact. But the Danish bishops were incapable of such enlightened action: with their great wealth, their connexions with the nobility, their rank in the hierarchy of the Church, they were entrenched in the existing system. They failed to see the need for religious revival, and they did not produce from their own body a man with the vision and leadership to control and to inspire the surging movement for reform. In this they were not different from their brethren in other lands. The absorption of the episcopate in political and administrative work was a characteristic of the Church in Europe in the centuries before the Reformation. "More and more the episcopal office was regarded as merely intended to restrain evil, to be mainly coercive; but not to be a spiritual inspiration, a great force for good. More and more the bishop's legal jurisdiction (exercised in his courts) was exalted, and his other duties depressed. The Episcopate, no less than the Papacy, was the plaything of ecclesiastical lawyers. . . . To them was largely due the indifference or even dislike with which many of the populace regarded religion."[1]

This was the situation which faced Paul Eliaesen in his efforts to eradicate the worst ecclesiastical abuses of the time and to inspire renewed life within the historic framework of the Church. But he was thwarted by something more powerful than the apathy or the opposition of the bishops: he was defeated by the forces of revolution. History has shown that in times of revolution the moderate men fail to make their voices prevail. Adrian VI and Erasmus were at one on the need for reform and might have agreed on some of the practical steps to be taken; but the forces of reaction within the Curia and the violence of the impetus let loose by Luther could not be overruled or controlled by an ailing Pope who wished for peaceful reform but lacked the power to achieve it. With the death of Adrian after a brief twenty months on the Papal throne

[1] J. P. Whitney, *The Episcopate and the Reformation*, p. 39.

passed away the last hope of any serious measures emanating from Rome, until—too late—the north was lost.

In no country in Europe did the men of moderate views succeed in carrying through their ideas of reform. Spain, for a time, seemed likely to adopt a policy of Erasmianism: Cardinal Ximenez had organized disciplinary reforms among the clergy, both secular and regular, and had encouraged learning; and a party of " Erasmistas " had actually been formed. But some of its prominent members were cited before the Inquisition and punished, and Erasmianism gradually died out in Spain. In southern Europe generally reforming ideas were generated by individuals or among groups, but were not adopted by the civil power or welcomed by the people: in consequence they were never strong enough to issue in revolution. When the civil power or the laity took the lead, as in Great Britain, Scandinavia, Germany and Switzerland, the result was not simply moderate reform but the Reformation itself—*i.e.*, revolution in religious, social and economic life. It may perhaps be suggested that those countries which thus experienced revolution in the sixteenth century got their troubles over early; while those lands in which, like Russia, the Reformation never came, or where, like France and Italy and Spain, reform was suppressed, had to pay the penalty by enduring the revolutions of the eighteenth, nineteenth and twentieth centuries.

Paul Eliaesen in failing to carry through a measure of conservative amendment in Denmark thus failed in company with the whole school of such reformers in the crisis of the sixteenth century. With most of them he had much in common, but with one Englishman in particular he may be profitably compared. There was much in his attitude to the changes of the time which resembled that of Bishop Fisher. The fruitful years of both were spent at Universities, Fisher at Cambridge and Eliaesen at Copenhagen. Both were ardent promoters of learning, and though not Greek scholars themselves they had the scholarly outlook of the Renaissance. Both strongly condemned the moral delinquencies of the clergy while firmly upholding the authority of the bishops. Both encouraged the reading of the Bible by students, while deprecating the wholesale circulation of the Scriptures in the vernacular. Both became forceful opponents of Lutheranism, which seemed to them to be destructive of the foundations of both Church and State. Perhaps their position may be summed up as that of reformers who disliked the Reformation, adherents both of the old religion and of the new learning. To say that such men failed is only to say that they were ahead of their time. As there were reformers before the Reformation of the sixteenth century, so the Reformation which is yet to be has had its precursors in those scholarly figures who hoped for reform without schism. In the spirit of those men " we can only look to the new Reformation to restore the unity which was shattered by the old ".[1]

[1] C. Beard, *The Reformation* (1883), p. 335.

CHAPTER VIII
CONCLUSION

COMPARING the relative speed of the Reformation movement in the three northern kingdoms of England, Sweden and Denmark, Bishop John Wordsworth wrote: " In Denmark, owing to its proximity to Germany and other causes, the process was most rapid. . . . In Sweden the change was much slower, and in England it was the slowest of all."[1] Taking Paul Eliaesen's lectures on the New Testament from 1519 onwards as initiating the movement and the passing of the *Church Ordinance* in 1539 as completing it, the whole process of reform in Denmark is thus comprised within a brief twenty years. Within that time the belief, worship and organization of the Danish Church was transformed from a Catholic to a Lutheran model.

At first the doctrine of the reformers did not take a credal or confessional form: emphasis was laid simply on the preaching of the Gospel and the necessity of faith. " The church ordinance [of 1539] settled no formal symbolical obligation, but its whole contents were decidedly Lutheran, and the *Confessio Augustana* was soon in practice acknowledged as the doctrinal standard. . . . It was really a Lutheranism much influenced by Melanchthon that conquered Denmark, and the influence of this great pedagogue through school and university was decisive."[2] The publication of the Danish Bible in 1550 helped to give the Danish Church the character of " a school striving at educational Christianity " and great importance was attached to uniformity of belief and of worship.[3] While it was not till 1574 that the original *Augsburg Confession* was adopted as the formal statement of the belief of the Danish Church,[4] yet that *Confession* had from the first been regarded as the true doctrinal standard; and this provides a link between the Church of Denmark and the Church of England, since Melanchthon's *Confession* both influenced the Anglican Articles and formed the standard of reference for Danish orthodoxy.

What was the inner significance of the doctrinal change which

[1] *The National Church of Sweden*, p. 238.
[2] J. O. Andersen, *Survey of the History of the Church in Denmark*, p. 23.
[3] Andersen, op. cit., p. 26.
[4] Kolderup-Rosenvinge, *Grundrids af den danske Kirkeret*, p. 29, *note* 2. " Den Augsburgske confession er først erkjendt som symbolsk Bog under Frederick den 2 *den* i en Befaling af 1574."

took place in Denmark? An historian of today describes it thus: "The whole anxious concern of the late Middle Ages had wrestled with the question, 'How can God be made gracious towards me?' And by the offering of prayers to the saints, by the founding of masses, by renunciation and good works, men strived to supply the answer. But to the question, 'When is God gracious?' never came the comforting word, 'It is enough'. Now the answer sounded: 'You already have a gracious God, if you believe on Him—simply because you believe!'"[1]

Here is the heart of the Lutheran gospel. "The new foundation of doctrine was simply the believer's justification by faith only, and, coupled with the supreme authority of the Word of God, his right as a priest to have access to it and to interpret it for himself."[2] The phrase so frequently met with in the Danish reformers, "God's Word and the Gospel", thus summarizes the essence of the new faith; and from these three roots—belief in the message of God's free grace, the supremacy of the Scriptures, and the priesthood of baptized Christians—springs the whole growth of later Lutheran orthodoxy.

The doctrinal innovation was one of form and emphasis rather than of content and substance. The *Augsburg Confession*, with other similar doctrinal statements of sixteenth-century Protestantism, "was the introduction to the Christian world of a new kind of creed".[3] Such confessional statements were both lengthy and controversial—*i.e.*, they dealt in detail with the points which were the subject of division and of debate. The *Augsburg Confession*, *e.g.*, assumed as true the strictly theological statements of the Nicene Creed as to the being of God, but elaborated with much care the position held with regard to free-will and to faith and good works. Though, however, the *Confession* was new both in its form and in its emphasis on the debated points of man's relation to God, it claimed that there was nothing in its doctrinal teaching inconsistent with Scripture or with the belief of the Catholic Church or even with that of the Roman Church, so far as that is known from its writers. Where the Lutheran reformers were impelled to make their protest was in the case of certain abuses in contemporary Church life, and the second part of the *Confession* defines in detail their views on communion in both kinds, on the marriage of the clergy, on the Mass, on confession, on the distinction of meats and traditions, on monastic vows, and on ecclesiastical and civil

[1] Fabricius, *Danmarks Kirkehistorie*, ii, p. 353.
[2] Kidd, *The Continental Reformation*, p. 107.
[3] C. Beard, *The Reformation*, p. 282.

authority. The position taken on these questions by men like Tausen and Laurenssen was closely similar to that of Melanchthon as recorded in this " venerable *Confession* " of the Lutherans.

In worship the medieval sacramental system gave way to a Lutheran ordering of the services. The substitution of Danish for Latin as the liturgical language was not the most significant change. Latin was indeed retained in certain parts of the Danish Mass as an alternative use to Danish, the intention being to encourage the study of Latin by its employment in church.[1] Even the introduction of Danish hymn-singing, though an innovation strongly criticized by a conservative stalwart like Paul Eliaesen,[2] was not in itself such a revolutionary change. The real break with medieval tradition was made by men like Tausen and Laurenssen, who repudiated the doctrine of the Mass as a sacrifice: the retention of much of the structure of the old service and of some of its externals, such as the vestments and lights, could not hide the fact that the *Messe* had been changed into the *Nadver*, or Supper, a change emphasized by the distribution of the elements in both species. Further, the importance attached to preaching led to the sermon occupying a definite and prominent part in the service, one result of which was a gradual change in the rationale of the liturgy. The part which led up to the sermon, with its hymns and prayers, came in time to be considered, with the sermon itself, as a complete service, even when not followed by the Communion; and as the zeal of the first years of the Reformation began to wane, and it frequently happened that no communicants presented themselves, this change in the character of the liturgy became permanent.[3]

[1] Engelstoft, *Liturgiens eller Alterbogens og Kirkeritualets Historie i Danmarks*, p. 79. " Skjønt det var en Hovedfortjeneste ved Reformationsvaerket at have tilbageført Modersmaalet i Gudstjenesten, holdt dog en stor Deel af den latiniske Kirketjeneste sig laenge; man frygtede det classiske Sprogs Tilsidesaettelse, hvis man ikke understyttede det ved kirkelig Brug."

[2] *Povl Eliesens Danske Skrifter*, p. 385.

[3] See Engelstoft, op. cit., p. 53. " Men snart fik Praediken sin faste Plads i Messen, og derved blev en anden Betragtning af Alter-tjenesten mulig. Den Deel af den, som laae foran Praediken, blev at ansee for en intergerende Deel af en Gudstjeneste i Almindelighed, et Partie af Sang og Bøn, som indledte Praediken, saaet Høimessen kunde blive betragtet som den høitidelige og fuldstaendige Gudstjeneste overhoved. Denne Overgang i Bregrebet viser sig vel endnu ikke i Luthers Liturgier eller i de første, som udkom paa Dansk, thi disse forudsaette, at der ril Høimesse stedse ere Communicanter, og give ingen Forskrivt for det modsatte Tilfaelde. Ogsaa efter Reformationens Indførelse vedblev der en tidlang at herske en saa stor relgiøs Iver, at det sjeldent kunde indtraeffe at en Høimesse holdtes uden Communionen. . . . Men efter et Par Decenniers Forløb omtaler en af de første Alterbøger dog slige Tilfaelde uden at characterisere dem som sjeldne, og allerede Ordinantsen havde forudseet det og derfor lagt Grunden til Høimessens Selvstaendighed uden Communion, idet ikke alene Messen før Praediken anordens uden at betinges ved en følgende Communion, men det endog tilladed at ' forfølge ' (fortsaette) Messen efter Praediken."

Thus, in contrast with what happened in the Church of England, the Danish Church retained as its chief Sunday service the liturgy, with collect, epistle and gospel, expository sermon and hymns, though, not infrequently, without the Communion; but it did not develop a service of the Word, like the Anglican Sunday Matins and Evensong, as an addition to the Sunday *Nadver*, or Lord's Supper.

Since Lutherans recognized the two Gospel sacraments only, the old sacramental system on which the life of the Christian in the Middle Ages had been built became a thing of the past. In Denmark Confirmation disappeared, to be revived later in a form different from that traditional in the Roman and Anglican Churches. "In the first formularies of the Lutheran Churches there are either no directions at all about Confirmation, or else the institution of a similar ceremony, differently conceived. The examination of the young and their introduction to first Communion, which is met with in certain formularies and was regarded by Luther as an allowable custom, were placed in connexion much more with Communion than with Baptism."[1]

The service of Baptism in Danish had been brought out by Tausen in 1528 in a rendering which adhered closely to the medieval form. This was followed in 1535 by a simpler ordering of the service published in the Malmø *Messebog* and based on Luther's *Baptismal Office* of 1524, which had omitted the old ceremonies. The *Church Ordinance* prescribed no special form but assumed that those in use would continue; but when Palladius published in his *Enchiridion* (1538) a close translation of Luther's service of 1524, his influence secured the gradual adoption of this simpler form of Baptism.[2]

The Occasional Offices of Marriage and Burial were continued in the reformed Church of Denmark, but with modifications. Luther's *Traubüchlein* became the model for the different versions of the Marriage Service which were in use in Denmark during the years of reconstruction. The Lutheran view that marriage was a civil matter diminished to some slight extent the importance of the Marriage Service and there is some little evidence in Palladius'

[1] Engelstoft, op. cit., p. 239. "I de lutherske Kirkens første Agender findes deels aldeles ingen Forskrivt om Confirmation, deels en lignende Handling, men anderledes betragtet. Thi den Overhørelse af Ungdommen og Introduction til den første Altergang, der forekommer i enkelte Agender og af Luther blev anseet for en ligegyldig Skik (Wercke 22, 569), bliver meget mere sat i Forbindelse med Nadveren end med Daaben."

[2] Engelstoft, op. cit., pp. 180-186.

Visitatsbog that people did not always seek the Church's blessing.[1] Similarly, the effect of the loss of belief in the medieval services was to make it a voluntary matter whether the parish priest was present at the burial of the dead, and Requiem Masses became of course things of the past. The *Ordinance* disallowed burial fees but required the parish priest to attend as a matter of Christian charity; and if he was present he was to give the funeral address. The custom of casting earth upon the coffin was continued through Reformation times, and there seems little doubt that the Lutheran clergy regarded it as their duty to be at the burial of their parishioners.[2]

The reorganization of the Danish Church took place in three stages. The first step was the decision of the Herredag at Odense in 1526 to cease applying to Rome for papal confirmation of newly appointed bishops, a decision of which probably the main motive was the King's determination to retain in his own hands the money payable to the Curia. Thus what was at first a financial expedient became ultimately a cause of severance from papal jurisdiction and a revolution in Church order.[3] The next stage in the reconstruction of the Danish Church was the abolition of the old episcopacy and the institution of the Superintendents nominated by the King and ordained by Bugenhagen. This was a change which not only entailed the loss of the episcopal succession, but which also involved a complete alteration in the status of the higher clergy. The old bishops had been territorial magnates, members of the royal Council and the equal of the highest in the land.[4] The new Superintendents were men of different origin, humble scholars, lecturers, canons or ex-monks; and their new office was a purely spiritual one, giving them no political power, except the right to be summoned, together with representatives of the clergy and of the other estates of the realm, to meetings of the *Rigsdage*.[5] Not only the status of the

[1] Engelstoft, op. cit., p. 292.
[2] Engelstoft, op. cit., p. 305.
[3] Helveg, *Den Danske Kirkes Historie*, iii, p. 690. "Saaledes kom det frem, hvad den var en gjennemgribende Forandring i den hele Kirkeorden, blot som en Pengesag, uden at Nogen indlod sig paa at drøfte Sporgmaalets aandelige Betydning."
[4] For the cleavage between the higher clergy (bishops, canons, abbots) and the lower ranks (parish priests, vicars, monks) during the Middle Ages see Engelstoft, *Om Geistligheden som Rigstand i Danmark efter Reformationen*, pp. 105 ff. (*Nyt historisk Tidsskrift* v, pt. 1).
[5] See J. E. Larsen, *Om Rigsdage og Provindsialforsamlinger samt Rigsraadet i Danmark*, p. 275 (*Historisk Tidsskrift*, i); and *cf.* H. Matzen, *Forelaesinger over den danske Retshistorie*, p. 51: "Da de romerske-katolske Biskopper bleve afskaffede, bleve deres Godser og Tiender inddragne i Statskassen, dog med Paalaeg om at anvende deraf til aandelige Formaal, vilket ogsaa skete, idet ikke blot de nye Biskopper for en vaesentlig Del ønnedes af dem, men ogsaa Universitet, Kommunitat, Skoler, Hospitaler og Praeste-

higher clergy was affected by this change: the authority of the whole clerical order was diminished, and the chief gainers, apart from the Crown, in this shifting of prestige and of power were the nobility. " In Catholic times the nobles and clergy were indeed in a special degree privileged classes; but at the Reformation the power of the clergy fell in proportion as that of the nobles rose. The eagerness which many of the nobility manifested for the introduction of the Reformation was often based on the desire, partly of being freed from the influence of the clergy, up till now their co-equals, partly of avoiding the payment of tithes; and it rested further on the hope of recovering the estates which their forefathers in earlier days had presented with pious intent as gifts to churches and monasteries."[1]

The withdrawal from the jurisdiction of the Pope and the change in the character of the higher clergy carried the Danish Church to its third stage of reshaping—viz., the predominance of the Crown in ecclesiastical affairs. No longer required to recognize a spiritual superior in the Pope, and no longer finding in the powerful prelacy of the old order a rival or an opponent, the King succeeded to some of the powers of both of these dispossessed authorities. The right of the Pope to confirm bishops being abrogated, its place was taken by the claim of the Crown to confirm the newly elected Superintendents. The Crown also became possessed of the bishops' rights of patronage and of the episcopal tithes, in addition to the immensely rich inheritance of the bishops' properties. Further, the character and abilities of Christian III and his achievement in engineering the ecclesiastical revolution enhanced

---

kald i betydelig Grad forsynedes ved Hjaelp af Konge-tiender. De evangelisk-lutherske Biskopper, der fra først af benaevnedes Superintendenter, vare Embedsmaend, hvis Embedsgjerning bestod i at føre det kirkelige Tilsyn i Stiftet. De sad ikke i Rigens Raad, men mødte fremdeles personlig paa Staenderforsamlinger." (" When the Roman Catholic bishops were abolished, their property and tithes were confiscated to the State, with the stipulation, however, that they should be used for spiritual purposes. This, in fact, was done, for not only was a substantial part of the new bishops' salaries thus provided, but also the royal tithes helped to a considerable degree in the maintenance of the University and communities, schools, hospitals and parish livings. The Lutheran bishops, who at first were called Superintendents, were officials whose duty was to exercise ecclesiastical supervision in the dioceses. They had no seat on the royal Council, though they still attended in person the assemblies of the Estates.")

[1] A. C. Bang, *Praestegaardsliv i Danmark*, pp. 233, 234. " I den katolske Tid havde Adel og Gejstlighed jo i saerlig Grad vaeret privilegerede Staender; men med Reformationen sank Gejstlighedens Magt i samme Grad, som Adelons Vaelde steg; og den Iver, som mange af Adelsmaend vistes for Reformationens Indførelse, har ofte hvilet paa Ønsket om, dels at fritages for den hidtil sideordnede Gejstligheds Indflydelse, dels at slippe for at yde Tiende, og tillige paa Haabet om at tilbageerhverve det Kirkegods, deres Forfaedre i tidligere Tid havde skaenket som Gaver i fromme Øjemed til Kirker og Klostre."

both for him and his successors the reputation and the influence of the Crown. Both in Denmark, in Sweden and in England the major changes of the Reformation were the result of the actions of the sovereigns in each country; but a particular contrast exists between the course of reform in Denmark and in England as affected by the personal character of the monarchs concerned. The English Reformation is a story of reactions. The Henrician reform was followed by its antithesis, the Edwardian, and that again by the counter-reform of Mary; and the Tudor drama of religious change was closed by the temporary reconciliation of opposing forces in the Elizabethan "settlement." The personal beliefs and dispositions of the four Tudors were in varying measures a chief factor in this welter of change. Similarly in Denmark the characters and religious outlook of Christian II, Frederick I and Christian III affected decisively the course of events in their respective reigns. But whereas in England the process of change was by way of reaction, in Denmark it was one of continuous development. The Reformation which made its tentative beginning under Christian II was continued under Frederick I and completed under Christian III. Although both the personal character and the religious policy of the three Kings differed greatly, the course of religious change—except for the brief period of the Interregnum—flowed on without serious reaction or setback.

Thus within these twenty years the ecclesiastical state of Denmark suffered a revolution. The Catholic Church in Denmark was transformed into the Danish State Church. This, rather than the creation of a completely new Church, is the conception entertained today of the significance of the Reformation changes. "The Church continued to exist in Denmark after 1536 as before, only reformed and newly ordered. The difference was merely that while, according to Catholic ideas, the State had hitherto been the subordinate partner of the great universal and international Church, now the Church became in every Protestant country the subordinate partner of the national State."[1] Yet this view requires qualification. "The Church was the State Church

[1] Arup, *Danmarks Historie*, ii, p. 507. "Kirken vedblev at bestaa i Danmark efter 1536 som før, kun at den reformeredes, nyordnedes. Forskellen var blot, at medens staten efter katolsk tankegang hidtil havde vaeret den store, almindelige internationale kirkes underordnede medarbejder, blev Kirken i hvert protestantisk land nu den nationale statsmagts underordnede medarbejder." *Cf.* J. O. Andersen, *Survey of the History*, etc., p. 22: "There was no more talk (at the Rigsdag of 1536) . . . about the 'establishment' of a 'new Church'. It is the organization and government of the existing Danish national Church which is laid down."

and yet it was something more. The congregation was granted indeed a voice in the election of its minister, though later this gave way to the patronage of the nobles and of the King. On the whole, the congregation was not the real supporter of the Church's work, but rather the object of the labours of the clergy, under the protection of the King. And yet the Church still remained the Church. The Kings, who made many mistakes, yet knew that the Word of God was the absolute standard. . . . The bishops—for this name quickly became usual again—both in their dioceses, which remained the same, and in their bishops' assemblies, were far more than German General superintendents, and carried besides so much upon their shoulders that the Church never became a mere department of the State."[1] Perhaps to some extent confirmatory of this and significant of a certain practical independence claimed for the Church of Denmark is the fact that its present-day title is " the Danish People's Church ".[2] Yet, however the ecclesiastical revolution be estimated, it is indisputable that doctrine, Church order, modes of worship, all were changed, not without occasional violence and some breach of continuity. Compared, however, with the events in England, the Danish Reformation was soon over, producing no martyrs,[3] leading to no bloody reprisals: and when Lutheranism had triumphed the vast majority of Danes quietly accepted the new order.

Outside the limits of Germany, Scandinavia was Lutheranism's sole permanent conquest: each of the three northern kingdoms yielded to it under pressure, aided by the zeal of a few convinced reformers, but without widespread popular enthusiasm. This uniform adoption of the Lutheran faith by the three Scandinavian kingdoms is again in striking contrast with what happened in the British Isles. Here the Reformation left in each kingdom a numerically preponderant Church, Anglican in England, Presbyterian in Scotland, Roman in Ireland; yet each country developed strong

[1] *Ekklesia*, ii, p. 31. " Die Kirche war Staatskirche und wurde es immer mehr. Man bewilligte zwar der Gemeinde einen Einfluss auf die Pfarrwahl; der ging aber später verloren zugunsten der adeligen Patrone und des Königs. Überhaupt war die Gemeinde nicht Trägerin der kirchlichen Arbeit, sondern Objekt der Arbeit der Geistlichkeit unter der Schutze des Königs. Und doch blieb die Kirche immer Kirche. Die Könige, die viele Fehler machten, wussten doch, dass das Wort Gottes die absolute Norm war. . . . Die Bischöfe—denn dieser Name wurde schnell wieder der übliche—waren in ihren Sprengeln, die dieselben blieben, und in der Bischofsversammlung weit mehr als deutsche Generalsuperintendenten und trugen viel dazu bei, dass die Kirche nie ein blosses Staatsdepartement wurde."

[2] " Den Danske Folkekirke."

[3] Fabricius, *Danmarks Kirkehistorie*, ii, p. 315. " Ingen, hverken katolsk eller evangeisk, led Martyr-døden her i Landet i hele vor Reformationshistorie."

and aggressive minorities whose ultimate destiny was to win toleration for themselves and so to advance the cause of religious freedom.

In the Denmark of Christian III, however, there was no toleration for those who were not Lutherans. It is true that Myles Coverdale, the translator of the Bible and former Bishop of Exeter, was welcomed and offered a benefice by Christian III when he came to Denmark in 1555 to escape the clutches of Queen Mary.[1] But very different had been the reception given to some other English exiles two years earlier. In November 1553 there arrived in Copenhagen two ships with about 150 English people on board who, under the leadership of the Polish nobleman John à Lasco, had fled from England on the accession of Mary and were now seeking refuge in Denmark. When their arrival was reported to the King his decision was that " no public worship could be permitted them in this kingdom, since both in doctrine and Church order they differed from the Danish Church, and the King feared that these differences would cause disturbances; but if they would change their opinions on these matters accommodation would be provided them ".[2] The exiles were Calvinists and would not compromise or yield: they were convinced that they could prove to their unwilling Danish hosts that their own faith and discipline were more in accordance with God's Word than those of the Danish Church. Such religious debate, however, Christian would not allow; and so the party of disappointed and embittered exiles sailed away, winter though it was, to Germany.

By exclusions such as these Denmark was preserved from the violent dissensions which disturbed less happier lands, but at a certain cost. Lutheranism has been called " a low-temperature religion,"[3] and in Denmark, where almost everyone was a Lutheran, the Church lacked the fires which smaller and more ardent sects could supply. That is not to say that in the years following the Reformation Church life in Denmark was quiescent. Controversy rose and fell, and currents of thought from Calvinism, pietism and rationalism flowed in and agitated the prevailing

[1] See Molbech, *Biskop Myles Coverdale og hans Ophold i Danmark*. This was Coverdale's second visit. He had come to Denmark from Germany some time within the years 1530-34 and may then have met Duke Christian. He had married a wife who was either Danish or German, or, according to another account, the sister of the wife of Johannes Maccabaeus. The reason why he declined Christian III's invitation was his ignorance of Danish.

[2] Helveg, *Den Danske Kirkes Historie*, iv, p. 91.

[3] H. A. L. Fisher, *A History of Europe*, ii, p. 507.

Lutheran orthodoxy. Nor can it be maintained that the Reformation in Denmark, any more than in other lands, fulfilled the expectations of its supporters: from Luther downwards disappointment was expressed at the failure of the hopes which shone so brightly when the movement first began. It can now be seen that in Denmark the spiritual apathy of the populace frustrated the labours of the most zealous of the reformers; that the new faith became hardened into the orthodoxy of confessionalism; and that the chief material gainers in the revolution were the Crown and nobility. Further, a certain narrowing of outlook ensued: cut off from the wider interests of an international Church the Danes became " still more Danish, still more home-made ".[1] It was not till early in the eighteenth century that the Danish Church entered on its first missionary enterprise overseas in the Lutheran mission to South India. Religious freedom, too, was long in coming: from the middle of the eighteenth century onwards concessions were gradually made to non-Lutheran bodies, until by the Fundamental Law of June 1849, revised in July 1866, full religious freedom was granted to all. " Much in the programme of the Reformation (even knowledge of the Bible) was thus only promises on paper, and the joy over ' the light of the pure doctrine ' could not in the end succeed in veiling its defects; only when the struggle of pietism against the dead ecclesiasticism of orthodoxy began in earnest did the question of the carrying on of the Reformation become the order of the day, since when the call has never wholly been forgotten."[2] Yet when all such admissions have been made it may reasonably be claimed that the Reformation changes, in bursting the bonds of the medieval Church, gave to the people of Denmark the type of religious faith and organization best adapted to the national temperament and character.

Arup, op. cit., ii, p. 512.

[2] J. O. Andersen, *Kirke-Leksikon*, iii, p. 718. " Meget i Ref.'s programmet (selv Bibelkundskaben) blev derfor Løfteparagrafer paa Papiret, og Glaeden over ' den rene Laeres Lys ' formaade efterhaanden ikke at daekke over Manglerne; men først Pietismens Kamp mod Ortodoksiens døde Kirkelighed satte for Alvor Spørgsmaalet om R.'s Fortsaettelse paa Dagsordenen; siden er Kravet aldrig helt glemt."

APPENDIX I

THE OLDENBORG LINE

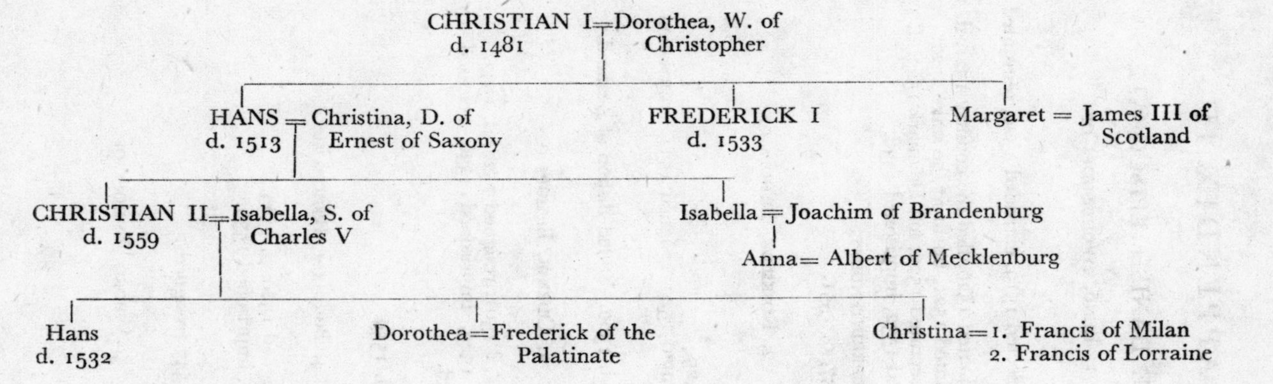

CHRISTIAN I = Dorothea, W. of Christopher
d. 1481
HANS = Christina, D. of Ernest of Saxony
d. 1513
FREDERICK I
d. 1533
Margaret = James III of Scotland
CHRISTIAN II = Isabella, S. of Charles V
d. 1559
Isabella = Joachim of Brandenburg
Anna = Albert of Mecklenburg
Hans
d. 1532
Dorothea = Frederick of the Palatinate
Christina = 1. Francis of Milan
2. Francis of Lorraine
FREDERICK I = 1. Anne, D. of John of Brandenburg
2. Sophia, D. of Bourgislav of Pomerania
d. 1533
CHRISTIAN III[1] = Dorothea, D. of Magnus of Saxe-Lauenburg
d. 1559
Dorothea[1] = Albert of Brandenburg
Hans[2]
Adolph[2]
Frederick[2]

APPENDIX II

THE DANISH EPISCOPATE

1. Lund, Archbishops of

Catholic:

Birgir, d. 1519.
Aage Jepsen Sparre, elected 1519, extruded 1520, reinstated 1526, resigned 1532, d. 1540.
Jørgen Skodborg, nominated 1520, fled the country 1521, d. 1551.
Didrik Slagheck, appointed 1521, burnt at the stake 1522.
Johann von Weze, consecrated 1522, left Denmark 1523, d. 1548.
Torben Bilde, appointed 1532, imprisoned 1536.

Lutheran Bishop or Superintendent:

Frans Vormordsen, 1537, d. 1551.

2. Roskilde, Bishops of

Catholic:

Jens Jepsen, d. 1512.
Lage Urne, 1513, d. 1529.
Joakim Rønnov, appointed 1529, resigned 1534, imprisoned 1536, d. 1544

Lutheran:

Peder Palladius, 1537, d. 1560. (Styled Bishop of Zealand.)

3. Odense, Bishops of

Catholic:

Jens Andersen Beldenak, ? 1501, resigned 1529, d. 1537.
Knud Gyldenstjerne, 1529, imprisoned 1536, released 1537, became a Lutheran and married.

Lutheran:

Jørgen Sadolin, 1537, d. 1559.

4. Børglum, Bishops of

Catholic:

Niels Stygge, 1486, resigned 1520, d. 1533.
Stygge Krumpen, 1520, imprisoned 1536.

Lutheran:

Peder Tomesen, 1537-1547 (resigned).

5. Viborg, Bishops of

Catholic:

Erik Kaas, d. 1520.
Jørgen Friis, 1520-1536.

Lutheran:

Jakob Skjønning, 1537, d. 1547.

6. Aarhus, Bishops of

Catholic:

Niels Klavssen, 1491, resigned 1520, d. 1531.
Ove Bilde, 1520-1536, d. 1555.

Lutheran:

Mads Lang, 1537, d. 1557.

7. Ribe, Bishops of

Catholic:

Iver Munk, 1499,? d. 1539.
Oluf Munk, coadjutor,? 1532-1536.

Lutheran:

Hans Vandal, 1537, d. 1541.
Hans Tausen, 1542, d. 1561.

APPENDIX III

BIBLIOGRAPHY

Allen, C. F., *De rebus Christiani Secundi*, Copenhagen, 1844.
Breve og Aktstykker til Oplysning af Christiern II og Frederick I Hist., Copenhagen, 1854.
De tre nordiske Rigers Historie, 5 vols., Copenhagen, 1864-72.
Historie de Danemark (tr. by E. Beauvois), Copenhagen, 1878.
Allen, P. S., *Erasmi Epistolæ*, Oxford, 1906.
Andersen, J. O., *Overfor Kirkebruddet*, Copenhagen, 1917.
Paulus Helie, Copenhagen, 1936.
Survey of the History of the Church of Denmark, Copenhagen, 1930.
Arup, E., *Danmarks Historie*, vol. ii, Copenhagen, 1932.
Bang, A. C., *Den lutherske Katechismus Historie*, vol. i, Christiana, 1893.
Bang, H. V. T. F., *Praestegaardsliv i Danmark og Norge*, Copenhagen, 1891.
Latinskoleliv og Studenterliv, Copenhagen, 1892.
Barford, F., *Danmarks Historie*, vol. ii, Copenhagen, 1885.
Brandt, C. J., *Om Lunde-Kanniken Christiern Pedersen og hans Skrifter*, Copenhagen, 1882.
Vore Danske Kirke-Salmebøger, Copenhagen, 1886.
Danske Bibeloversaettelsers Historie, Copenhagen, 1889.
En kristelig Undervisning om Skriftemaal og Sakramentet, Copenhagen, 1884.
Brandt, C. J., and Fenger, R. T., *Christiern Pedersens Danske Skrifter*, 5 vols., Copenhagen 1850-56.
Brewer, J. S., *Letters and Papers of Henry VIII*, London, 1867.
Bruun, C., *Viser fra Reformationstiden*, Copenhagen, 1864.
Psalmebøger fra Reformationstiden I, II, Copenhagen, 1865-66.
Cambridge Modern History, vol. ii, Cambridge, 1907.
Cornelius, C. A., *Handbok i Svenska Kyrkans Historia*, Upsala, 1867.
Daugaard, J. B., *Om de danske Klostre i Middelalderen*, Copenhagen, 1830.
Ekklesia, vol. 2, *Die Kirche in Dänemark*, Leipzig, 1937.
Engelstoft, C. T., *Reformantes et Catholici*, Copenhagen, 1836.
Liturgiens eller Alterbogens og Kirkeritualets Historie i Danmark, Copenhagen, 1840.
Paulus Eliae, in *Nyt historisk Tidsskrift II*, Copenhagen, 1848.
Om Geistligheden som Rigstand, in *Nyt historisk Tidsskrift IV*, Copenhagen, 1852.
Odense Byes Sognehistorie, in *Nyt historisk Tidsskrift VI*, Copenhagen, 1856.
Fabricius, L. P., *Danmarks Kirkehistorie*, vol. ii, Copenhagen, 1936.
Gau, J., *The Richt Vay to the Kingdom of Heuine*, ed. A. F. Mitchell, Edinburgh, 1887.
Geijer, E. G., *History of the Swedes* (Eng. tr. by J. H. Turner), London, 1845.
Gerset, K., *History of the Norwegian People*, New York, 1927.
Grundtvig, S., *Peder Smed*, Copenhagen, 1880.
Heden, H., *Studier till Danmarks Reformations Historie*, Goteborg, 1903.

Heise, A., "Herredagen i Kjobenhavn 1533" in *Historisk Tidsskrift*, series 4, vol. iii, Copenhagen 1840.
"Wulfgang von Utenhof", in *Historisk Tidsskrift*, vol. vi, Copenhagen, 1840.
Kristiern den anden i Norge og hans Faengsling, Copenhagen, 1877.
Diplomatarium Vibergense, Breve og Aktstykker, Copenhagen, 1879.
Skibykrøniken, Copenhagen, 1890.

Helveg, L. N., *Den Danske Kirkes Historie*, 5 vols., Copenhagen 1870.

Hering, H. *Doktor Pomeranus, Johannes Bugenhagen*, Halle, 1888.

Jacobsen, L., *Peder Palladius' Danske Skrifter*, 5 vols. Copenhagen, 1911-26.
Peder Palladius' Visitatsbog, Copenhagen, 1925.

Jørgensen, G., *Reformationen i Danmark*, Copenhagen, 1919.

Karup, W. J., *Geschichte der katholischen Kirke in Dänemark*, Münster, 1863.

Kent, H., *Braendpunkter i Reformationstidens Gudstjeneste-ordning*, Copenhagen, 1937.

Kidd, B. J., *Documents of the Continental Reformation*, Oxford, 1911.

Kirkehistoriske Samlinger (Selskabet for Danmarks Kirkehistorie), Copenhagen, 1849.

Knudsen, H., Joachim Rønnow, Copenhagen, 1840.
Bidrag til Oplysning af den Danske Reformationshistorie, in *Annaler for Nordisk . . . Historie*, Copenhagen, 1847.
"En gammel Krønike om Graabrodrenes Udjagelse", *Kirkehistoriske Samlinger I*, Copenhagen, 1849.

Koch, L., and Rørdam, H. F., *Fortaellinger af Danmarks Kirkehistorie*, Copenhagen, 1889.

Kolderup-Rosenvinge, J. L. A., *Grundrids af den danske Kirkeret*. Copenhagen, 1851.

Kornerup, B., *Hans Tausens Postil*, 2 vols., Copenhagen, 1934.
Reformationen i Danmark, Copenhagen, 1936.

Larsen, J. E., "Rigsdage og Provindsialforsamlinger", in *Historisk Tidsskrift I*, Copenhagen, 1840.

Lau, G. T. J., *Gestchichte der Einführung und Verbreitung der Reformation in den Herzogthümern Schleswig-Holstein*, Hamburg, 1867.

Laurence, R., *The Visitation of the Saxon Reformed Church*, Dublin, 1839.

Luthers Werke, *Kritische Gesamtausgabe*, Weimar, 1883.

Martin, C. R., *Sveriges Første Svenska Massa*, Upsala, 1901.

Mason, A. J., "Loss of the Succession in Denmark", *Church Quarterly Review*, London, 1891.

Matzen, H., *Forelaesninger over den danske Retshistorie*, Copenhagen, 1893-97.

Molbech, C., *Bidrag til en Historie af de danske Bibeloversaettelse*, Copenhagen, 1840.
Biskop Myles Coverdale og hans Ophold i Danmark, in *Historisk Tidsskrift V*, Copenhagen, 1844.

Müller, P. E., *Vita Lagonis Urne*, Copenhagen 1831-33.

Münter, F., *Den Danske Reformationshistorie*, 2 vols., Copenhagen 1802.
Kirchengeschichte von Dänemark und Norwegen, Leipzig, 1833.

Nielsen, F., and Andersen, J. O., *Kirke-Leksikon for Norden*, Copenhagen, 1900-29.

Oman, C., *The Sixteenth Century*, London, 1936.

Ordinatio Ecclesiastica Regnorum Daniæ et Norwegiæ, Copenhagen, 1537.

Palladius, P., *Alterbogen*, Copenhagen, 1555.

Paludan-Müller, C., *Grevens Feide*, Copenhagen, 1853.
De Første Konger af den Oldenborgsk Slaegt, Copenhagen 1874.

Ranke, L. von, *History of the Reformation in Germany* (tr. by S. Austin), London, 1905.

Resen, P. H., *Kong Christians den Andens Danske Lov-Bøger*, Copenhagen, 1684.

Richter, A. L. *Die evangelischen Kirchenordnungen*, vol. i, Leipzig, 1871.

Rørdam, H. F., *Smaaskrifter af Hans Tausen*, Copenhagen, 1870.
Monumenta Historiæ Danicæ, Copenhagen, 1873.
Malmøbogen af Peder Laurenssen, Copenhagen, 1868.
Kjøbenhavns Universitets Historie, Copenhagen, 1869-77.
Danmarks christelige Praedikanters Gjensvar, Copenhagen, 1885.
Peder Laurenssens En stakket Undervisning, Copenhagen, 1890.

Schmitt, L., *Paulus Heliä*, Freiburg-im-Breisgau, 1893.
Johann Tausen, Koln, 1894.

Schnell, J., *Die Dänische Kirchenordnung von* 1542, Breslau, 1927.

Secher, C. E., *Povel Eliaesens Danske Skrifter*, Copenhagen, 1855.

Severinsen, P., *Dansk Salmedigtning i Reformationstiden*, Copenhagen, 1904.
Hvordan Reformationen indførtes i Danmark, Copenhagen, 1936.

Steinberg, S. H., *Short History of Germany*, Cambridge, 1944.

Suhr, J. S. B., *Tausens Levnet*, Ribe, 1836.

Svanström and Palmstierna, *A Short History of Sweden*, Oxford, 1934.

Wace and Buchheim, *Luther's Primary Works*, London, 1883.

Werlauff, E. C., *Kiøbenhavns Universitet fra dets Stiftelse indtil Reformationen*, Copenhagen, 1850.

Willson, T. B., *History of the Church and State in Norway*, London, 1903.

Wordsworth, J., *The National Church of Sweden*, London, 1911.

INDEX

M

N

O

P

R

S